NAUTICAL RULES OF THE ROAD

CORNELL MARITIME PRESS
A Division of Schiffer Publishing, Ltd.

4880 Lower Valley Road, Atglen, Pennsylvania 19310

NAUTICAL RULES
OF THE ROAD

The International and Inland Rules

Fourth Edition

Revised and updated by
Steven D. Browne

Based on previous editions by
B. A. Farnsworth
Larry C. Young

CORNELL MARITIME PRESS
A Division of Schiffer Publishing, Ltd.
4880 Lower Valley Road, Atglen, PA 19310

Library of Congress Cataloging-in-Publication Data
Browne, Steven D.
    Nautical rules of the road : the international and inland rules / revised and updated
by Steven D. Browne ; based on previous editions by B. A. Farnsworth, Larry C.
Young.—4th ed.
        p. cm.
    Includes bibliographical references and index.
    ISBN-13: 978-0-87033-578-5 (alk. paper)
    1. Inland navigation—Law and legislation. 2. Rule of the road at sea. I. Farnsworth,
B. A., 1949– Nautical rules of the road. II. Title.
    K4188.F37 2006
    343.09'64—dc22
                                                    2006016851
Manufactured in the United States of America
First edition, 1991; fourth edition, 2006

Schiffer Books are available at special
discounts for bulk purchases for sales
promotions or premiums. Special editions,
including personalized covers, corporate
imprints, and excerpts can be created in
large quantities for special needs. For more
information contact the publisher:

Published by Schiffer Publishing Ltd.
4880 Lower Valley Road
Atglen, PA 19310
Phone: (610) 593-1777; Fax: (610) 593-2002
E-mail: Info@schifferbooks.com

For the largest selection of fine reference books
on this and related subjects, please visit our
web site at **www.schifferbooks.com**
We are always looking for people to write

books on new and related subjects. If you have
an idea for a book please contact us at the
above address.

This book may be purchased from the publisher.
Include $5.00 for shipping.
Please try your bookstore first.
You may write for a free catalog.

In Europe, Schiffer books are distributed by
Bushwood Books
6 Marksbury Ave.
Kew Gardens
Surrey TW9 4JF England
Phone: 44 (0) 20 8392-8585;
Fax: 44 (0) 20 8392-9876
E-mail: info@bushwoodbooks.co.uk
Website: www.bushwoodbooks.co.uk

Contents

First Edition Acknowledgments vii

Fourth Edition Acknowledgments. viii

Introduction ix

Introduction to U.S. Coast Guard Commandant Instruction M16672.2D xi

Legal Citations xiii

Conversion of Metric to U.S. Customary/Imperial Units xv

Part A   General (Rules 1–3) 2

Part B   Steering and Sailing Rules 16
                Section/Subpart I—Conduct of Vessels in
                    Any Condition of Visibility (Rules 4–10). 16
                Section/Subpart II—Conduct of Vessels in
                    Sight of One Another (Rules 11–18). 38
                Section/Subpart III—Conduct of Vessels in
                    Restricted Visibility (Rule 19) 52

Part C   Lights and Shapes (Rules 20–31) 56

Part D   Sound and Light Signals (Rules 32–37) 96

Part E   Exemptions (Rule 38). 108

Annex I   Positioning and Technical Details of Lights and Shapes 114

Annex II   Additional Signals for Fishing Vessels Fishing in
                    Close Proximity. 126

Annex III   Technical Details of Sound Signal Appliances. 128

Annex IV   Distress Signals. 134

Annex V   Pilot Rules. 137

Related Government Regulations 143
                International Interpretative Rules (33 CFR 82) 143
                Inland Interpretative Rules (33 CFR 90) 143

Contents

COLREGS Demarcation Lines (33 CFR 80) 144

Penalty Provisions 164

Alternative Compliance 168

Waters Specified by the Secretary 170

Vessel Bridge-to-Bridge Radiotelephone Regulations
(33 CFR 26). 171

Appendix A   Questions on the Rules of the Road 178

Appendix B   Study Outline for Rules of the Road. 203

Index 205

Bibliography 209

About the Authors 211

First Edition Acknowledgments

In the preparation of the first edition of this book, we received assistance from a number of quarters, but we are particularly grateful to the following individuals for the professional expertise, comments, and constructive criticism they so willingly rendered to make this book into a useful tool for the mariner.

Captain J. E. Ferguson, USCG, Commanding Officer, U.S. Coast Guard Institute; Commander E. J. Geissler, Master Mariner, Maine Maritime Academy; Lieutenant Commander J. L. Hassall, USCG, Master Mariner, Chief Deck Branch, U.S. Coast Guard Institute; Lieutenant Commander W. J. Theroux, USCG, Nautical Science Department, Section Chief, Advanced Nautical Science, U.S. Coast Guard Academy.

The opinions or assertions contained herein, however, are our own and are not to be construed as official or reflecting the views of the Commandant or the Coast Guard at large.

B. A. Farnsworth
Larry C. Young

Fourth Edition Acknowledgments

I would like to thank Captain Jim Buckley, Captain Peter Hayes, and Captain Sam Pecota, my colleagues at California Maritime Academy, for their helpful comments and excellent suggestions on this text. It is a better book because they read it. I am most thankful for the encouragement and patience of my loving wife. Without her, this project would not have been attempted.

Steven D. Browne

Introduction

This year marks the 25th anniversary of the first edition of *Nautical Rules of the Road*. The appeal of the book over the years has been its simplicity. It is a straightforward presentation of the Rules designed to be useful for all who need to learn and apply the Rules of the Road. It is hoped that the fourth edition will be as enlightening and informative for the recreational boater, maritime student, and professional mariner as the first three have been.

The aim of this book is to make learning the Rules as easy as possible. To achieve this aim, the text of the Rules is printed on the left-hand pages. The authors' comments are printed on the right-hand pages. In cases where the International Rules and the Inland Rules differ from each other, those differences are bold.

The Code of Federal Regulations (CFR) requires vessels 12 meters or more in length to have an up-to-date copy of the Rules of the Road aboard. This book, containing the latest changes to the Rules as of the date of printing, will meet that requirement. Any subsequent changes to the text of the Rules will be published in the Notices to Mariners and should be entered by the mariner.

Appendix A contains practice Rules of the Road questions. These questions are intended to help prepare students who must sit for a Rules of the Road exam in order to earn a U.S. Coast Guard license. But, they would be of value to anyone who wants to test their knowledge and deepen their understanding of the Rules.

Appendix B is a recommended study plan for learning the Rules. Although the Rules are organized in a logical manner, they were not arranged with ease of learning in mind. The typical student will start with Rule 1 and read straight through to Rule 28 and the Annexes, but this is not necessarily the best way to study them. For example, in order to grasp the meaning of the Rules, it is necessary to understand the terms that are used in the Rules. But key terms are not defined until Rules 3, 21, and 32. Any study of the Rules, then, would best be started there. The outline of study presented in Appendix B starts with the definition Rules and then builds from there.

A Very Brief History of the Rules of the Road

Rules concerning the prevention of collisions at sea have been around for hundreds of years. For the most part, they were local laws or international traditions without legal force. In the days of wooden sailing vessels, ships were slow and major collisions were rare. The advent of fast steamships in the nineteenth century resulted in an increasing number of serious collisions with catastrophic loss of life and cargo. In 1863, with hopes of preventing such collisions, Great Britain and France drew up a set of collision regulations known as the Articles. By 1864, over

30 countries, including the United States, adopted the rules for vessels operating in international waters.

Several international conventions were convened in subsequent years to revise the rules. In 1972, the rules underwent a major modification and reorganization at a convention convened by the Inter-Governmental Maritime Consulting Organization (IMCO), which is now known as the International Maritime Organization (IMO). The result was the International Regulations for the Prevention of Collisions at Sea (COLREGS). The COLREGS are commonly known as the International Rules in the United States because a different set of rules applies in U.S. inland waters. The International Rules came into effect in 1977 and were amended in 1981, 1987, 1989, 1993, and 2001. Those amendments are included in this book.

In the past there were three very different sets of rules for U.S. inland waters. Each set of rules covered a different geographic area: Great Lakes, Western Rivers, and other Inland waters. Following the ratification of the COLREGS in 1972, an effort was made to unify the three sets of U.S. Inland Rules and to make them conform as closely as possible to the International Rules. The result was the Inland Navigational Rules Act of 1980, which came into effect in 1981. Although the unified Inland Rules still retain a few differences based on location within U.S. waters, and there are some major differences from the International Rules, they largely agree with the COLREGS and, in most cases, agree word-for-word.

Introduction to U.S. Coast Guard Commandant Instruction M16672.2D

International Rules

The International Rules in this book were formalized in the Convention on the International Regulations for Preventing Collisions at Sea, 1972, and became effective on July 15, 1977. The Rules (commonly called 72 COLREGS) are part of the Convention, and vessels flying the flags of states ratifying the treaty are bound to the Rules. The United States has ratified this treaty and all U.S. flag vessels must adhere to these Rules where applicable. President Gerald R. Ford proclaimed the 72 COLREGS and the Congress adopted them as the International Navigational Rules Act of 1977.

The 72 COLREGS were developed by the Inter-Governmental Maritime Consultative Organization (IMCO), which in May 1982 was renamed the International Maritime Organization (IMO). In November 1981, IMO's Assembly adopted 55 amendments to the 72 COLREGS that became effective on June 1, 1983. The IMO also adopted nine more amendments that became effective on November 19, 1989. The International Rules in this book contain these amendments.

These Rules are applicable on waters outside of established navigational lines of demarcation. The lines are called COLREGS Demarcation Lines and delineate those waters upon which mariners shall comply with the Inland and International Rules. COLREGS Demarcation Lines are contained in this book.

Inland Rules

The Inland Rules in this book replace the old Inland Rules, Western Rivers Rules, Great Lakes Rules, their respective pilot rules and interpretive rules, and parts of the Motorboat Act of 1940. Many of the old navigation rules were originally enacted in the last century. Occasionally, provisions were added to cope with the increasing complexities of water transportation. Eventually, the navigation rules for U.S. inland waterways became such a confusing patchwork of requirements that in the 1960s several attempts were made to revise and simplify them. These attempts were not successful.

Following the signing of the Convention on the International Regulations for Preventing Collisions at Sea, 1972, a new effort was made to unify and update the various inland navigation rules. This effort culminated in the enactment of the Inland Navigational Rules Act of 1980. This legislation sets out Rules 1 through 38—the main body of the Rules. The five Annexes were published as regulations. It is important to note that with the exception of Annex V to the Inland Rules, the International and Inland Rules and Annexes are very similar in both content and format.

The effective date for the Inland Navigation Rules was December 24, 1981, except for the Great Lakes where the effective date was March 1, 1983.

Legal Citations

72 COLREGS

International Navigational Rules Act of 1977	Public Law 95-75; 91 Stat. 308; 33 U.S.C. 1601–1608
COLREGS Demarcation Lines	33 CFR 80
72 COLREGS: Implementing Rules	33 CFR 81
72 COLREGS: Interpretative Rules	33 CFR 82
Amendments to 72 COLREGS effective June 1, 1983	48 FR 28634

Inland Rules

Inland Navigational Rules Act of 1980	Public Law 96-591; 94 Stat. 3415; 33 U.S.C. 2001–2038
Annex 1: Positioning and Technical Details of Lights and Shapes	33 CFR 84
Annex II: Additional Signals for Fishing in Close Proximity	33 CFR 85
Annex III: Technical Details of Sound Signal Appliances	33 CFR 86
Annex IV: Distress Signals	33 CFR 87
Annex V: Pilot Rules	33 CFR 88
Inland Navigation Rules: Implementing Rules	33 CFR 89
Inland Navigation Rules: Interpretative Rules	33 CFR 90

Vessel Bridge-to-Bridge Radiotelephone

Vessel Bridge-to-Bridge Radiotelephone Act	Public Law 92-63; 85 Stat. 164; 33 U.S.C. 1201–1208

Vessel Bridge-to-Bridge Radiotelephone Regulations   **33 CFR 26**
    (Coast Guard regulations)

Radiotelephone Stations Provided for Compliance with the Vessel
    Bridge-to Bridge Radiotelephone Act (Federal Communications
    Commission regulations)   **47 CFR 80.1001–80.1023**

Other FCC regulations pertaining to vessel bridge-to-bridge radiotelephone communications
    are contained in various sections of 47 CFR 80.

Boundary Lines   **46 CFR 7**

Conversion of Metric to
U.S. Customary/Imperial Units

Metric Measure	U.S. Customary/Imperial Units (approx.)
1,000 Meters (M)	3,280.8 ft
500 M	1,640.4 ft
200 M	656.2 ft
150 M	492.1 ft
100 M	328.1 ft
75 M	246.1 ft
60 M	196.8 ft
50 M	164.0 ft
25 M	82.0 ft
20 M	65.6 ft
12 M	39.4 ft
10 M	32.8 ft
8 M	26.2 ft
7 M	23.0 ft
6 M	19.7 ft
5 M	16.4 ft
4.5 M	14.8 ft
4.0 M	13.1 ft
3.5 M	11.5 ft
2.5 M	8.2 ft
2.0 M	6.6 ft
1.5 M	4.9 ft
1 M	3.3 ft
.9 M	35.4 in
.6 M	23.6 in
.5 M	19.7 in
300 mm	11.8 in
200 mm	7.9 in

NAUTICAL RULES OF THE ROAD

INTERNATIONAL	INLAND
PART A *GENERAL*	*PART A* *GENERAL*

RULE 1. Application

(a) These Rules shall apply to all vessels upon the high seas and in all waters connected therewith navigable by seagoing vessels.

RULE 1. Application

(a) These Rules apply to all vessels upon the inland waters of the United States, and to vessels of the United States on the Canadian waters of the Great Lakes to the extent that there is no conflict with Canadian law.

(b) Nothing in these Rules shall interfere with the operation of special rules made by an appropriate authority for roadsteads, harbors, rivers, lakes or inland waterways connected with the high seas and navigable by seagoing vessels. Such special rules shall conform as closely as possible to these Rules.

(b)(i) These Rules constitute special rules made by an appropriate authority within the meaning of Rule 1(b) of the International Regulations.
(ii) All vessels complying with the construction and equipment requirements of the International Regulations are considered to be in compliance with these Rules.

(c) Nothing in these Rules shall interfere with the operation of any special rules made by the **Government of any State** with respect to additional station or signal lights, shapes or whistle signals for ships of war and vessels proceeding under convoy, or with respect to additional station or signal lights or shapes for fishing vessels engaged in fishing as a fleet. These addi-

(c) Nothing in these Rules shall interfere with the operation of any special rules made by the **Secretary of the Navy** with respect to additional station or signal lights and shapes or whistle signals for ships of war and vessels proceeding under convoy, **or by the Secretary** with respect to additional station or signal lights and shapes for fishing vessels engaged in fishing as a

COMMENTS

Part A, Rules 1–3, contains general rules that apply at all times.

Rule 1

(a) The International Rules (COLREGS) apply to all vessels on the high seas and connecting waters. The high seas are those areas outside of the territorial waters of any nation, generally more than twelve miles from the coastline. The COLREGS also apply to territorial and inland waters of nations unless "special rules" cover them (see Rule 1(b)).

The Inland Rules apply to vessels navigating the inland waters of the United States. Inland waters lay inside COLREGS demarcation lines as set forth in 33 CFR (Code of Federal Regulations), Part 80, and are reproduced in the back of this book. Demarcation lines are drawn and identified on most United States charts.

Note that there are several areas of internal U.S. waters that do not fall under the Inland Rules. The COLREGS are followed on the waters of Alaska and Puerto Rico and parts of Hawaii, Washington, California, Florida, and the New England states. Check the chart and U.S. Coast Pilots carefully before proceeding into an unfamiliar U.S. port to determine which set of rules applies.

The Inland Rules also apply to United States vessels on "Canadian waters of the Great Lakes to the extent that there is no conflict with Canadian law." The two nations have worked together to ensure that their laws are very similar.

Note that "Inland Waters," as the term is defined by the Rules of the Road, are not the same as "Inland Waters" for the purpose of Coast Guard licensing. For licensing purposes, any waters shoreward of the boundary line (as delineated in 46 CFR Part 7) are inland waters no matter whether the COLREGS or Inland Rules apply. Therefore, you must pass an examination on the COLREGS to be able to operate on all Inland Waters of the United States.

(b) The U.S. Inland Rules "constitute special rules made by an appropriate authority" as allowed Rule 1(b) of the COLREGS. Though there are some significant differences between the two sets of rules, they are generally written in the same format and the same order and, in many cases, match exactly. This is a great boon to the student who can concentrate on the similarities of the two sets of rules, rather than on the many differences.

Paragraph (ii) enables vessels that meet the construction and equipment standards of the International Rules to operate inside the demarcation lines without undergoing modification.

(c) The Navy is allowed by the Inland Rules to make "special rules with respect to additional station or signal lights, shapes, or whistle signals" for their vessels. These additional signals can be found in 32 CFR Part 706. There are also provisions regarding rules for special lights for fishing vessels. These rules are to be made by the secretary of the department in which the Coast Guard is operating. At the present time, this is the Secretary of Homeland Security. The additional rules for fishing vessels can be found in 33 CFR Part 80 and in Annex II of the Inland Rules.

INTERNATIONAL	INLAND

tional station or signal lights, shapes or whistle signals shall, so far as possible, be such that they cannot be mistaken for any light, shape or signal authorized elsewhere under these Rules.[1]

fleet. These additional station or signal lights and shapes or whistle signals shall, so far as possible, be such that they cannot be mistaken for any light, shape, or signal authorized elsewhere under these Rules. **Notice of such special rules shall be published in the Federal Register and, after the effective date specified in such notice, they shall have effect as if they were a part of these Rules.**[1]

(d) Traffic separation schemes may be **adopted by the Organization** for the purpose of these Rules.

(d) Traffic separation schemes may be **established** for the purposes of these Rules. **Vessel traffic service regulations may be in effect in certain areas.**

(e) Whenever the **Government concerned shall have determined t**hat a vessel of special construction or purpose cannot comply fully with the provisions of any of these Rules with respect to the number, position, range or arc of visibility of lights or shapes, as well as to the disposition and characteristics of sound-signalling appliances, such vessel shall comply with such other provisions in regard to the number, position, range or arc of visibility of lights or shapes, as well as to the disposition and characteristics of sound-signalling appliances, **as her Government** shall have determined to be the closest possible compliance with these Rules in respect to that vessel.

(e) Whenever the **Secretary determines that a vessel or class of vessels** of special construction or purpose cannot comply fully with the provisions of any of these Rules with respect to the number, position, range, or arc of visibility of lights or shapes, as well as to the disposition and characteristics of sound-signalling appliances, the vessel shall comply with such other provisions in regard to the number, position, range, or arc of visibility of lights or shapes, as well as to the disposition and characteristics of sound-signalling appliances, as **the Secretary** shall have determined to be the closest possible compliance **with these Rules. The Secretary may issue a certificate of alternative compliance for a vessel or class of vessels specifying the closest possible compliance with these Rules. The Secretary of the**

---

[1] Submarines may display, as a distinctive means of identification, an intermittent flashing amber (yellow) beacon with a sequence of operation of one flash per second for three (3) seconds followed by a three (3) second off-period. Other special rules made by the Secretary of the Navy with respect to additional station and signal lights are found in Part 707 of Title 32, Code of Federal Regulations (32 CFR 707).

(d) International. For an explanation of Traffic Separation Schemes, see the comments on Rule 10.

Inland. Vessel Traffic Service (VTS) regulations are in existence for certain ports in the United States. They will generally be explained by a note on current editions of charts for the affected area. Promulgated by the Coast Guard, the regulations differ from area to area, but they usually require, at least, that vessels monitor a certain radio channel or frequency and make periodic position reports to the Coast Guard's VTS headquarters. A small booklet is published for each area, containing information and regulations for the use of that service. U.S. VTS regulations are denoted in 33 CFR Part 161. Portions of these regulations are reproduced in the back of this book. Worldwide VTS guides are available at http://www.worldvtsguide.org.

(e) In this Rule authority is granted to allow vessels of special construction or purpose to be in less than full compliance with the Rules. However, these vessels must still comply as closely as possible and must be issued a certificate of alternative compliance. This is obtained from the Secretary of the Navy for naval vessels and from the Secretary of Homeland Security for all other vessels. These regulations can be found in 33 CFR Part 89.

INTERNATIONAL	INLAND
	Navy shall make these determinations and issue certificates of alternative compliance for vessels of the Navy.
	(f) The Secretary may accept a certificate of alternative compliance issued by a contracting party to the International Regulations if he determines that the alternative compliance standards of the contracting party are substantially the same as those of the United States.
RULE 2. Responsibility	RULE 2. Responsibility
(a) Nothing in these Rules shall exonerate any vessel, or the owner, master or crew thereof, from the consequences of any neglect to comply with these Rules or of the neglect of any precaution which may be required by the ordinary practice of seamen, or by the special circumstances of the case.	(a) Nothing in these Rules shall exonerate any vessel, or the owner, master or crew thereof, from the consequences of any neglect to comply with these Rules or of the neglect of any precaution which may be required by the ordinary practice of seamen, or by the special circumstances of the case.

Rule 2

The rest of the Rules cover common situations regularly experienced between vessels and mandate appropriate action. But, no set of Rules can cover every possible circumstance. Rule 2 is the general catchall that applies when all others fail. The wording is the same in the COLREGS and the Inland Rules.

(a) Rule 2(a) is commonly known as the "Rule of Good Seamanship." It gets its name from the fact that it mandates "any precaution that may be required by the ordinary practice of seamen, or by the special circumstances of the case."

Rule 2(a) requires: (1) obedience to the Rules (all of them), (2) precautions that an ordinary, prudent mariner would take in similar circumstances, and (3) any extra precautions that might be required in more demanding, dangerous, or unusual circumstances.

Among other things, good seaman should:

- Obey the Rules of the Road
- Obey other governing rules, such as SOLAS, STCW, local speed limits, routing requirements, etc.
- Take the best possible actions to avoid collision
- Take action to lessen the effects of collision
- Use the radiotelephone properly
- Plan ahead
- Monitor weather reports
- Not get underway with uncorrected charts and navigation publications
- Test steering, communication equipment, etc., prior to getting underway
- Predict and compensate for the effects of currents and tide
- Ensure the bridge is adequately manned with trained and licensed personnel
- Know the use and limitations of bridge equipment
- Give other vessels adequate sea room so there will be time to correct for any equipment failure or lapsed judgment
- Know the maneuvering characteristics of the vessel
- Switch to manual steering when appropriate
- Give proper, clear helm commands
- Give wide berth to anchored and moored vessels
- Give wide berth to vessels in the vicinity of pilot stations
- Anchor in a safe area outside channels and fairways
- Pay out enough anchor chain to avoid dragging

(b) In construing and complying with these Rules due regard shall be had to all dangers of navigation and collision and to any special circumstances, including the limitations of the vessels involved, which may make a departure from these Rules necessary to avoid immediate danger.

RULE 3. General Definitions

For the purpose of these Rules, except where the context otherwise requires:

(a) The word "vessel" includes every description of water craft, including nondisplacement craft, **WIG craft** and seaplanes, used or capable of being used as a means of transportation on water.

(b) In construing and complying with these Rules due regard shall be had to all dangers of navigation and collision and to any special circumstances, including the limitations of the vessels involved, which may make a departure from these Rules necessary to avoid immediate danger.

RULE 3. General Definitions

For the purpose of these Rules **and this Chapter,** except where the context otherwise requires:

(a) The word "vessel" includes every description of water craft, including nondisplacement craft and seaplanes, used or capable of being used as a means of transportation on water;

COMMENTS

Extra precautions are required in times of "special circumstances." For example, a prudent mariner faced with low visibility and an unreliable radar set might choose to remain anchored until repairs are complete or conditions improve.

Special circumstances are also mentioned in Rule 2(b).

(b) Rule 2(b) is known as the "General Prudential Rule." It requires the mariner to keep in mind all hazards to navigation, the danger of collision, the characteristics of the vessels involved in a situation, any unusual circumstances, and the fact that it may become necessary to violate the Rules to avoid immediate danger.

When a vessel is confronted with immediate danger, such as imminent grounding or collision, and it is impossible to escape that danger without violating the Rules, Rule 2(b) authorizes (and requires) departure from the Rules. Any vessel that ran aground or collided with another vessel because she rigidly adhered to the other Rules would be in violation of Rule 2(b). The Rules cannot be disregarded for the sake of convenience or schedule but only out of necessity.

Rules 2(a) and 2(b) both mention "special circumstances." Special circumstances are subject to court interpretation, but include:

- Situations not covered by the other Rules, such as
  - A vessel backing down
  - A power-driven vessel approaching a rowboat
  - A vessel not under command meeting a vessel restricted in her ability to maneuver
  - More than 2 vessels approaching with risk of collision
- The *in extremis* situation in which action by both vessels is necessary in order to avoid a collision
- The presence of shallow water or another vessel that makes it impossible for a vessel to maneuver as required
- When action contrary to the Rules is proposed by one vessel and accepted by another

The purpose of the Rules is to prevent collisions at sea. If obedience to the Rules would result in a collision or other disaster, a mariner has a "duty to depart" from the Rules. This action can be taken only when the danger is immediate and only to the extent necessary to avoid the hazard.

Rule 3

This Rule gives the general definitions of terms used in various parts of the Rules themselves. The definitions for lights are given in Rule 21 and those for whistle signals in Rule 32.

(a) The Rules of the Road apply to *vessels*, so this term is defined. The definition covers virtually any craft on the water. It specifically includes nondisplacement craft (hydrofoils and hovercraft) and seaplanes and the COLREGS mentions Wing-in-Ground (WIG) craft. A wing-in-ground (WIG) craft is a vessel capable of operating completely above the surface of the water using the ground effect of the air trapped between the vessel and the water's surface. WIG craft can operate at speeds of more than 100 knots. Though not specifically stated by the Inland Rules, the term "vessel" certainly includes WIG craft on inland waters as well.

(b) The term "power-driven ves sel" means any vessel propelled by machinery.

(b) The term "power-driven vessel" means any vessel propelled by machinery;

(c) The term "sailing vessel" means any vessel under sail provided that propelling machinery, if fitted, is not being used.

(d) The term "vessel engaged in fishing" means any vessel fishing with nets, lines, trawls or other fishing apparatus which restrict maneuverability, but does not include a vessel fishing with trolling lines or other fishing apparatus which do not restrict maneuverability.

(e) The word "seaplane" includes any aircraft designed to maneuver on the water.

(f) The term "vessel not under command" means a vessel which through some exceptional circumstance is unable to maneuver as required by these Rules and is therefore unable to keep out of the way of another vessel.

(g) The term "vessel restricted in her ability to maneuver" means a vessel which from the nature of her work is restricted in her ability to maneuver as required by these Rules and is therefore unable to keep out of the way of another vessel.

(c) The term "sailing vessel" means any vessel under sail provided that propelling machinery, if fitted, is not being used;

(d) The term "vessel engaged in fishing" means any vessel fishing with nets, lines, trawls, or other fishing apparatus which restricts maneuverability, but does not include a vessel fishing with trolling lines or other fishing apparatus which do not restrict maneuverability;

(e) The word "seaplane" includes any aircraft designed to maneuver on the water;

(f) The term "vessel not under command" means a vessel which through some exceptional circumstance is unable to maneuver as required by these Rules and is therefore unable to keep out of the way of another vessel;

(g) The term "vessel restricted in her ability to maneuver" means a vessel which from the nature of her work is restricted in her ability to maneuver as required by these Rules and is therefore unable to keep out of the way of another vessel; **vessels restricted in**

COMMENTS

It is very important to be careful of definitions, how the Rules apply them, and how the Coast Guard and the courts interpret them. For instance, while almost everything on the water is a vessel, there may be some exceptions. For example, while a barge is "capable of being used as transportation on water," if that barge is being used as a restaurant, casino, or band platform, she may not be required to show typical lights, depending on how she is moored. And a Mobile Offshore Drilling Unit (MODU) that must be lighted as a vessel while underway, is considered a fixed platform, not a vessel, once the unit is attached to the Outer Continental Shelf for drilling. It is interesting to note that the term "seaplane" is defined separately, but is included under the definition of the term "vessel." Therefore, any rule that addresses itself to a "vessel" applies to seaplanes as well, although Rule 18 (d) states: "A seaplane on the water shall, in general, keep well clear of all vessels."

(b) A "power-driven vessel" is one with mechanical means of propulsion in use. A motorboat under oars with the engine secured would not be "power-driven" while a sailboat under sail with the engine running would be. It is interesting to note that some rules that apply to power-driven vessels don't necessarily apply to all vessels propelled by machinery. For example, a vessel restricted in her ability to maneuver will sound a different fog signal than that sounded by a power-driven vessel, even though she, too, may be propelled by machinery.

(d) To be considered "engaged in fishing," a vessel must be using gear that restricts maneuverability. For this reason, most vessels fishing with trolling lines, such as charter boats, are not considered engaged in fishing. If, however, the vessels are using trolling lines that do hamper their ability to comply with the Rules then they, too, would fall in this category. To qualify as "engaged in fishing," the restrictive gear must actually be in use. A fishing vessel proceeding to or from the fishing grounds with gear stowed would be considered a "power-driven vessel," if mechanically propelled.

(f) To qualify as "not under command" (NUC), a vessel must be unable to maneuver as required due to an unusual circumstance that is out of the control of the vessel's operator. A vessel with steering or propulsion failure would be NUC while a vessel drifting with functioning, though secured, engines would not be. The drifting vessel could maneuver, if necessary. A low powered vessel in severe weather that must maintain course to avoid loss of the vessel could also be considered NUC as would a becalmed sailing vessel.

(g) In defining the term "vessel restricted in her ability to maneuver" (RAM), the Rules are self-explanatory. To qualify as such, a vessel must be unable to maneuver as required and that must be due to her present work. She must be currently engaged in her task. A dredge in transit wouldn't be considered RAM but one "engaged in dredging" would.

Both sets of Rules give a list of vessels that are restricted in their ability to maneuver, but the Rules state that the vessels "include, but are not limited to" those in the

INTERNATIONAL	INLAND
The term "vessels restricted in their ability to maneuver" shall include but not be limited to:	**their ability to maneuver include, but are not limited to:**

The term "vessels restricted in their ability to maneuver" shall include but not be limited to:

(i) a vessel engaged in laying, servicing or picking up a navigation mark, submarine cable or pipeline;
(ii) a vessel engaged in dredging, surveying or underwater operations;
(iii) a vessel engaged in replenishment or transferring persons, provisions or cargo while underway;
(iv) a vessel engaged in the launching or recovery of aircraft;
(v) a vessel engaged in mineclearance operations;
(vi) a vessel engaged in a towing operation such as severely restricts the towing vessel and her tow in their ability to deviate from their course.

(h) The term "vessel constrained by her draft" means a power-driven vessel which, because of her draft in relation to the available depth and width of navigable water is severely restricted in her ability to deviate from the course she is following.

their ability to maneuver include, but are not limited to:

(i) a vessel engaged in laying, servicing, or picking up a navigation mark, submarine cable, or pipeline;
(ii) a vessel engaged in dredging, surveying, or underwater operations;
(iii) a vessel engaged in replenishment or transferring persons, provisions, or cargo while underway;
(iv) a vessel engaged in the launching or recovery of aircraft;
(v) a vessel engaged in mineclearance operations; **and**
(vi) a vessel engaged in a towing operation such as severely restricts the towing vessel and her tow in their ability to deviate from their course.

(i) The word "underway" means that a vessel is not at anchor, or made fast to the shore, or aground.

(h) The word "underway" means that a vessel is not at anchor, or made fast to the shore, or aground;

(j) The words "length" and "breadth" of a vessel means her length overall and greatest breadth.

(i) The words "length" and "breadth" of a vessel means her length overall and greatest breadth;

12

list. This may lead to a question about what additional vessels might be included in the list. It might also lead to a situation in which an operator decides that, due to the nature of the work, the vessel falls into this category. Any ideas of this nature should be discouraged. In case of a collision, the vessel involved would have the burden of proof that she was "restricted in her ability to maneuver" as defined by the Rules. However, this is not to declare decisively that the given list is exhaustive, but rather that one should think twice before deeming his ship to be in this category.

Though the maneuverability of a vessel engaged in fishing is restricted due to her work, she is not "restricted in ability to maneuver" under the Rules. This is an important distinction because Rule 18(c) requires that "A vessel engaged in fishing shall, so far as possible, keep out of the way of . . . a vessel restricted in her ability to maneuver."

It should also be pointed out at this juncture that Rule 3(g)(vi) states that vessels engaged in towing operations may be considered restricted in their ability to maneuver. The requirement for this designation is that their work must "severely restrict" them in their ability to make course changes. The Rule does not specify what type of towing is involved, thereby allowing the definition to apply to these vessels whether they are towing astern, alongside, or by pushing ahead.

Although a vessel that is "not under command" certainly has restricted maneuverability, she is not "restricted in her ability to maneuver" as defined by the Rules because that restriction is due to exceptional circumstances, not the nature of her work.

(h) International. The International Maritime Organization (IMO) has published a clarification of the definition of a "vessel constrained by her draft" that reads as follows:

> Not only the depth of water but also the available navigable water should be used as a factor to determine whether a vessel may be regarded as constrained by her draft. When determining this due account should also be taken of the vessel and thus her ability to deviate from the course she is following. A vessel navigating in an area with a small under-keel clearance but with adequate space to take avoiding action should not be regarded as a vessel constrained by her draft.

In other words, the *width* of the navigable water available is as important as the *depth*. If a vessel can alter her course to avoid another vessel without shortly running aground, she shouldn't claim to be "constrained by her draft."

The term "vessel constrained by her draft" is not included in the Inland Rules. Since the inland waters are more congested, it might be a great temptation for a vessel to consider herself "constrained by her draft" and perhaps to assume a right of way that is not hers. The International Rules direct vessels to "avoid impeding" a vessel constrained by her draft (see Rule 18) but do not give the constrained vessel the right of way. In congested waters, where several vessels are operating in a channel, this could become a very confusing situation.

(i) International/(h) Inland. The term "underway" should not be confused with "making way," or moving through the water. To be considered anchored, and, therefore, not underway, a vessel's anchor must be down and holding. A vessel moored to a buoy is also not underway.

INTERNATIONAL	INLAND

INTERNATIONAL

(k) Vessels shall be deemed to be in sight of one another only when one can be observed visually from the other.

(l) The term "restricted visibility" means any condition in which visibility is restricted by fog, mist, falling snow, heavy rainstorms, sandstorms or any other similar causes.

(m) The term "Wing-In-Ground (WIG) craft" means a multimodal craft which, in its main operational mode, flies in close proximity to the surface by utilizing surface-effect action.

INLAND

(j) Vessels shall be deemed to be in sight of one another only when one can be observed visually from the other;

(k) The term "restricted visibility" means any condition in which visibility is restricted by fog, mist, falling snow, heavy rainstorms, sandstorms, or any other similar causes;

(l) "Western Rivers" means the Mississippi River, its tributaries, South Pass, and Southwest Pass, to the navigational demarcation lines dividing the high seas from harbors, rivers, and other inland waters of the United States, and the Port Allen-Morgan City Alternate Route, and that part of the Atchafalaya River above its junction with the Port Allen-Morgan City Alternate Route including the Old River and the Red River;

(m) "Great Lakes" means the Great Lakes and their connecting and tributary waters including the Calumet River as far as the Thomas J. O'Brien Lock and Controlling Works (between mile 326 and 327), the Chicago River as far as the east side of the Ashland Avenue Bridge (between mile 321 and 322), and the Saint Lawrence River as far east as the lower exit of Saint Lambert Lock;

(n) "Secretary" means the Secretary of the department in which the Coast Guard is operating;

(o) "Inland Waters" means the navigable waters of the United States shoreward of the navigational demarcation lines dividing the high

(k) International/(j) Inland. This is a very important definition because the application of entire sections of the Rules depends on whether or not vessels are in sight of one another. Vessels are in sight if one *can* be observed *visually* from the other. A vessel is in sight even if you don't see it but could if you looked in the correct direction. And, it is visual observation, by naked eye, binoculars or other visual aid, that counts. A vessel that can be detected by radar alone isn't "in sight."

(l) International/(k) Inland. "Similar causes" would include smoke, dust, and volcanic ash.

(l) Inland. The term "Western Rivers" is used in Rules 9 (a)(ii), 15(b) and 24(i), and includes the entire Mississippi River system south to the COLREGS demarcation lines.

(m) Inland. The term "Great Lakes" is defined in this paragraph and is used in Rules 1(a), 9(a)(ii), 15(b), and 23(d).

(o) Inland. The term "Inland Waters" includes the Great Lakes (on the United States side of the boundary) and the Western Rivers for the purposes of these Rules. Where exceptions are made for these waters, as in Rule 15(b), they are specifically

INTERNATIONAL	INLAND
	seas from harbors, rivers, and other inland waters of the United States and the waters of the Great Lakes on the United States side of the International Boundary;
	(p) "Inland Rules" or "Rules" mean the Inland Navigational Rules and the annexes thereto, which govern the conduct of vessels and specify the lights, shapes, and sound signals that apply on inland waters; and
	(q) "International Regulations" mean the International Regulations for Preventing Collisions at Sea, 1972, including annexes currently in force for the United States.

PART B
STEERING AND SAILING RULES

Section I
Conduct of Vessels in Any Condition
of Visibility

RULE 4. Application
  Rules in this **Section** apply to any
condition of visibility.

PART B
STEERING AND SAILING RULES

Subpart I
Conduct of Vessels in Any Condition
of Visibility

RULE 4. Application
  Rules in this **subpart** apply in any
condition of visibility.

RULE 5. Look-out
  Every vessel shall at all times maintain a proper look-out by sight and hearing as well as by all available means appropriate in the prevailing circumstances and conditions so as to make a full appraisal of the situation and of the risk of collision.

RULE 5. Look-out
  Every vessel shall at all times maintain a proper look-out by sight and hearing as well as by all available means appropriate in the prevailing circumstances and conditions so as to make a full appraisal of the situation and of the risk of collision.

stated. Demarcation lines are specified in 33 CFR Part 80 and are reproduced at the back of this book.

PART B
STEERING AND SAILING RULES

Rule 4

There are three sections (International) or subparts (Inland) to the Steering and Sailing Rules. Section (Subpart) I of Part B applies to "any condition of visibility" and includes Rules 4 through 10. These Rules must be followed *at all times*. Section (Subpart) II includes Rules 11 through 18 and applies to vessels "in sight of one another." Section (Subpart) III applies to vessels in "restricted visibility" and is comprised of Rule 19.

Rule 5

This Rule is very short, but very, very important. A quick read through some National Transportation Safety Board collision reports or the excellent book, *Collisions and Their Causes* will reveal that in the case of almost every collision between ships, failure to keep a proper lookout was cited as a contributing cause. The purpose of the Rules is to prevent collisions; the purpose of maintaining a proper lookout is to collect the information necessary to make the right decisions in order to avoid those collisions.

In this short Rule, there are several key words and phrases that should be drawn to the mariner's attention.

- *Every vessel*—Rule 5 applies to all vessels, without exception. Cruise ships, aircraft carriers, tankers, recreational vessels, and single-handed sailboats must maintain a lookout.
- *Shall at all times maintain*—No breaks are allowed, and there is no situation or condition when a proper lookout is not required. Whether in clear

COMMENTS

weather or fog, day or night, coastal or ocean waters, a proper lookout must be kept.

- *Proper*—The lookout must be good and effective. If the watch officer has enough information to make a *full appraisal of the situation and of the risk of collision,* then the lookout is proper. However, the standards of what constitute *proper* will change with the circumstances.

The Rule gives no specifics as to the number of people required on watch to maintain a proper lookout. Neither does it state where they must be posted nor the state of visibility or the time of day when they are needed. This is left up to the master's best judgment. A prudent master would keep in mind "the ordinary practice of seamen" (tradition) and court interpretations of the Rule.

In some cases, the watch officer can be the sole lookout. Operators of small vessels with 360 degree unobstructed views, such as tugs, fishing vessels, and ski boats, will normally be the only lookout. For ships on the open ocean, with light traffic during daylight there may be circumstances in which officers of the watch can safely act as the sole lookout, but only after careful assessment of each situation. Even then, IMO (International Maritime Organization) states, "assistance must be immediately available." Extra lookout(s) should be posted to assist the watch officer:

- At night
- At times of restricted visibility
- In high traffic areas
- When the watch officer is distracted by other duties

The IMO Recommendations on Navigational Watch-keeping, which provide more guidance in this area, state that keeping a lookout involves making "a full appraisal of the situation, and of the risk of collision, stranding and other hazards to navigation." The duties of a lookout also include "the detection of ships or aircraft in distress, shipwrecked persons, wrecks, and debris."

In order to maintain a proper lookout, the assigned individual must be trained. Don't use an inexperienced seaman. Lookouts need to know the meaning of lights and be able to recognize ships, navigation aids, and navigation hazards such as shoal water. They should receive basic training on the Rules so that they can identify ships' navigation lights and aspects. And they should know enough to be able to recognize when something is wrong and feel empowered to report it.

Where should lookouts be posted? The Rule doesn't say, but it is advisable to have a lookout separate from the bridge watch, and as close to the bow as possible. If lookouts are low on the vessel and close to the water, rather than aloft, they can also get a better sense of the direction of fog signals. Such a position will remove them from the distracting noises of diesel engines and other machinery. However, it is the common practice on many vessels to post a lookout on the bridge wing under close supervision by the watch officer. The master must use good judgment in stationing the lookout at the location best suited for the vessel and the circumstances.

The task of a lookout is not something to be taken lightly. All attention must be devoted to the job. For this reason the IMO recommendations state that:

1. No duties shall be assigned or undertaken that would interfere with the keeping of a proper lookout;

RULE 6. Safe Speed

Every vessel shall at all times proceed at a safe speed so that she can take proper and effective action to avoid collision and be stopped within a distance appropriate to the prevailing circumstances and conditions. In determining a safe speed the following factors shall be among those taken into account:

(a) By all vessels:

(i) the state of visibility;

(ii) the traffic density including concentrations of fishing vessels or any other vessels;

(iii) the maneuverability of the vessel with special reference to stopping distance and turning ability in the prevailing conditions;

(iv) at night, the presence of background light such as from shore lights or from back scatter of her own lights;

(v) the state of wind, sea and current, and the proximity of navigational hazards;

(vi) the draft in relation to the available depth of water.

(b) Additionally, by vessels with operational radar:

(i) the characteristics, efficiency and limitations of the radar equipment;

(ii) any constraints imposed by the radar range scale in use;

(iii) the effect on radar detection of the sea state, weather and other sources of interference;

RULE 6. Safe Speed

Every vessel shall at all times pro ceed at a safe speed so that she can take proper and effective action to avoid collision and be stopped within a distance appropriate to the prevailing circumstances and conditions. In determining a safe speed the following factors shall be among those taken into account:

(a) By all vessels:

(i) the state of visibility;

(ii) the traffic density including concentrations of fishing vessels or any other vessels;

(iii) the maneuverability of the vessel with special reference to stopping distance and turning ability in the prevailing conditions;

(iv) at night, the presence of background light such as from shore lights or from back scatter of her own lights;

(v) the state of wind, sea and current, and the proximity of navigational hazards;

(vi) the draft in relation to the available depth of water.

(b) Additionally, by vessels with operational radar:

(i) the characteristics, efficiency and limitations of the radar equipment;

(ii) any constraints imposed by the radar range scale in use;

(iii) the effect on radar detection of the sea state, weather and other sources of interference;

COMMENTS

2. The duties of the lookout and helmsman are separate, and a helmsman who is steering is not a lookout.

A proper lookout must be kept by use of "sight and hearing" and "all available means appropriate" to do the job. Those available means often include:

- Binoculars
- Radar/ARPA
- VHF radio
- Vessel Traffic Service (VTS)
- Automatic Identification System (AIS)

Rule 6

The location of this Rule in Section (Subpart) I of the Steering and Sailing Rules indicates that the Rule applies in any condition of visibility. The Rule states that vessels "shall at all times proceed at a safe speed." At midnight or noon, in fair weather or fog, in inland or coastal waters, or upon the high seas, a vessel must be operated at a safe speed.

How fast is safe speed? The Rule doesn't specify. It is left to the good judgment of the mariner (or of the judge, should a collision occur). The Rule merely states that all vessels must be operated at such a speed that will allow her to avoid collision and stop in an appropriate distance. Safe speed is neither too fast nor so slow that the vessel loses steerageway.

How do you determine what safe speed is? The Rule gives six factors for every vessel to consider and six additional ones for those fitted with radar. The state of visibility is often the most important consideration. As visibility drops, so too does safe speed. The vessel operator must have time to react when another vessel or object is detected late. Even vessels fitted with radar should slow because small objects might not be detected until the last moment, if at all. The old rule of thumb was that vessels should proceed at such a speed so that they might be stopped in half the distance of visibility. So, if visibility was one mile, the vessel would be operated at the speed at which she could be stopped within a half mile. This isn't the law, but it is certainly a good idea for those vessels without radar.

Safe speed includes those factors of safety affecting a vessel as well as other vessels or structures in the vicinity. A VLCC (very large crude carrier) may be able to operate safely at a speed of 15 knots, but if in restricted or congested waters, she may be a hazard to smaller vessels or to piers and other shore structures. Even the wake of relatively small vessels may cause a good deal of damage to small anchored vessels, vessels in crowded waters, or vessels tied up at a marina. In most cases, vessel operators or owners are held liable for damages caused by their wake.

The last point made in the Rule pertains to the use of radar. A vessel might well be able to determine precisely the distance of visibility by noting the distance shown by radar at the time of visual sighting of an object. There will also be instances, especially at night, when a strong radar target is picked up, but cannot be sighted visually. This will notify the watch officer that visibility is restricted (perhaps more so than expected), and that closer attention to lookout duties, and perhaps a change in the vessel's speed, is in order. By using the radar to its full capacity and knowing the maneuvering characteristics of his vessel, the ship's officer can make a better assessment of what is a safe speed than an officer on a vessel that is not radar-equipped. Safe

INTERNATIONAL	INLAND
(iv) the possibility that small vessels, ice and other floating objects may not be detected by radar at an adequate range;	(iv) the possibility that small vessels, ice and other floating objects may not be detected by radar at an adequate range;
(v) the number, location and movement of vessels detected by radar;	(v) the number, location and movement of vessels detected by radar; **and**
(vi) the more exact assessment of the visibility that may be possible when radar is used to determine the range of vessels or other objects in the vicinity.	(vi) the more exact assessment of the visibility that may be possible when radar is used to determine the range of vessels or other objects in the vicinity.
RULE 7. Risk of Collision	**RULE 7. Risk of Collision**
(a) Every vessel shall use all available means appropriate to the prevailing circumstances and conditions to determine if risk of collision exists. If there is any doubt such risk shall be deemed to exist.	(a) Every vessel shall use all available means appropriate to the prevailing circumstances and conditions to determine if risk of collision exists. If there is any doubt such risk shall be deemed to exist.
(b) Proper use shall be made of radar equipment if fitted and operational, including long-range scanning to obtain early warning of risk of collision and radar plotting or equivalent systematic observation of detected objects.	(b) Proper use shall be made of radar equipment if fitted and operational, including long-range scanning to obtain early warning of risk of collision and radar plotting or equivalent systematic observation of detected objects.
(c) Assumptions shall not be made on the basis of scanty information, especially scanty radar information.	(c) Assumptions shall not be made on the basis of scanty information, especially scanty radar information.
(d) In determining if risk of collision exists the following considerations shall be among those taken into account:	(d) In determining if risk of collision exists the following considerations shall be among those taken into account:
(i) such risk shall be deemed to exist if the compass bearing of an approaching vessel does not appreciably change;	(i) such risk shall be deemed to exist if the compass bearing of an approaching vessel does not appreciably change; **and**
(ii) such risk may sometimes exist even when an appreciable bearing change is evident, particularly when approaching a very large vessel or a tow or when approaching a vessel at close range.	(ii) such risk may sometimes exist even when an appreciable bearing change is evident, particularly when approaching a very large vessel or a tow or when approaching a vessel at close range.

speed is often higher for a vessel with radar than a vessel without, but it isn't necessarily full speed. Radar is not a tool to be used as an excuse for excessive speed in conditions of restricted visibility.

All vessels must maintain safe speed at all times. Safe speed changes due to circumstances and constant reappraisal is necessary. If in doubt, slow down!

Rule 7

Several of the Steering and Sailing Rules that follow apply only when risk of collision exists. If there is no risk of collision, there is no head-on situation (Rule 14) or crossing situation (Rule 15). Likewise, without risk of collision, neither Rule 12, nor Rules 16 or 17 apply. Therefore, when evaluating a situation between vessels, the watch officer must first determine if risk of collision exists and then decide which Rule applies, if any.

When does risk of collision exist? First of all, vessels must be "approaching," that is, getting closer to each other. Second, the compass bearing of the other vessel must be constant or nearly constant. When in a constant bearing, decreasing range (CBDR) situation, a collision is inevitable if neither vessel maneuvers. If the compass bearing to the other vessel is constant, the passing distance or closest point of approach (CPA) will be zero. If the bearing is changing, the CPA will be somewhat further apart. The faster the rate of bearing change, the greater the passing distance will be. Note that risk of collision might sometimes exist even if the bearing is changing, especially for vessels in close proximity. Though the bearing to the bow of a large containership may be changing rapidly, you might still collide with her stern. And a changing bearing on the pilot house of a tug isn't necessarily an indication that you won't collide with the tow cable or the barge behind her.

The Rule doesn't specify the range at which risk of collision begins to exist. If two vessels are 20 miles apart but approaching with constant bearing is there risk of collision? Surely not yet. The range risk begins depends on the circumstances and is left to the good judgment of the mariner. While two small motorboats might approach within a few hundred yards of each other without risk, two supertankers might have risk of collision when still 10 miles apart. The simple fact is that often the time when "risk of collision" comes into effect is determined by the court after the collision occurred. As a general rule, risk of collision begins to exist at the point in time when a maneuver contrary to any of the Rules will result in the danger of collision, either by the maneuver alone or by the interpretation of that maneuver by the other vessel.

How close of a CPA is needed for risk of collision to exist? Some seem to think that as long as they don't scrape the paint off of the other vessel's hull, they passed far enough apart without need for maneuver. The Rule doesn't specify a CPA for risk of collision; this too is left up to the judgment of the mariner and varies with the circumstances. Small, maneuverable vessels might safely pass at hailing distance while for large ships risk of collision might exist when set up to pass a mile or more apart. If you have any doubt

RULE 8. Action to Avoid Collision   RULE 8. Action to Avoid Collision

(a) Any action to avoid collision shall **be taken in accordance with the Rules of this Part and** shall, if the circumstances of the case admit, be positive made in ample time and with due regard to the observance of good seamanship.

(a) Any action taken to avoid collision shall, if the circumstances of the case admit, be positive, made in ample time and with due regard to the observance of good seamanship.

(b) Any alteration of course and/or speed to avoid collision shall, if the circumstances of the case admit, be large enough to be readily apparent to another vessel observing visually or by radar; a succession of small alterations of course and/or speed should be avoided.

(b) Any alteration of course or speed to avoid collision shall, if the circumstances of the case admit, be large enough to be readily apparent to another vessel observing visually or by radar; a succession of small alterations of course or speed should be avoided.

(c) If there is sufficient sea room, alteration of course alone may be the most effective action to avoid a close-quarters situation provided that it is made in good time, is substantial and

(c) If there is sufficient sea room, alteration of course alone may be the most effective action to avoid a close-quarters situation provided that it is made in good time, is substantial and

COMMENTS

whether or not there is risk of collision, assume it does and react accordingly.

The Rule requires the use of "all available means" to determine if risk of collision exists. The available means include visual lookout, radar, ARPA if fitted, VHF bridge-to-bridge radio, the Automatic Identification System (AIS), if fitted, etc. "Proper use" must be made of radar. Proper use means that it is turned on, tuned, on the correct range scale for the situation, closely observed by a trained operator, and plotting is being conducted either manually or automatically (ARPA).

Rule 8

This Rule applies to vessels in all conditions of visibility. The previous rules in this section told how to detect dangerous situations: by keeping a proper lookout and determining if there is risk of collision. This Rule, and several that follow, tell what to do about those situations. Rule 8 doesn't state which vessel needs to maneuver, or which direction to turn, but it does explain how to do so safely.

(a) A recent change in the International Rules requires that any action to avoid collision shall be taken "in accordance with the Rules of this Part." Though this phrase is absent in the Inland Rules, it is certainly their intent, as well. In other words, this Rule should be applied in conjunction with, and not separate from, the other Steering and Sailing Rules.

Action taken to avoid collision must be "positive," that is, effective, beneficial to the situation, and result in a large safety margin. Also, it must be made "in ample time," not at the last moment. Fortunately, the Rule recognizes that in some circumstances, such as when in congested waters, in narrow channels, or in the proximity of navigation hazards, a vessel might not be able to take action as positively or as early as would otherwise be required.

(b) This paragraph provides guidelines to use when taking action to avoid collision. It is important that the other vessel in the situation be able to determine what your vessel is doing. If your vessel is the give-way vessel, your evasive action should be such that the stand-on vessel will be certain that you are taking appropriate action. Otherwise, she may take action that, although not contrary to the Rules, may certainly confuse the situation and make your task of keeping clear more difficult.

When you have the option, make one large course change. If you make a series of small course changes and another vessel is plotting you on radar, your maneuvers may not be readily apparent to her. (See Figure 1.)

A substantial course change would let the other vessel know that you are definitely taking action. (See Figure 2.)

In clear visibility, a course change of more than 10° would be advisable. But, if at all possible, make a course change substantial enough to change the aspect of your vessel from the observer's viewpoint, that is, to show her the opposite bow during daylight, or the opposite sidelight at night. In restricted visibility, it is especially important to make any course changes substantial. A prudent mariner would likely alter course by 30° or even 60° should conditions allow.

(c) In many cases alteration of course is to be preferred over a speed change because:

- A change in course can usually be accomplished more quickly than a change in speed, especially on large commercial vessels;
- In clear visibility a substantial course change is usually "readily apparent" to the eye, while a speed change is difficult to detect visually;

INTERNATIONAL	INLAND
does not result in another close-quarters situation.	does not result in another close-quarters situation.
(d) Action taken to avoid collision with another vessel shall be such as to result in passing at a safe distance. The effectiveness of the action shall be carefully checked until the other vessel is finally past and clear.	(d) Action taken to avoid collision with another vessel shall be such as to result in passing at a safe distance. The effectiveness of the action shall be carefully checked until the other vessel is finally past and clear.

COMMENTS

- Altering course will generally change the relative motion line on an observing vessel's radar faster than a change of speed and will be easier to detect by radar plotting.

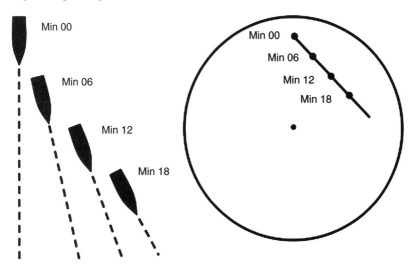

Figure 1. A series of small course changes.

(d) The vessel taking action in accordance with this Rule is responsible to ensure the vessels pass at a "safe distance." Like many terms used by the Rules, "safe distance" isn't defined. You must use your good judgment. What is considered safe depends on the circumstances. In a channel, a passing distance of a couple hundred yards might be safe while in the open ocean a couple of miles might be too close. Whenever possible, leave a generous safety margin so that the other vessel will feel no need to maneuver to get more room.

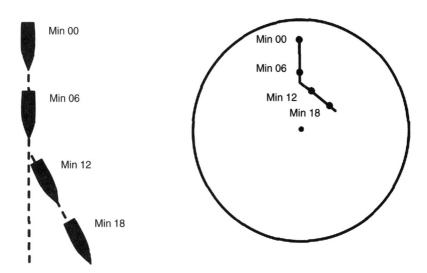

Figure 2. One large course change.

(e) If necessary to avoid collision or allow more time to assess the situation, a vessel shall slacken her speed or take all way off by stopping or reversing her means of propulsion.

(e) If necessary to avoid collision or allow more time to assess the situation, a vessel shall slacken her speed or take all way off by stopping or reversing her means of propulsion.

(f)(i) A vessel which, by any of these rules, is required not to impede the passage or safe passage of another vessel shall, when required by the circumstances of the case, take early action to allow sufficient sea room for the safe passage of the other vessel.
(ii) A vessel required not to impede the passage or safe passage of another vessel is not relieved of this obligation if approaching the other vessel so as to involve risk of collision and shall, when taking action, have full regard to the action which may be required by the rules of this part.
(iii) A vessel, the passage of which is not to be impeded remains fully obliged to comply with the rules of this part when the two vessels are approaching one another so as to involve risk of collision.

(f)(i) A vessel which, by any of these rules, is required not to impede the passage or safe passage of another vessel shall, when required by the circumstances of the case, take early action to allow sufficient sea room for the safe passage of the other vessel.
(ii) A vessel required not to impede the passage or safe passage of another vessel is not relieved of this obligation if approaching the other vessel so as to involve risk of collision and shall, when taking action, have full regard to the action which may be required by the rules of this part.
(iii) A vessel, the passage of which is not to be impeded remains fully obliged to comply with the rules of this part when the two vessels are approaching one another so as to involve risk of collision.

COMMENTS

Any action taken should be checked and rechecked for effectiveness. Don't maneuver and then forget about the other vessel. Closely observe her until "past and clear." A workable definition of "past and clear" would be that point at which:

- The vessels are a suitable distance apart for the conditions;
- The distance between them is increasing;
- Any reasonable maneuver by either vessel would not create another situation involving risk of collision between those two vessels.

(e) Though a change of course is generally the preferred maneuver to avoid collision, sometimes this isn't an option, particularly when operating in restricted waters. In those cases, a change of speed is mandatory. The Rules do not prohibit an increase in speed to avoid collision, but the general tone of the Rules is to favor speed reductions. A vessel must at all times proceed at a "safe speed," and, therefore, a vessel's authority to increase speed is limited by Rule 6. Also, a speed increase in a crossing situation would likely result in the give-way vessel crossing ahead of the stand-on vessel, a violation of Rule 15.

We are also to slow or stop if necessary to "allow more time to assess the situation." We are required by Rule 5 to maintain a proper lookout so as to "make a full appraisal of the situation." If excess speed renders our lookout process ineffective, Rule 8 (and Rule 6) requires us to slow or take all way off.

(f) Rules 9, 10, and 18 direct some vessels to "not impede" or "avoid impeding" others. "Impede" means to hinder, delay, or to block another vessel.

At first glance, the Rules may appear to contradict themselves in places. For example, if a loaded tanker proceeds down a channel, and a fishing vessel is crossing ahead from starboard to port, who has the right-of-way? The fishing vessel has (Rule 18(a)). But at the same time the fishing vessel is directed "not to impede" the passage of the tanker (Rule 9(c)). Does that mean that the roles are now reversed and the fishing vessel must give way and the tanker must stand-on? Rule 8 tells us that isn't the case.

Before risk of collision exists, the vessel "required not to impede" must take action to prevent the risk from developing and to allow the other vessel safe passage (Paragraph f (i)). The Rule recognizes the fact that small vessels have an easier time maneuvering in such a situation and places upon them a requirement to give sufficient sea room to the vessel within the channel. If risk of collision develops anyway, the vessel "required not to impede" must still take action to allow safe passage (Paragraph f (ii)). If the other vessel is required by the Rules to "keep out of the way" when risk of collision exists, she must give-way, even though she is "not to be impeded." In other words, when risk of collision exists, both vessels may need to maneuver.

If collision occurred, and it was determined that one of the vessels (in this case the fishing vessel) could operate safely outside the channel, that vessel would most likely be held at fault. However, the Rule does not change the status of a give-way vessel to that of a stand-on vessel within the meaning of the Rules. (See further discussion of this term in Rule 9.)

INTERNATIONAL	INLAND
RULE 9. Narrow Channels	RULE 9. Narrow Channels

(a) A vessel proceeding along the course of a narrow channel or fairway shall keep as near to the outer limit of the channel or fairway which lies on her starboard side as is safe and practicable.

(a)(i) A vessel proceeding along the course of a narrow channel or fairway shall keep as near to the outer limit of the channel or fairway which lies on her starboard side as is safe and practicable.

(ii) Notwithstanding paragraph (a)(i) and Rule 14(a), a power-driven vessel operating in narrow channels or fairways on the Great Lakes, Western Rivers, or waters specified by the Secretary, and proceeding downbound with a following current shall have the right-of-way over an upbound vessel, shall propose the manner and place of passage, and shall initiate the maneuvering signals prescribed by Rule 34(a)(i), as appropriate. The vessel proceeding upbound against the current shall hold as necessary to permit safe passing.

(b) A vessel of less than 20 meters in length or a sailing vessel shall not impede the passage of a vessel which can safely navigate only within a narrow channel or fairway.

(b) A vessel of less than 20 meters in length or a sailing vessel shall not impede the passage of a vessel that can safely navigate only within a narrow channel or fairway.

COMMENTS

Rule 9

This Rule applies to vessels in narrow channels or fairways. Neither of those terms is defined. The rule doesn't specify how narrow the channel needs to be to qualify. It is a relative term. The same channel could be narrow for a supertanker but wide for a small fishing vessel. The decision of what constitutes "narrow" is left up to the judgment of the mariner, or to the judge if a collision occurs. A fairway can be defined as an open area of water on which navigation is restricted due to regulations or obstructions. Though the wording is a bit ambiguous, this Rule applies to narrow fairways, not every fairway.

(a) Rule 9(a) requires that we keep our vessels to the starboard side of narrow channels. "Shall keep" means that is true even if no other vessel is around. We must keep as far to starboard as is "safe and practicable." No need to hit the buoys or run aground.

Inland (a)(ii) starts with the term "notwithstanding paragraph a(i) and Rule 14(a)." Another way to say it could be "despite what it says in paragraph a(i) and Rule 14(a)." Inland (a)(ii) overrides those paragraphs for vessels operating with a current on the "Great Lakes, Western Rivers, or waters specified by the Secretary" and permits starboard to starboard passages when agreed upon.

Great Lakes and Western Rivers are defined in Rule 3. "Waters specified by the Secretary" are mentioned Inland Rules 9(a)(ii), 14(d), and 15(b). According to 33 CFR §89.25, they are:

a. Tennessee-Tombigbee Waterway;
b. Tombigbee River;
c. Black Warrior River;
d. Alabama River;
e. Coosa River;
f. Mobile River above the Cochrane Bridge at St. Louis Point;
g. Flint River;
h. Chattahoochee River; and
i. The Apalachicola River above its confluence with the Jackson River.

In narrow channels on those waters, vessels operating downbound with a following current have the right-of-way over upbound vessels. The downbound vessel is generally less maneuverable than the upbound one. With the right-of-way comes the responsibility for proposing the manner and place of passage and for initiating the maneuvering signals required by Rule 34(a)(i). The upbound vessel must agree unless the proposal isn't safe. If necessary, the upbound vessel shall hold her position until the other vessel is clear.

(b) Rule 9 puts the term "not to impede," to which we were just introduced in Rule 8, into actual practice in a situation. Paragraph (b) states that vessels of any type that are less than 20 meters in length and sailing vessels of any size shall not impede vessels that can safely navigate only within a narrow channel or fairway. How can we know whether another vessel is limited to the channel? In international waters, vessels constrained by their draft should show distinguishing lights and day shapes. (See Rule 28.) In inland waters there are no equivalent lights or shapes. Therefore, it is

(c) A vessel engaged in fishing shall not impede the passage of any other vessel navigating within a narrow channel or fairway.

(d) A vessel shall not cross a narrow channel or fairway if such crossing impedes the passage of a vessel which can safely navigate only within such channel or fairway. The latter vessel **may** use the **sound** signal prescribed in Rule 34(d) if in doubt as to the intention of the crossing vessel.

(e)(i) In a narrow channel or fairway when **overtaking can take place only if the vessel to be overtaken has to take action to permit safe passing, the vessel intending to overtake shall indicate her intention by sounding the appropriate signal prescribed in Rule 34(c)(i). The vessel to be overtaken shall, if in agreement, sound the appropriate signal prescribed in Rule 34(c)(ii) and take steps to permit safe passing.** If in doubt she **may** sound the signals prescribed in Rule 34(d).

(ii) This Rule does not relieve the overtaking vessel of her obligation under Rule 13.

(f) A vessel nearing a bend or an area of a narrow channel or fairway where other vessels may be obscured by an intervening obstruction shall navigate with particular alertness and caution and shall sound the appropriate signal prescribed in Rule 34(e).

(g) Any vessel shall, if the circumstances of the case admit, avoid anchoring in a narrow channel.

(c) A vessel engaged in fishing shall not impede the passage of any other vessel navigating within a narrow channel or fairway.

(d) A vessel shall not cross a narrow channel or fairway if such crossing impedes the passage of a vessel which can safely navigate only within that channel or fairway. The latter vessel **shall** use the **danger** signal prescribed in Rule 34(d) if in doubt as to the intention of the crossing vessel.

(e)(i) In a narrow channel or fairway when overtaking, **the power-driven vessel intending to overtake another power-driven vessel shall indicate her intention by sounding the appropriate signal prescribed in Rule 34(c) and take steps to permit safe passing. The power-driven vessel being overtaken, if in agreement, shall sound the same signal and may, if specifically agreed to take steps to permit safe passing.** If in doubt she **shall** sound the **danger** signal prescribed in Rule 34(d).

(ii) This Rule does not relieve the overtaking vessel of her obligation under Rule 13.

(f) A vessel nearing a bend or an area of a narrow channel or fairway where other vessels may be obscured by an intervening obstruction shall navigate with particular alertness and caution and shall sound the appropriate signal prescribed in Rule 34(e).

(g) Every vessel shall, if the circumstances of the case admit, avoid anchoring in a narrow channel.

COMMENTS

imperative that watch officers keep a close eye on the characteristics and movements of other vessels in the vicinity. If there is any doubt in the situation, the vessel should assume the need to avoid impeding and keep well clear of the vessel in the channel.

(c) Fishing vessels of any size are to not impede any vessel operating in channel whether restricted to the channel or not. It is typically OK to fish in the channel, but you must move out of the way if any vessel approaches.

(d) No vessel of any size or any category shall cross a narrow channel if she might impede a vessel that can't operate outside of the channel.

It is interesting to note that the Inland Rules state that if the vessel restricted to the channel is in doubt of the crossing vessel's intention she "shall use the danger signal" while the International Rules say that she "may" do so. This naturally leads to the conclusion that the danger signal is optional in international waters. But, Rule 34(d)(International) states that if "from *any* cause either vessel fails to understand the intentions or actions of the other, or is in doubt whether sufficient action is being taken by the other to avoid collision, the vessel in doubt *shall* immediately indicate such doubt by giving at least five short and rapid blasts on the whistle." A prudent mariner in this situation should, therefore, sound the signal despite the use of the word "may" in Rule 9(d).

(e) Rule 13 addresses overtaking in general. 9(e) addresses overtaking in narrow channels. International 9(e)(i) applies only if the vessel being overtaken has to "take action to permit safe passing." Inland 9(e)(i) applies to power-driven vessels in overtaking situations in a narrow channel whether or not the overtaking vessel needs help to pass clear.

It should be noted that even though this Rule applies in any condition of visibility, the prescribed whistle signals shall be sounded only when the vessels are in sight of one another. (See the discussion of the whistle signals under Rule 34.)

There are no special whistle signals in the Inland Rules for overtaking in narrow channels when the overtaken vessel has to take action to facilitate passage. The signals are identical to those sounded anytime one power-driven vessel is overtaking another.

When required, an agreement must be reached before the overtaking maneuver can be completed. Both vessels must sound whistle signals. Each vessel must be certain that the other agrees with the maneuver. If the vessel being overtaken responds to the overtures of the overtaking vessel with the danger/doubt signal, the overtaking vessel should hold back and not attempt to pass. It may be that the lead vessel wishes to be passed on the opposite side, or it may be that she considers any overtaking situation dangerous for the time being. Since signals should be initiated by the overtaking vessel in this situation, that vessel may try again. She may sound the same signal as before and hope for a favorable response, or she may indicate an intention to pass on the opposite side. Again, she must have permission before proceeding with the maneuver.

We will, in passing, mention the term "cross-signals." Although this term is not found in the Rules, it has come to mean a situation in which the answering vessel gives the opposite signal to that of the initiating vessel. Just because there is no allowance for such signals in the Rules does not mean they will never take place.

In the situation in Rule 9, cross-signals should be very unlikely in international waters, because the answering signal is completely different from the initiating signal. The vessel being overtaken can either answer the proposal with one prolonged,

RULE 10. Traffic Separation Schemes

(a) This Rule applies to traffic separation schemes adopted **by the Organization** and does not relieve any vessel of her obligation under any other rule.

(b) A vessel using a traffic separation scheme shall:

(i) proceed in the appropriate traffic lane in the general direction of traffic flow for that lane;

(ii) so far as practicable keep clear of a traffic separation line or separation zone;

(iii) normally join or leave a traffic lane at the termination of the lane, but when joining or leaving from either side shall do so at as small an angle to the general direction of traffic flow as practicable.

(c) A vessel shall, so far as practicable, avoid crossing traffic lanes but if obliged to do so shall cross on a heading as nearly as practicable at right angles to the general direction of traffic flow.

(d)(i) A vessel shall not use an inshore traffic zone when she can safely use the appropriate traffic lane within the adjacent traffic separation scheme. However, vessels of less than 20 meters in length, sailing vessels and vessels engaged in fishing may use the inshore traffic zone.

(ii) Notwithstanding subparagraph (d)(i), a vessel may use an inshore traffic zone when en route to or

RULE 10. Traffic Separation Schemes

(a) This Rule applies to traffic separation schemes and does not relieve any vessel of her obligation under any other Rule.

(b) A vessel using a traffic separation scheme shall:

(i) proceed in the appropriate traffic lane in the general direction of traffic flow for that lane;

(ii) so far as practicable keep clear of a traffic separation line or separation zone;

(iii) normally join or leave a traffic lane at the termination of the lane, but when joining or leaving from either side shall do so at as small an angle to the general direction of traffic flow as practicable.

(c) A vessel shall, so far as practicable, avoid crossing traffic lanes but if obliged to do so shall cross on a heading as nearly as practicable at right angles to the general direction of traffic flow.

(d)(i) A vessel shall not use an inshore traffic zone when she can safely use the appropriate traffic lane within the adjacent traffic separation scheme. However, vessels of less than 20 meters in length, sailing vessels, and vessels engaged in fishing may use the inshore traffic zone.

(ii) Notwithstanding subparagraph (d)(i), a vessel may use an inshore traffic zone when en route to or

COMMENTS

one short, one prolonged, and one short blast, or with the danger signal. If she answers with any other kind of signal, the overtaking vessel had better stay clear because it reflects a serious lack of knowledge of the Rules.

In inland waters, the overtaken vessel is supposed to answer, if in agreement, with the same signal. If she answers one blast with two blasts, that is a cross-signal that is confusing, is illegal, and doesn't mean anything. The overtaking vessel cannot assume that the lead vessel is suggesting passing on the other side. She may just have made a mistake. The overtaking vessel should hold back, wait a bit, and try initiating another signal. This process must go on until a signal has been initiated by the overtaking vessel and answered by the same signal from the vessel being overtaken. The overtaking vessel is the one still responsible for the success of the maneuver (Rule 13).

Rule 10

Traffic separation schemes are designed to promote safe traffic flow in congested areas. They are not the same as narrow channels or fairways, therefore, Rule 9 does not apply to them.

A watch officer should be sure that he understands the terms used in the Rule. IMO gives us a helping hand by defining the following terms in Resolution A. 284 (viii):

- Traffic Separation Scheme—A scheme that separates traffic proceeding in opposite or nearly opposite directions by the use of a separation zone or line, traffic lanes, or by other means.
- Traffic Lane—An area within definite limits inside which one-way traffic is established.
- Separation Zone or Line—A zone or line separating traffic proceeding in one direction from traffic proceeding in another direction. A separation zone may also be used to separate a traffic lane from the adjacent inshore traffic zone.
- Inshore Traffic Zone—A designated area between the landward boundary of a traffic separation scheme and the adjacent coast intended for coastal traffic.

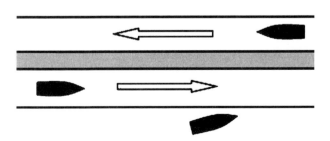

Figure 3. Join a traffic lane at as small an angle as practicable.

from a port, offshore installation or structure, pilot station or any other place situated within the inshore traffic zone, or to avoid immediate danger.

(e) A vessel other than a crossing vessel or a vessel joining or leaving a lane shall not normally enter a separation zone or cross a separation line except:

(i) in cases of emergency to avoid immediate danger;

(ii) to engage in fishing within a separation zone.

(f) A vessel navigating in areas near the terminations of traffic separation schemes shall do so with particular caution.

(g) A vessel shall so far as practicable avoid anchoring in a traffic separation scheme or in areas near its terminations.

(h) A vessel not using a traffic separation scheme shall avoid it by as wide a margin as is practicable.

(i) A vessel engaged in fishing shall not impede the passage of any vessel following a traffic lane.

(j) A vessel of less than 20 meters in length or a sailing vessel shall not impede the safe passage of a power-driven vessel following a traffic lane.

(k) A vessel restricted in her ability to maneuver when engaged in an operation for the maintenance of safety of navigation in a traffic separation scheme is exempted from complying with this Rule to the extent necessary to carry out the operation.

(l) A vessel restricted in her ability to maneuver when engaged in an operation for the laying, servicing or picking up of a submarine cable, within a traffic separation scheme, is exempted from complying with this Rule to the extent necessary to carry out the operation.

from a port, offshore installation or structure, pilot station, or any other place situated within the inshore traffic zone, or to avoid immediate danger.

(e) A vessel other than a crossing vessel or a vessel joining or leaving a lane shall not normally enter a separation zone or cross a separation line except:

(i) in cases of emergency to avoid immediate danger; or

(ii) to engage in fishing within a separation zone.

(f) A vessel navigating in areas near the terminations of traffic separation schemes shall do so with particular caution.

(g) A vessel shall so far as practicable avoid anchoring in a traffic separation scheme or in areas near its terminations.

(h) A vessel not using a traffic separation scheme shall avoid it by as wide a margin as is practicable.

(i) A vessel engaged in fishing shall not impede the passage of any vessel following a traffic lane.

(j) A vessel of less than 20 meters in length or a sailing vessel shall not impede the safe passage of a power-driven vessel following a traffic lane.

(k) A vessel restricted in her ability to maneuver when engaged in an operation for the maintenance of safety of navigation in a traffic separation scheme is exempted from complying with this Rule to the extent necessary to carry out the operation.

(l) A vessel restricted in her ability to maneuver when engaged in an operation for the laying, servicing, or picking up of a submarine cable, within a traffic separation scheme, is exempted from complying with this Rule to the extent necessary to carry out the operation.

COMMENTS

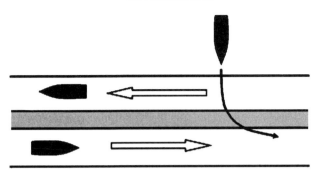

Figure 4. Cross traffic lanes at right angles.

(f) We need to be particularly vigilant near the terminations of traffic separation schemes. Several vessels traveling in multiple directions are likely to be converging to join or leave the schemes and special circumstances are likely to develop.

(h) When in the area of a traffic separation scheme, a vessel should either use the scheme or avoid it "by as wide a margin as is practicable." This policy will save the consequences of any confusion resulting when applying the more vaguely worded parts of the Rule.

(i) Vessels are allowed to engage in fishing in traffic separation schemes. However, they must:

- proceed in the general direction of traffic flow, if fishing in a traffic lane; and
- not impede the passage of any vessel following a traffic lane.

Again, we have a situation where the fishing vessel is directed "not to impede" the passage of other vessels. This obligation would include the vessel and any working gear that may be extending from her. Fishermen should take great care to ascertain their position correctly when operating in areas around the schemes. See discussion of the "not to impede" situation in Rule 8(f).

INTERNATIONAL

Section II
Conduct of Vessels in Sight of One Another

RULE 11. Application

Rules in this **section** apply to vessels in sight of one another.

RULE 12. Sailing Vessels

(a) When two sailing vessels are approaching one another, so as to involve risk of collision, one of them shall keep out of the way of the other as follows:

(i) when each has the wind on a different side, the vessel which has the wind on the port side shall keep out of the way of the other;

(ii) when both have the wind on the same side, the vessel which is to windward shall keep out of the way of the vessel which is to leeward;

(iii) if a vessel with the wind on the port side sees a vessel to windward and cannot determine with certainty whether the other vessel has the wind on the port or on the starboard side, she shall keep out of the way of the other.

(b) For the purposes of this Rule the windward side shall be deemed to be the side opposite to that on which the mainsail is carried or, in the case of a square-rigged vessel, the side opposite to that on which the largest fore-and-aft sail is carried.

INLAND

Subpart II
Conduct of Vessels in Sight of One Another

RULE 11. Application

Rules in this **subpart** apply to vessels in sight of one another.

RULE 12. Sailing Vessels

(a) When two sailing vessels are approaching one another, so as to involve risk of collision, one of them shall keep out of the way of the other as follows:

(i) when each has the wind on a different side, the vessel which has the wind on the port side shall keep out of the way of the other;

(ii) when both have the wind on the same side, the vessel which is to windward shall keep out of the way of the vessel which is to leeward;

(iii) if a vessel with the wind on the port side sees a vessel to windward and cannot determine with certainty whether the other vessel has the wind on the port or on the starboard side, she shall keep out of the way of the other.

(b) For the purposes of this Rule the windward side shall be deemed to be the side opposite to that on which the mainsail is carried or, in the case of a square-rigged vessel, the side opposite to that on which the largest fore-and-aft sail is carried.

COMMENTS

Rule 11

This is the first Rule in Section II which includes Rules 11–18. Section II applies only when vessels are "in sight of one another." Remember that this term is defined in Rule 3(k) as existing "only when one can be observed visually from the other." A radar contact is not a visual contact. If vessels are not "in sight," Section III (Rule 19) applies.

Rule 12

When two sailing vessels are approaching with risk of collision, one (not both) of them is required to maneuver to keep clear.

When the sailing vessels have the wind on different sides, the one with the wind to port (on a "port tack") must keep out of the way of the one with the wind to starboard (on a "starboard tack"). What if the wind is directly astern? Paragraph (b) instructs us that the windward side would be considered to be the side opposite to that on which to the mainsail or the largest sail is carried.

If both vessels are on the same tack, the one to windward must keep clear. She is the more maneuverable of the two, because she could "steal the wind" of the leeward vessel.

Paragraph (a)(iii) describes a potentially ambiguous case (likely at night). A vessel on the port tack sees a vessel to windward on an unknown tack. If the vessel to windward is also on the port tack, the windward vessel would give-way. However, if the vessel to windward has the wind to starboard, the vessel to leeward would keep clear. If in doubt assume that you must keep clear and act accordingly.

There are exceptions to Rule 12. If one sailing vessel is overtaking another, the overtaking vessel must keep clear no matter what tack she is on or which vessel is to windward (Rule 13). If one sailing vessel is restricted to a narrow channel, one outside the channel must not impede her progress (Rule 9(b)). If a sailing vessel is burdened (fishing, restricted in ability to maneuver, or not under command), another sailing vessel would have to keep clear (Rule 18).

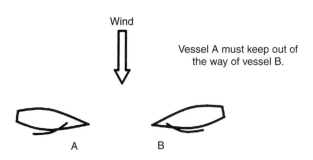

Wind

Vessel A must keep out of the way of vessel B.

A   B

Figure 5. Two sailing vessels on opposite tack.

RULE 13. Overtaking

(a) Notwithstanding anything contained in **the Rules of Part B, Sections I and II,** any vessel overtaking any other shall keep out of the way of the vessel being overtaken.

(b) A vessel shall be deemed to be overtaking when coming up with another vessel from a direction more than 22.5 degrees abaft her beam, that is, in such a position with reference to the vessel she is overtaking, that at night she would be able to see only the sternlight of that vessel but neither of her sidelights.

(c) When a vessel is in any doubt as to whether she if overtaking another, she shall assume that this is the case and act accordingly.

(d) Any subsequent alteration of the bearing between the two vessels shall not make the overtaking vessel a crossing vessel within the meaning of these Rules or relieve her of the duty of keeping clear of the overtaken vessel until she is finally past and clear.

RULE 13. Overtaking

(a) Notwithstanding anything contained in **Rules 4 through 18,** any vessel overtaking any other shall keep out of the way of the vessel being overtaken.

(b) A vessel shall be deemed to be overtaking when coming up with another vessel from a direction more than 22.5 degrees abaft her beam; that is, in such a position with reference to the vessel she is overtaking, that at night she would be able to see only the sternlight of that vessel but neither of her sidelights.

(c) When a vessel is in any doubt as to whether she is overtaking another, she shall assume that this is the case and act accordingly.

(d) Any subsequent alteration of the bearing between the two vessels shall not make the overtaking vessel a crossing vessel within the meaning of these Rules or relieve her of the duty of keeping clear of the overtaken vessel until she is finally past and clear.

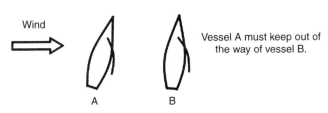

Wind

Vessel A must keep out of
the way of vessel B.

A   B

Figure 6. Two sailing vessels on the same tack.

Rule 13

The use of "notwithstanding" indicates that Rule 13 takes precedence over any other Rule in Sections (or, Subparts) I and II. Any vessel overtaking any other must give way, as long as the vessels are in sight of one another. A vessel not under command must keep out of the way of a power-driven vessel she is overtaking. A sailing vessel overtaking another must keep clear no matter who is to windward or on the port tack.

When does an overtaking situation exist? First of all, a vessel must be "coming up," that is getting closer. A vessel that is moving away from another cannot be overtaking her. The second requirement is that the vessel is approaching another from a direction more than $22.5°$ (2 points of the compass) abaft the beam. At night it should be fairly easy to determine if you are overtaking another vessel; you would see her sternlight but not her sidelights. During the day it can be more difficult to determine. If the aspect (your relative bearing from the other vessel) of the vessel ahead isn't visually obvious it can be calculated if you know her course. ($R = T - S$. Your **R**elative bearing = your **T**rue bearing – her **S**hip's heading.) If there is any doubt about whether or not you are overtaking, assume that you are and keep out of the way (Paragraph (c)).

We must be particularly wary in borderline crossing/overtaking cases. What type of situation is it when one power-driven vessel is approaching another from $21°$ abaft the starboard beam with risk of collision? Technically, it is a crossing situation (Rule 15) and the vessel to port should keep clear. If, however, the vessel to starboard is in doubt about the situation, she might assume that she is overtaking and, therefore, would maneuver. If both vessels alter to attempt to cross the other's stern a very dangerous situation would quickly develop! Alternatively, the vessel to port might feel she is being overtaken while the one to starboard thinks they are crossing. In this case, both vessels might stand-on with equally bad results! It should be clear that in this situation we must be extra cautious,

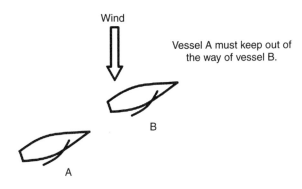

Wind

Vessel A must keep out of
the way of vessel B.

B

A

Figure 7. Overtaking situation.

RULE 14. Head-on Situation

(a) When two power-driven vessels are meeting on reciprocal or nearly reciprocal courses so as to involve risk of collision each shall alter her course to starboard so that each shall pass on the port side of the other.

(b) Such a situation shall be deemed to exist when a vessel sees the other ahead or nearly ahead and by night she could see the masthead lights of the other in a line or nearly in a line and/or both sidelights and by day she observes the corresponding aspect of the other vessel.

(c) When a vessel is in any doubt as to whether such a situation exists she shall assume that it does exist and act accordingly.

RULE 14. Head-on Situation

(a) **Unless otherwise agreed,** when two power-driven vessels are meeting on reciprocal or nearly reciprocal courses so as to involve risk of collision each shall alter her course to starboard so that each shall pass on the port side of the other.

(b) Such a situation shall be deemed to exist when a vessel sees the other ahead or nearly ahead and by night she could see the masthead lights of the other in a line or nearly in a line or both sidelights and by day she observes the corresponding aspect of the other vessel.

(c) When a vessel is in any doubt as to whether such a situation exists she shall assume that it does exist and act accordingly.

(d) Notwithstanding paragraph (a) of this Rule, a power-driven vessel operating on the Great Lakes, Western Rivers, or waters specified by the Secretary, and proceeding downbound with a following current shall have the right-of-way over an upbound vessel, shall propose the manner of passage, and shall initiate the maneuvering signals prescribed by Rule 34(a)(i), as appropriate.

COMMENTS

use the VHF bridge-to-bridge radio early and clearly, sound whistle signals to communicate our actions or intentions, and take early and substantial action to remain well clear.

Rule 13(d) states that an overtaking vessel cannot become a crossing vessel once a situation has been established. The reason for this is that otherwise an overtaking vessel might change her status from give-way to stand-on.

The overtaking vessel is not finished with her obligation to keep clear until "finally past and clear." The distance between the two vessels must be increasing with no risk of collision.

Rule 14

This Rule applies in very limited circumstances. This Rule is in Section II of Part B, so the vessels must be in sight of one another. If not, see Rule 19. Two vessels need to be involved and they both must be power-driven. If one or both fall into a different category, we must look to other Rules. In addition, they must be meeting on reciprocal or nearly reciprocal courses. And, the situation must involve risk of collision. (See Rule 7.)

Paragraph (b) gives additional criteria to help us evaluate when head-on situations exist. The vessels must see each other ahead or nearly ahead. If that is so, because they are on reciprocal courses (or nearly so), they would be able to see each other's masts in a line, and/or both her sidelights at night. Annex I, 9(a)(i) states that sidelights should be visible between 1° and 3° outside their prescribed sector. Accordingly, it is possible that one could see both sidelights when within 3° of either bow. A definition of "nearly ahead," then, could be "within 3° of the bow." A vessel seeing both sidelights at an angle of more than 3° or 4° on either bow should determine that she is not involved in a head-on situation. A vessel seeing only a single sidelight dead ahead should come to the same conclusion.

The one circumstance that can lead to confusion in a head-on situation involves a vessel or vessels being affected by wind or current. In this case, the course made good may differ substantially from the vessel's heading. It is clear from the Rule that the head-on situation is determined by the vessel's head, and not the course made good. Watch officers and vessel operators should make every attempt to be aware of prevailing current, so that they can make a better assessment of the situation. Course changes may have to be larger than normal to compensate for the leeway encountered.

When in a head-on situation in international waters, both vessels must maneuver. There is no stand-on vessel. Both are required to alter to starboard and pass port to port, even if they were initially on each other's starboard bow. Under International Rules, there is no provision for anything other than a port to port passing in this situation.

The Inland Rules allow for a few more options. Paragraph (a) begins with "unless otherwise agreed." If an agreement is made by bridge-to-bridge radio or by whistle, vessels meeting in inland waters can pass starboard to starboard. When power-driven vessels are meeting on the Great Lakes, Western Rivers, or waters specified by the Secretary (see Rule 9 comments) with a current, the downbound vessel has the right of way and shall propose the manner of passage. And that manner of passage is *not* limited to port to port.

How does 14(d) differ from Rule 9(a)(ii)? Rule 9 applies only to narrow channels while Rule 14(d) is not as limited. Rule 9(a)(ii) enables downbound vessels to propose the place of passage in addition to the manner. Also, Rule 9 states that the upbound vessel "shall hold as necessary" while Rule 14 does not.

43

RULE 15. Crossing Situation

When two power-driven vessels are crossing so as to involve risk of collision, the vessel which has the other on her own starboard side shall keep out of the way and shall, if the circumstances of the case admit, avoid crossing ahead of the other vessel.

RULE 15. Crossing Situation

(a) When two power-driven vessels are crossing so as to involve risk of collision, the vessel which has the other on her starboard side shall keep out of the way and shall, if the circumstances of the case admit, avoid crossing ahead of the other vessel.

(b) Notwithstanding paragraph (a), on the Great Lakes, Western Rivers, or water specified by the Secretary, a power-driven vessel crossing a river shall keep out of the way of a power-driven vessel ascending or descending the river.

RULE 16. Action by Give-way Vessel

Every vessel which is directed to keep out of the way of another vessel

RULE 16. Action by Give-way Vessel

Every vessel which is directed to keep out of the way of another vessel

COMMENTS

Both power-driven vessels must come to starboard
and pass port to port.

Figure 8. Head-on situation between power-driven vessels.

If there is any doubt as to whether a head-on situation exists, the watch officer shall assume that it does and react accordingly.

Rule 15

A crossing situation is defined by the process of elimination. When risk-of-collision exists between two power-driven vessels in sight of one another, if the situation does not meet the requirements of an overtaking situation (Rule 13) or a head-on situation (Rule 14), then it must be a crossing situation.

In a crossing situation, the vessel that has the other to starboard shall keep out of the way. In other words, she is the give-way vessel (Rule 16) and the vessel to starboard would stand-on (Rule 17). Whenever possible, the give-way vessel is directed to avoid crossing ahead. Most often, then, she should alter to starboard, slow down or stop as necessary to pass clear astern of the other vessel.

This Rule equally applies to vessels that are underway but not making way. Such a vessel is not allowed to show any special signals or take any special privileges. Therefore, that vessel must be prepared to keep out of the way when involved in a crossing situation as the give-way vessel.

When applying this Rule, it will help to keep in mind the situations that are affected by other Rules as well as this one. In a narrow channel, Rule 9(b) and (d) require small vessels and crossing vessels not to impede vessels that can navigate only within the channel. And, according to Rule 10(j), a vessel of less than 20 meters in length shall not impede a power-driven vessel in a traffic separation scheme. "Not impede" is not the same as "keep out of the way," so those Rules don't automatically give vessels in the channel or separation scheme the right-of-way. See the comments on Rules 9 and 10 for a discussion of this point.

The Inland Rules gives an exception to the Rule. When vessels are in crossing situations on the waters mentioned, a power-driven vessel ascending or descending a river is granted right of way over a vessel crossing the river, no matter which is to starboard. This differs from Rule 9(d). Rule 15(b) applies only in crossing situations while Rule 9(d) applies to other situations as well. Rule 9(d) applies to vessels of any category while Rule 15(b) applies only to power-driven vessels. And Rule 9(d) applies only when one vessel can safely navigate only in a narrow channel while Rule 15(b) applies to any power-driven vessel ascending or descending a river on the specified waters, not just those that are limited to the channel.

Rule 16

This rule is entitled "Action by Give-way Vessel." Although "give-way vessel" isn't explicitly defined anywhere in the Rules, it is clear that the give-way vessel is one that is required to "keep out of the way of another vessel." Four of the other

INTERNATIONAL	INLAND
shall, so far as possible, take early and substantial action to keep well clear.	shall, so far as possible, take early and substantial action to keep well clear.

RULE 17. Action by Stand-on Vessel

(a)(i) Where one of two vessels is to keep out of the way the other shall keep her course and speed.

(ii) The latter vessel may however take action to avoid collision by her maneuver alone, as soon as it becomes apparent to her that the vessel required to keep out of the way is not taking appropriate action in compliance with these Rules.

(b) When, from any cause, the vessel required to keep her course and speed finds herself so close that collision cannot be avoided by the action of the give-way vessel alone, she shall take such action as will best aid to avoid collision.

(c) A power-driven vessel which takes action in a crossing situation in accordance with subparagraph (a)(ii) of this Rule to avoid collision with another power-driven vessel shall, if the circumstances of the case admit, not alter course to port for a vessel on her own port side.

RULE 17. Action by Stand-on Vessel

(a)(i) Where one of two vessels is to keep out of the way, the other shall keep her course and speed.

(ii) The latter vessel may, however, take action to avoid collision by her maneuver alone, as soon as it becomes apparent to her that the vessel required to keep out of the way is not taking appropriate action in compliance with these Rules.

(b) When, from any cause, the vessel required to keep her course and speed finds herself so close that collision cannot be avoided by the action of the give-way vessel alone, she shall take such action as will best aid to avoid collision.

(c) A power-driven vessel which takes action in a crossing situation in accordance with subparagraph (a)(ii) of this Rule to avoid collision with another power-driven vessel shall, if the circumstances of the case admit, not alter course to port for a vessel on her own port side.

COMMENTS

B

Vessel A must keep out of
the way of vessel B.

A

Figure 9. Crossing situation between power-driven vessels.

Steering and Sailing Rules direct vessels to keep out of the way of another: Rule 12—Sailing Vessels, Rule 13—Overtaking, Rule 15—Crossing Situation, and Rule 18— Responsibilities Between Vessels.

Action taken in accordance with this Rule must also comply with the other applicable Rules. The action must fall within the guidelines of Rule 8, since Rule 8 applies in any condition of visibility. Consequently, the action taken must be positive, made in ample time, be readily apparent, result in a safe passing distance, and be checked for effectiveness until the other vessel is clear. Although Rule 16 states only that the vessel must keep clear, she must make certain not to violate any of the other Rules while doing so.

Rule 17

In a situation involving two vessels, when one vessel is required to "keep out of the way of another" that vessel is the "give-way" vessel (see comments on Rule 16). The other vessel in the situation is the "stand-on" vessel. (Rules 2, 14, and 19 don't direct a vessel to "keep out of the way," so in special circumstances, head-on situations and in restricted visibility when vessels aren't in sight of one another there is no stand-on vessel.)

The basic duty of the stand-on vessel is to maintain her course and speed. By doing so, she makes the job of the give-way vessel relatively easy. "Keep her course and speed" means just that in open waters. In rivers or channels the stand-on vessel must maneuver as expected in the situation. If the channel turns, the stand-on vessel must turn to keep in the channel.

At first glance, the job of the stand-on vessel seems very straightforward: maintain course and speed. It is a bit more complicated than that, however. There can be up to four distinct stages in a situation involving Risk of Collision and the duties and/or options of the stand-on vessel differ in each stage.

The first stage occurs before risk of collision exists. While the vessels are still a good distance apart, the would-be stand-on vessel is free to maneuver. So, if you are coming up on a waypoint and a crossing vessel is still 15 miles to port, go ahead and turn. Risk of Collision doesn't exist yet, so Rule 17 doesn't apply yet. (Note, though, that Rule 7 doesn't specify the range that Risk of Collision begins to exist. So, this is left to the good judgment of the mariner or the judge, should a collision occur.)

The second stage begins once Risk of Collision exists. At that time, the stand-on vessel must maintain course and speed. The give-way vessel must have an adequate opportunity to take appropriate action to keep out of the way. If the stand-on vessel takes action other than to hold course and speed in this stage, it will undoubtedly be held liable for any subsequent catastrophe resulting from that action.

47

(d) This Rule does not relieve the give-way vessel of her obligation to keep out of the way.

RULE 18. Responsibilities Between Vessels

Except where Rules 9, 10 and 13 otherwise require:

(d) This Rule does not relieve the give-way vessel of her obligation to keep out of the way.

RULE 18. Responsibilities Between Vessels

Except where Rules 9, 10, and 13 otherwise require:

COMMENTS

A stand-on vessel *may* take action to avoid collision as soon as it becomes apparent to her that the give-way vessel is not taking appropriate action in the situation. This is the third stage. The give-way vessel is required to "take early and substantial action to keep well clear." (Rule 16) If the give-way vessel's action isn't early or substantial enough, the stand-on vessel is permitted, not required, to act.

This Rule does not mention sounding the signal of doubt (danger signal) prescribed in Rule 34(d). However, the stand-on vessel would usually be in doubt as to whether the give-way vessel is taking sufficient action before becoming certain that she is not. In this case, the vessel in doubt must sound at least five short and rapid blasts on the whistle (Rule 34(d)). When sounded by a stand-on vessel in an approaching situation, this signal may alert the other vessel to the fact that reasonable doubt exists as to whether she is fulfilling her obligations according to the Rules. If the danger signal just described has the desired effect, further action by the stand-on vessel may be unnecessary.

When the stand-on vessel has determined that the give-way vessel is not taking appropriate action to avoid collision, she may herself maneuver to achieve that end. The only restriction placed on this action is that, if she is power-driven, she should avoid altering course to port for a power-driven vessel on her own port side. One obvious reason for this requirement is that, since the give-way vessel may still decide to take action, and since the Rules discourage the give-way vessel from crossing ahead of the other (Rule 15), she would likely change course to starboard. If the stand-on vessel was simultaneously changing course to port, the result could be most unfortunate.

It should be noted that though the stand-on vessel isn't required to maneuver at this stage, if a collision did ultimately occur, she might well be found at least partly at fault for not doing so.

The final stage is when the stand-on vessel "finds herself so close that collision cannot be avoided by the action of the give-way vessel alone." This is the point known as "in extremis," and it should be pointed out that at this point collision can still be avoided, but not by the action of the give-way vessel only. Once in extremis, and only then, the stand-on vessel is required by the Rules to take action. At that point there are no forbidden actions. The stand-on vessel must maneuver as necessary to avoid the collision or at least minimize the resulting damage.

To summarize: While the vessels are still a good distance apart, both vessels are free to maneuver. Once Risk of Collision exists, the stand-on vessel must maintain course and speed. Once it becomes apparent that the give-way vessel is not taking appropriate action, the stand-on vessel *may* maneuver as long as she doesn't turn to port for a vessel on her own port side. Once the vessels are "in extremis" the stand-on vessel *must* take whatever action is needed to avoid the collision or lessen its effects.

Paragraph (d) of this Rule reminds the give-way vessel that, regardless of actions taken by the stand-on vessel, nothing relieves the give-way vessel of her obligation to keep clear and, under normal circumstances, to bear most, if not all, the blame for any resulting mishap.

Rule 18

This is the final rule of Section II of the Steering and Sailing Rules and applies when vessels are in sight of one another. It establishes a "pecking order," that is, a hierarchy of responsibilities between vessels, directing some to "keep out of the way" of others based on their inherent maneuvering limitations. The Rule begins with the

(a) A power-driven vessel underway shall keep out of the way of:
    (i) a vessel not under command;
    (ii) a vessel restricted in her ability to maneuver;
    (iii) a vessel engaged in fishing;
    (iv) a sailing vessel.

(b) A sailing vessel underway shall keep out of the way of:
    (i) a vessel not under command;
    (ii) a vessel restricted in her ability to maneuver;
    (iii) a vessel engaged in fishing.

(c) A vessel engaged in fishing when underway shall, so far as possible, keep out of the way of:
    (i) a vessel not under command;
    (ii) a vessel restricted in her ability to maneuver.

(d)(i) Any vessel other than a vessel not under command or a vessel restricted in her ability to maneuver shall, if the circumstances of

---

(a) A power-driven vessel underway shall keep out of the way of:
    (i) a vessel not under command;
    (ii) a vessel restricted in her ability to maneuver;
    (iii) a vessel engaged in fishing; and
    (iv) a sailing vessel.

(b) A sailing vessel underway shall keep out of the way of:
    (i) a vessel not under command;
    (ii) a vessel restricted in her ability to maneuver; and
    (iii) a vessel engaged in fishing.

(c) A vessel engaged in fishing when underway shall, so far as possible, keep out of the way of:
    (i) a vessel not under command; and
    (ii) a vessel restricted in her ability to maneuver.

phrase "except where Rules 9, 10, and 13 otherwise require." The Rule, then, does not cover all situations involving the vessels mentioned. Rule 9 states that sailing vessels and crossing vessels shall not impede vessels that can only navigate safely in a narrow channel and that vessels engaged in fishing not impede any vessel at all in a channel. Rule 10, Traffic Separation Schemes, prohibits vessels less than 20 meters in length and sailing vessels from impeding power-driven vessels following a traffic lane while vessels engaged in fishing shouldn't impede any vessels in a lane. And, Rule 13 requires a vessel to keep out of the way of any vessel she is overtaking.

In order to claim a privilege by virtue of Rule 18, a vessel must meet the appropriate definition of Rule 3. In addition she must be showing the appropriate lights and/or shapes so that other vessels can readily recognize her condition. Since special lights and shapes are sometimes difficult to distinguish, the stand-on vessel in these situations should be aware that the other vessel may not recognize the situation and should be ready to sound the danger signal (Rule 34(d)) if the give-way vessel does not seem to be taking appropriate action.

Because of the operational restrictions present in any situation involving any of the vessels mentioned by this Rule, the give-way vessel cannot reasonably expect that the stand-on vessel will be able to hold its course and speed as required by Rule 17(a)(ii), unless the hampered vessel is dead in the water. The give-way vessel should give as wide a berth as possible in these situations, realizing that the stand-on vessel may not have much control over its own movements, and that the entire burden of avoiding collision may well fall to the give-way vessel.

(a) A power-driven vessel shall keep out of the way of all other categories of vessels except seaplanes on the surface, wing-in-ground vessels taking off and landing (International Rules), and any vessel overtaking her. This applies anytime the power-driven vessel is underway, even if she is dead in the water. If such a vessel sees a vessel with greater precedence approaching, she must make way to keep clear.

(b) To qualify as a sailing vessel, the vessel needs to be propelled by sail alone. A sailboat using her engine for propulsion is a power-driven vessel. If under sail alone, she would keep out of the way of a vessel not under command, a vessel restricted in her ability to maneuver, a vessel engaged in fishing, and a power-driven vessel she is overtaking (Rule 13).

(c) Under most circumstances a vessel engaged in fishing could consider herself the stand-on vessel. However, she should not take her privilege for granted, but should keep a sharp lookout lest the other vessel involved be even more privileged (such as a vessel restricted in her ability to maneuver).

Paragraph (c) states that a fishing vessel "shall, so far as possible, keep out of the way . . . ." The Rule recognizes that a vessel engaged in fishing may find it almost impossible to keep out of the way of another vessel. This depends, usually, on the type of gear employed by the fishing vessel. If the fishing vessel is indeed unable to keep out of the way as required, the situation would qualify as a special circumstance.

(d) The International Rules require that vessels other than vessels not under command or restricted in ability to maneuver avoid impeding a vessel constrained by her draft. As discussed in Rule 8, this does not make the vessel constrained by her draft the stand-on vessel. Rule 3(h) states that a vessel constrained by her draft must be

INTERNATIONAL	INLAND

the case admit, avoid impeding the safe passage of a vessel constrained by her draft, exhibiting the signals in Rule 28.
(ii) A vessel constrained by her draft shall navigate with particular caution having full regard to her special condition.

(e) A seaplane on the water shall, in general, keep well clear of all vessels and avoid impeding their navigation. In circumstances, however, where risk of collision exists, she shall comply with the Rules of this Part.

(f)(i) A WIG craft shall, when taking off, landing and in flight near the surface, keep well clear of all other vessels and avoid impeding their navigation;

(ii) a WIG craft operating on the water surface shall comply with the Rules of this Part as a power-driven vessel.

(d) A seaplane on the water shall, in general, keep well clear of all vessels and avoid impeding their navigation. In circumstances, however, where risk of collision exists, she shall comply with the Rules of this Part.

Section III
Conduct of Vessels in Restricted Visibility

Subpart III
Conduct of Vessels in Restricted Visibility

RULE 19. Conduct of Vessels in Restricted Visibility

(a) This Rule applies to vessels not in sight of one another when navigating in or near an area of restricted visibility.

(b) Every vessel shall proceed at a safe speed adapted to the prevailing circumstances and conditions of restricted visibility. A power-driven vessel shall have her engines ready for immediate maneuver.

RULE 19. Conduct of Vessels in Restricted Visibility

(a) This Rule applies to vessels not in sight of one another when navigating in or near an area of restricted visibility.

(b) Every vessel shall proceed at a safe speed adapted to the prevailing circumstances and conditions of restricted visibility. A power-driven vessel shall have her engines ready for immediate maneuver.

power-driven. In a situation involving a sailing vessel and a vessel constrained by her draft, the sailing vessel must avoid impeding the deep draft vessel, while the constrained vessel must keep out of the way of the sailing vessel once risk of collision occurs. It is important to note that local rules might apply to this situation. In some areas, a vessel constrained by her draft is given the right of way. See Rule 8 comments for further discussion of this point.

There is no order of precedence between a vessel restricted in ability to maneuver and a vessel not under command; they have equal status. A situation involving two hampered vessels when responsibility between them isn't specified in the Rules (e.g., two fishing vessels or a vessel not under command and a vessel restricted in her ability to maneuver) would be a special circumstance. The vessels should take whatever action is necessary to avoid collision. Most often, a course change to starboard would be the best option.

(e) International/(d) Inland. Seaplanes on the water should keep clear of everyone. The exception would be if the seaplane was being overtaken.

(f) A Wing in Ground (WIG) craft while taking off or landing has the lowest precedence of all vessels. Rule 23 (c) (International) requires such craft to exhibit an all-around flashing red light to indicate her status. While operating on the surface, her status (and lights) changes to that of a power-driven vessel.

Rule 19

Rule 19 is the first and only rule in Section III of Part B. It applies anytime vessels are not in sight of one another because of restricted visibility. We may tend to think this Rule applies at any time visibility is restricted, but such is not the case. If, when operating in restricted visibility, the other vessel can be seen visually, this Rule does not apply. Therefore, it is vital that we employ the Rule only when we cannot visually observe the other vessel. If another vessel is detected by radar or hearing alone, Rule 19 must be followed. But, the moment that the other vessel breaks out of the fog bank and is sighted the other Steering and Sailing Rules come into effect.

Rule 19 applies to vessels "navigating in or near an area of restricted visibility." This means that if you are in an area of good visibility but can see a fog bank, rainstorm, or other area of restricted visibility, you are responsible to abide by the provisions of this Rule. Remember, there may be a vessel in the fog bank not aware of your presence.

The Rule addresses the subject of safe speed, which is to be "adapted to the prevailing circumstances and conditions of restricted visibility." This paragraph is

INTERNATIONAL	INLAND
(c) Every vessel shall have due regard to the prevailing circumstances and conditions of restricted visibility when complying with **the Rules of Section I of this Part.**	(c) Every vessel shall have due regard to the prevailing circumstances and conditions of restricted visibility when complying with **Rules 4 through 10.**
(d) A vessel which detects by radar alone the presence of another vessel shall determine if a close-quarters situation is developing and/or risk of collision exists. If so, she shall take avoiding action in ample time, provided that when such action consists of an alteration of course, so far as possible the following shall be avoided:	(d) A vessel which detects by radar alone the presence of another vessel shall determine if a close-quarters situation is developing or risk of collision exists. If so, she shall take avoiding action in ample time, provided that when such action consists of an alteration of course, so far as possible the following shall be avoided:
(i) an alteration of course to port for a vessel forward of the beam, other than for a vessel being overtaken;	(i) an alteration of course to port for a vessel forward of the beam, other than for a vessel being overtaken; **and**
(ii) an alteration of course towards a vessel abeam or abaft the beam.	(ii) an alteration of course toward a vessel abeam or abaft the beam.

redundant because Rule 6 already required all vessels to proceed at safe speed at all times and the state of visibility is the first factor to be considered in determining what that speed is. Rule 19 reminds us of that requirement and calls to our attention the fact that safe speed is likely to be slower as visibility drops. Since to apply Rule 19 we have already admitted that the visibility is restricted to such a degree that we cannot see other vessels, we must admit that when we adapt the safe speed of Rule 6 to the visibility conditions required by Rule 19, the result is a reduced speed requirement. In almost every case of a collision in fog, one or both of the vessels is cited for proceeding at an excessive rate of speed for the existing visibility conditions.

The speed requirement is coupled with the requirement that "a power-driven vessel shall have her engines ready for immediate maneuver." This requirement should be considered to apply to any vessel fitted with an engine, including fishing vessels, vessels restricted in ability to maneuver, and vessels not under command. Remember, Rule 18 doesn't apply in restricted visibility, so hampered vessels get no special privileges.

Paragraph (c) is a reminder that, since the Rules (4 through 10) in Section I apply in any condition of visibility, Rule 19 applies in addition to (and not separate from) those Rules when visibility is restricted. We need to maintain a proper lookout (Rule 5) and determine if risk of collision exists (Rule 6) using "all available means appropriate in the prevailing circumstances." As visibility drops, our vigilance must increase. Watch officers should keep a close watch on the radar and plot as necessary. An extra lookout should be posted at the bow. Any action taken to avoid collision in restricted visibility should, when possible, be taken earlier and result in a greater passing distance than would be necessary when in sight. Any course change taken should be large enough to be readily apparent on radar. (Rule 8)

Paragraph (d) addresses the problem of a situation involving risk of collision in restricted visibility. Such a situation can be detected only by radar. If you can determine by radar that a close-quarters situation is developing, you are required to "take avoiding action in ample time." It does not matter where the other vessel is located, or whether your vessel would ordinarily have the right of way. There is no right of way, no stand-on vessel, no give-way vessel, and no time for playing waiting games.

This Rule takes the negative approach and tells you what you should avoid doing. The options available to you are the following:

1. If the vessel is anywhere forward of either beam, you may

- adjust your speed
- alter course to starboard
- do both of the above in any proportion you see fit

The Rule states that the exception to this course of action is an instance when you are overtaking another vessel. To overtake another vessel in visibility restricted to the extent that you cannot see her is an extremely hazardous maneuver and should be avoided. When it is determined that such a situation exists, the overtaking vessel should take early action to give the other vessel plenty of sea room. Rule 13, Overtaking, applies only when vessels are in sight of one another. In restricted visibility, a vessel being overtaken isn't required to stand-on and should be prepared to maneuver as necessary to ensure a safe passing distance.

(e) Except where it has been determined that a risk of collision does not exist, every vessel which hears apparently forward of her beam the fog signal of another vessel, or which cannot avoid a close-quarters situation with another vessel forward of her beam, shall reduce her speed to the minimum at which she can be kept on her course. She shall if necessary take all her way off and in any event navigate with extreme caution until danger of collision is over.	(e) Except where it has been determined that a risk of collision does not exist, every vessel which hears apparently forward of her beam the fog signal of another vessel, or which cannot avoid a close-quarters situation with another vessel forward of her beam, shall reduce her speed to the minimum at which she can be kept on course. She shall if necessary take all her way off and, in any event, navigate with extreme caution until danger of collision is over.

PART C
LIGHTS AND SHAPES

RULE 20. Application

(a) Rules in this Part shall be complied with in all weathers.

(b) The Rules concerning lights shall be complied with from sunset to sunrise, and during such times no other lights shall be exhibited, except such lights as cannot be mistaken for the lights specified in these Rules or do not impair their visibility or distinctive character, or interfere with the keeping of a proper look-out.

(c) The lights prescribed by these Rules shall, if carried, also be exhibited from sunrise to sunset in restricted visibility and may be exhibited in all other circumstances when it is deemed necessary.

PART C
LIGHTS AND SHAPES

RULE 20. Application

(a) Rules in this Part shall be complied with in all weathers.

(b) The Rules concerning lights shall be complied with from sunset to sunrise, and during such times no other lights shall be exhibited, except such lights as cannot be mistaken for the lights specified in these Rules or do not impair their visibility or distinctive character, or interfere with the keeping of a proper look-out.

(c) The lights prescribed by these Rules shall, if carried, also be exhibited from sunrise to sunset in restricted visibility and may be exhibited in all other circumstances when it is deemed necessary.

COMMENTS

2. If the vessel is abaft your beam, you may

- adjust your speed
- alter course away from the vessel
- do both of the above in any proportion you see fit

The actions recommended by this Rule will result in the same passing processes as the actions required by vessels in sight of one another. They are simply being stated in a different way.

Remember that when the vessels come in sight of one another, Rule 19 no longer applies, and the vessels must then apply the Rules for vessels in sight.

Paragraph (e) requires that, unless you have determined that there is no risk of collision, anytime you hear a fog signal that is apparently coming from a direction forward of the beam, you are to slow to bare steerageway and take all way off your vessel, if necessary. It is sometimes a temptation to alter course away from a fog signal. This temptation should be avoided at all costs. Fog signals should not be used to determine a vessel's position. A fog signal's direction may be especially deceptive if the person hearing the sound is high on the vessel. Vessels are also to slow or stop as necessary if a close quarters situation can't be avoided with a vessel forward of the beam, even when that situation is detected by radar. This could occur when the vessels involved cannot alter course because of lack of sea room. If nothing else, slowing or stopping will greatly minimize the damage if a collision actually occurred.

Vessels that are required by paragraph (e) to slow or stop are also required to "navigate with extreme caution until danger of collision is over." Therefore, a vessel that, upon hearing a fog signal forward of the beam, came to a stop for a few seconds and then immediately went full head again would be violating both the spirit and the letter of the Rule.

Rule 20

Rule 20 is the first Rule of Part C (Rules 20–31). A thorough understanding of lights (and shapes) is vital because they communicate the size, type, and direction of travel of vessels, all details we must know in order to apply the Steering and Sailing Rules of Part B.

This Rule seems fairly clear. First of all, Rules 20–31 must be complied with in all weathers; in other words, all the time. The lights required by Part C must be exhibited at night or any time when the visibility is restricted. Many vessels leave their lights on anytime they are underway: day or night, clear or foul. That is a practice that is hard to fault. Other lights may be on as well, as long as they can't be mistaken for the required lights, don't block or overpower the required lights, or interfere with the keeping of a proper lookout.

Required shapes must be displayed during the day even when visibility is restricted.

Annex I of the Rules contains the technical specifications of the required lights, including intensity, color, location, and spacing.

For convenience the many Rules with lighting requirements for vessels have been arranged in the form of the table that follows.

INTERNATIONAL	INLAND
(d) The Rules concerning shapes shall be complied with by day.	(d) The Rules concerning shapes shall be complied with by day.
(e) The lights and shapes specified in these Rules shall comply with the provisions of Annex I **to** these **Regulations.**	(e) The lights and shapes specified in these Rules shall comply with the provisions of Annex I **of** these **Rules.**

COMMENTS

Vessel	Underway and Making Way	Underway and Stopped	At Anchor
Power-driven vessel ≥ 50 m (International and Inland)	• Forward masthead light • After masthead light • Sidelights • Sternlight	• Forward masthead light • After masthead light • Sidelights • Sternlight	• Forward all-round white light • After all-round white light • Working lights (optional for vessels < 100 m)
Power-driven vessel < 50 m (International and Inland)	• Forward masthead light • After masthead light (optional) • Sidelights • Sternlight	• Forward masthead light • After masthead light (optional) • Sidelights • Sternlight	• All-round white light where best seen or, • Forward all-round white light • After all-round white light • Working lights (optional)
Power-driven vessel < 12 m (International and Inland)	• Forward masthead light • After masthead light (optional) • Sidelights • Sternlight or, • All-round white light • Sidelights	• Forward masthead light • After masthead light (optional) • Sidelights • Sternlight or, • All-round white light • Sidelights	• All-round white light where best seen or, • Forward all-round white light • After all-round white light • Working lights (optional)
Power-driven vessel < 7 m with maximum speed < 7 knots (International)	• Forward masthead light • After masthead light (optional) • Sidelights (if practicable) • Sternlight or, • All-round white light • Sidelights (if practicable)	• Forward masthead light • After masthead light (optional) • Sidelights (if practicable) • Sternlight or, • All-round white light • Sidelights (if practicable)	• All-round white light where best seen or, • Forward all-round white light • After all-round white light • Working lights (optional)
Air cushion vessel in the nondisplacement mode (International and Inland)	• Forward masthead light • After masthead light (optional < 50 m) • Sidelights • Sternlight • All-round flashing yellow light	• Forward masthead light • After masthead light (optional < 50 m) • Sidelights • Sternlight • All-round flashing yellow light	• Not applicable
Power-driven vessel (Great Lakes only)	• Forward masthead light • After masthead light (optional < 50 m) • Sidelights • Sternlight or, • Forward masthead light • All-round white light • Sidelights	• Forward masthead light • After masthead light (optional < 50 m) • Sidelights • Sternlight or, • Forward masthead light • All-round white light • Sidelights	• All-round white light where best seen (if < 50 m) or, • Forward all-round white light • After all-round white light • Working lights (optional if < 100 m)

Vessel	Underway and Making Way	Underway and Stopped	At Anchor
Power-driven vessel < 50 m towing astern. Length of tow ≤ 200 m	• Two masthead lights in a vertical line instead of either the forward or after masthead light • After masthead light (optional) • Sidelights • Sternlight • Towing light above the sternlight	• Two masthead lights in a vertical line instead of either the forward or after masthead light • After masthead light (optional) • Sidelights • Sternlight • Towing light above the sternlight	• Not applicable
Power-driven vessel ≥ 50 m towing astern. Length of tow ≤ 200 m	• Two masthead lights in a vertical line instead of either the forward or after masthead light • Forward or after masthead light • Sidelights • Sternlight • Towing light above the sternlight	• Two masthead lights in a vertical line instead of either the forward or after masthead light • Forward or after masthead light • Sidelights • Sternlight • Towing light above the sternlight	• Not applicable
Power-driven vessel < 50 m towing astern. Length of tow > 200 m	• Three masthead lights in a vertical line instead of either the forward or after masthead light • After masthead light (optional) • Sidelights • Sternlight • Towing light above the sternlight	• Three masthead lights in a vertical line instead of either the forward or after masthead light • After masthead light (optional) • Sidelights • Sternlight • Towing light above the sternlight	• Not applicable
Power-driven vessel ≥ 50 m towing astern. Length of tow > 200 m	• Three masthead lights in a vertical line instead of either the forward or after masthead light • Forward or after masthead light • Sidelights • Sternlight • Towing light above the sternlight	• Three masthead lights in a vertical line instead of either the forward or after masthead light • Forward or after masthead light • Sidelights • Sternlight • Towing light above the sternlight	• Not applicable
Power-driven vessel < 50 m pushing ahead or towing alongside (International)	• Two masthead lights in a vertical line instead of either the forward or after masthead light • After masthead light (optional) • Sidelights • Sternlight	• Two masthead lights in a vertical line instead of either the forward or after masthead light • After masthead light (optional) • Sidelights • Sternlight	• All-round white light where best seen or, • Forward all-round white light • After all-round white light • Working lights (optional)

Vessel	Underway and Making Way	Underway and Stopped	At Anchor
Power-driven vessel ≥ 50 m pushing ahead or towing alongside (International)	• Two masthead lights in a vertical line instead of either the forward or after masthead light • Forward or after masthead light • Sidelights • Sternlight	• Two masthead lights in a vertical line instead of either the forward or after masthead light • Forward or after masthead light • Sidelights • Sternlight	• Forward all-round white light • After all-round white light • Working lights (optional for vessels < 100 m)
Power-driven vessel < 50 m pushing ahead or towing alongside (Inland)	• Two masthead lights in a vertical line instead of either the forward or after masthead light • After masthead light (optional) • Sidelights • Two towing lights	• Two masthead lights in a vertical line instead of either the forward or after masthead light • After masthead light (optional) • Sidelights • Two towing lights	• All-round white light where best seen or, • Forward all-round white light • After all-round white light • Working lights (optional)
Power-driven vessel ≥ 50 m pushing ahead or towing alongside (Inland)	• Two masthead lights in a vertical line instead of either the forward or after masthead light • Forward or after masthead light • Sidelights • Two towing lights	• Two masthead lights in a vertical line instead of either the forward or after masthead light • Forward or after masthead light • Sidelights • Two towing lights	• Forward all-round white light • After all-round white light • Working lights (optional for vessels < 100 m)
Power-driven vessel pushing ahead or towing alongside (Western Rivers)	• Sidelights • Two towing lights	• Sidelights • Two towing lights	• All-round white light where best seen (if < 50 m) or, • Forward all-round white light • After all-round white light • Working lights (optional if < 100 m)
Vessel being towed astern (International and Inland)	• Sidelights • Sternlight	• Sidelights • Sternlight	• Not applicable
Note: Any number of vessels being towed should be lighted as one vessel.			
Vessel being towed alongside (International)	• Sidelights • Sternlight	• Sidelights • Sternlight	• Not applicable
Note: Any number of vessels being towed should be lighted as one vessel.			
Vessel being towed alongside (Inland)	• Sidelights • Sternlight • Special flashing light forward	• Sidelights • Sternlight • Special flashing light forward	• Not applicable
Note: Any number of vessels being towed should be lighted as one vessel.			

COMMENTS

Vessel	Underway and Making Way	Underway and Stopped	At Anchor
Vessel being pushed ahead (International)	• Sidelights	• Sidelights	• Not applicable
Note: Any number of vessels being towed should be lighted as one vessel.			
Vessel being pushed ahead (Inland)	• Sidelights • Special flashing light forward	• Sidelights • Special flashing light forward	• Not applicable
Note: Any number of vessels being towed should be lighted as one vessel. See Rule 24 (e), (f), (g), and (h) for additional requirements for vessels being towed.			
Sailing vessels (International and Inland)	• Sidelights • Sternlight • Red over green all-round lights on the mast (optional)	• Sidelights • Sternlight • Red over green all-round lights on the mast (optional)	• All-round white light where best seen (if < 50 m) or, • Forward all-round white light • After all-round white light • Working lights (optional if < 100 m)
On sailing vessels < 20 m, sidelights and sternlights may be combined into one lantern carried on the mast. If lights are in a combined lantern, the red over green lights may not be carried. Sailing vessels < 7 m may show a white light in time to prevent a collision, instead of the lights, above.			
Vessel engaged in trawling (International and Inland)	• Green over white all-round lights • Masthead light abaft and higher than the green light (optional < 50 m) • Sidelights • Sternlight	• Green over white all-round lights • Masthead light abaft and higher than the green light (optional < 50 m)	• Green over white all-round lights • Masthead light abaft and higher than the green light (optional < 50 m)
Vessel engaged in fishing other than trawling (International and Inland)	• Red over white all-round lights • If gear extends > 150 m, an all-round white light in direction of the gear • Sidelights • Sternlight	• Red over white all-round lights • If gear extends > 150 m, an all-round white light in direction of the gear	• Red over white all-round lights • If gear extends > 150 m, an all-round white light in direction of the gear
Vessel not under command (International and Inland)	• Red over red all-round lights • Sidelights • Sternlight	• Red over red all-round lights	• Not applicable—vessel must be underway
Vessel restricted in her ability to maneuver (except mineclearance) (International and Inland)	• Red over white over red all-round lights • Masthead light(s) • Sidelights • Sternlight	• Red over white over red all-round lights	• All-round white light where best seen (if < 50 m) or, • Forward all-round white light • After all-round white light • Working lights (optional if < 100 m) and, • Red over red all-round lights

Vessel	Underway and Making Way	Underway and Stopped	At Anchor

Vessel engaged in mineclearance (International and Inland)	• Masthead light(s)
	• Sidelights
	• Sternlight
	• Three green lights, one at foremast head and one at each end of the foreyard
		• Masthead light(s)
		• Sidelights
		• Sternlight
		• Three green lights, one at foremast head and one at each end of the foreyard
			• All-round white light where best seen (if < 50 m)
			  or,
			• Forward all-round white light
			• After all-round white light
			• Working lights (optional if < 100 m)
			  and,
			• Three green lights, one at foremast head and one at each end of the foreyard

Vessel towing, unable to deviate from her course (International and Inland)	• Red over white over red all-round lights in addition to the lights required of a towing vessel	• Red over white over red all-round lights in addition to the lights required of a towing vessel	• Not applicable
Vessel engaged in dredging or underwater operations (International and Inland)	• Red over white over red all-round lights • Masthead light(s) • Sidelights • Sternlight • Two red lights in a vertical line on the obstructed side • Two green lights in a vertical line on the clear side	• Red over white over red all-round lights • Two red lights in a vertical line on the obstructed side • Two green lights in a vertical line on the clear side	• Red over white over red all-round lights • Two red lights in a vertical line on the obstructed side • Two green lights in a vertical line on the clear side
Vessel constrained by her draft (International only)	• Forward masthead light • After masthead light (optional < 50 m) • Sidelights • Sternlight • Three red lights in a vertical line	• Forward masthead light • After masthead light (optional < 50 m) • Sidelights • Sternlight • Three red lights in a vertical line	• All-round white light where best seen (if < 50 m) or, • Forward all-round white light • After all-round white light • Working lights (optional if < 100 m)

Pilot Vessel	• White over red all-round lights
	• Sidelights
	• Sternlight
		• White over red all-round lights
		• Sidelights
		• Sternlight
			• All-round white light where best seen (if < 50 m)
			  or,
			• Forward all-round white light
			• After all-round white light
			• Working lights (optional if < 100 m)
			  and,
			• White over red all-round lights

INTERNATIONAL	INLAND

RULE 21. Definitions

RULE 21. Definitions

(a) "Masthead light" means a white light placed over the fore and aft centerline of the vessel showing an unbroken light over an arc of the horizon of 225 degrees and so fixed as to show the light from right ahead to 22.5 degrees abaft the beam on either side of the vessel.

(a) "Masthead light" means a white light placed over the fore and aft centerline of the vessel showing an unbroken light over an arc of the horizon of 225 degrees and so fixed as to show the light from right ahead to 22.5 degrees abaft the beam on either side of the vessel, **except that on a vessel of less than 12 meters in length the masthead light shall be placed as nearly as practicable to the fore and aft centerline of the vessel.**

(b) "Sidelights" means a green light on the starboard side and a red light on the port side each showing an unbroken light over an arc of the horizon of 112.5 degrees and so fixed as to show the light from right ahead to 22.5 degrees abaft the beam on its respective side. In a vessel of less than 20 meters in length the sidelights may be combined in one lantern carried on the fore and aft centerline of the vessel.

(b) "Sidelights" mean a green light on the starboard side and a red light on the port side each showing an unbroken light over an arc of the horizon of 112.5 degrees and so fixed as to show the light from right ahead to 22.5 degrees abaft the beam on its respective side. On a vessel of less than 20 meters in length the sidelights may be combined in one lantern carried on the fore and aft centerline of the vessel, **except that on a vessel of less than 12 meters in length, the sidelights when combined in one lantern shall be placed as nearly as practicable to the fore and aft centerline of the vessel.**

(c) "Sternlight" means a white light placed as nearly as practicable at the stern showing an unbroken light over an arc of the horizon of 135 degrees and so fixed as to show the light 67.5 degrees from right aft on each side of the vessel.

(c) "Sternlight" means a white light placed as nearly as practicable at the stern showing an unbroken light over an arc of the horizon of 135 degrees and so fixed as to show the light 67.5 degrees from right aft on each side of the vessel.

(d) "Towing light" means a yellow light having the same characteristics as the "sternlight" defined in paragraph (c) of this Rule.

(d) "Towing light" means a yellow light having the same characteristics as the "sternlight" defined in paragraph (c) of this Rule.

COMMENTS

Rule 21

This Rule defines terms that will be used in Parts C and D.

(a) Annex I 9(a)(ii) allows masthead lights, sternlights, and sidelights at 22.5° abaft of the beam (but, not forward) to show up to 5° outside the prescribed sectors. The lights potentially overlap, then, allowing an observer around 22.5° abaft another vessel's beam to see masthead lights and a sidelight at the same time as the sternlight.

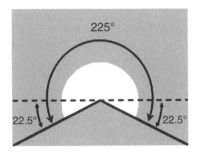

Figure 10. Masthead light.

(b) Annex I 9(a)(i) states that the cutouts for sidelights shall be between 1° and 3° outside the prescribed sector. This ensures that the lights will overlap in the forward direction so that vessels dead ahead at close range will see both lights.

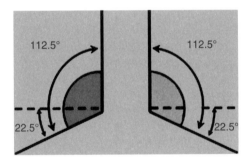

Figure 11. Sidelights.

(c) The sternlight shall be "placed as nearly as practicable at the stern." This acknowledges that it isn't always practicable or possible for craft such as towing vessels, fishing vessels, and vessels of special construction to place the sternlight at the centerline.

(e) "All-round light" means a light showing an unbroken light over an arc of the horizon of 360 degrees.

(f) "Flashing light" means a light flashing at regular intervals at a frequency of 120 flashes or more per minute.

(e) "All-round light" means a light showing an unbroken light over an arc of the horizon of 360 degrees.

(f) "Flashing light" means a light flashing at regular intervals at a frequency of 120 flashes or more per minute.

(g) "Special flashing light" means a yellow light flashing at regular intervals at a frequency of 50 to 70 flashes per minute, placed as far forward and as nearly as practicable on the fore and aft centerline of the tow and showing an unbroken light over an arc of the horizon of not less than 180 degrees nor more than 225 degrees and so fixed as to show the light from right ahead to abeam and no more than 22.5 degrees abaft the beam on either side of the vessel.

RULE 22. Visibility of Lights

The lights prescribed in these Rules shall have an intensity as specified in **Section 8 of** Annex I to these **Regula-**

RULE 22. Visibility of Lights

The lights prescribed in these Rules shall have an intensity as specified in

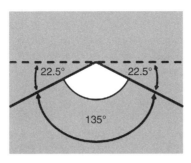

Figure 12. Sternlight.

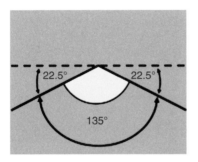

Figure 13. Towing light.

(e) Annex I 9(b)(i) allows an all-roundlight to be obscured up to 6°. If obscured by more than 6°, two lights may be used if they appear as one at a distance of one mile.

Rule 22

See Annex I for vertical and horizontal spacing and intensity requirements for the lights specified. The required minimum ranges are summarized in the following table:

INTERNATIONAL	INLAND
tions so as to be visible at the following minimum ranges:	Annex I to these **Rules,** so as to be visible at the following minimum ranges:

INTERNATIONAL

tions so as to be visible at the following minimum ranges:

(a) In **vessels** of 50 meters or more in length:
— a masthead light, 6 miles;
— a sidelight, 3 miles;
— a sternlight, 3 miles;
— a towing light, 3 miles;
— a white, red, green or yellow all-round light, 3 miles.

(b) In **vessels** of 12 meters or more in length but less than 50 meters in length:
— a masthead light, 5 miles; except that where the length of the vessel is less than 20 meters, 3 miles;
— a sidelight, 2 miles;
— a sternlight, 2 miles;
— a towing light, 2 miles;
— a white, red, green or yellow all-round light, 2 miles.

(c) In **vessels** of less than 12 meters in length:
— a masthead light, 2 miles;
— a sidelight, 1 mile;
— a sternlight, 2 miles;
— a towing light, 2 miles;
— a white, red, green or yellow all-round light, 2 miles.

(d) In inconspicuous, partly submerged **vessels or objects** being towed:
— a white all-round light, 3 miles.

RULE 23. Power-driven Vessels Underway

(a) A power-driven vessel underway shall exhibit:
(i) a masthead light forward;
(ii) a second masthead light abaft of and higher than the forward one; except that a vessel of less than 50 meters in length shall not be obliged to exhibit such light but may do so;
(iii) sidelights; and

INLAND

Annex I to these **Rules,** so as to be visible at the following minimum ranges:

(a) In **a vessel** of 50 meters or more in length:
— a masthead light, 6 miles;
— a sidelight, 3 miles;
— a sternlight, 3 miles;
— a towing light, 3 miles;
— a white, red, green or yellow all-round light, 3 miles; **and**
— **a special flashing light, 2 miles.**

(b) In **a vessel** of 12 meters or more in length but less than 50 meters in length:
— a masthead light, 5 miles; except that where the length of the vessel is less than 20 meters, 3 miles;
— a sidelight, 2 miles;
— a sternlight, 2 miles;
— a towing light, 2 miles;
— a white, red, green or yellow all-round light, 2 miles; **and**
— **a special flashing light, 2 miles.**

(c) In **a vessel** of less than 12 meters in length:
— a masthead light, 2 miles;
— a sidelight, 1 mile;
— a sternlight, 2 miles;
— a towing light, 2 miles;
— a white, red, green or yellow all-round light, 2 miles; **and**
— **a special flashing light, 2 miles.**

(d) In **an** inconspicuous, partly submerged **vessel or object** being towed:
— a white all-round light, 3 miles.

RULE 23. Power-driven Vessels Underway

(a) A power-driven vessel underway shall exhibit:
(i) a masthead light forward;
(ii) a second masthead light abaft of and higher than the forward one; except that a vessel of less than 50 meters in length shall not be obliged to exhibit such light but may do so;
(iii) sidelights; and

COMMENTS

TABLE 1
Range of Visibility of Lights

Length of vessel	≥ 50 m	< 50 m, ≥ 20 m	< 20 m, ≥ 12 m	< 12 m
Masthead Lights	6 nm	5 nm	3 nm	2 nm
Sidelights	3 nm	2 nm	2 nm	1 nm
Sternlight	3 nm	2 nm	2 nm	2 nm
Towing Light	3 nm	2 nm	2 nm	2 nm
All-round Light	3 nm	2 nm	2 nm	2 nm
Special Flashing	2 nm	2 nm	2 nm	2 nm

Lights on inconspicuous, partly submerged objects being towed shall be visible for 3 nm.

Rule 23

Lights required for power-driven vessels depend on the size of the vessel, the location (Great Lakes vs. everywhere else) and mode (displacement or non-displacement). In addition to the lights mentioned here, a power-driven vessel engaged in towing or pushing ahead would also exhibit the lights required by Rule 24.

INTERNATIONAL	INLAND

(iv) a sternlight.

(b) An air-cushion vessel when operating in the nondisplacement mode shall, in addition to the lights prescribed in paragraph (a) of this Rule, exhibit an all-round flashing yellow light.

(c) A WIG craft only when taking off, landing and in flight near the surface shall, in addition to the lights prescribed in paragraph (a) of this Rule, exhibit a high intensity all-round flashing red light.

(d)**(i)** A power-driven vessel of less than 12 meters in length may in lieu of the lights prescribed in paragraph (a) of this Rule exhibit an all-round white light and sidelights;

(ii) a power-driven vessel of less than 7 meters in length whose maximum speed does not exceed 7 knots may in lieu of the lights prescribed in paragraph (a) of this Rule exhibit an all-round white light and shall, if practicable, also exhibit sidelights;

(iii) the masthead light or all-round white light on a power-driven vessel of less than 12 meters in length may be displaced from the fore and aft centerline of the vessel if centerline fitting is not practicable, provided that the sidelights are combined in one lantern which shall be carried on the fore and aft centerline of the vessel or located as nearly as practicable in the same fore and aft line as the masthead light or the all-round white light.

(iv) a sternlight.

(b) An air-cushion vessel when operating in the nondisplacement mode shall, in addition to the lights prescribed in paragraph (a) of this Rule, exhibit an all-round flashing yellow light **where it can best be seen.**

(c) A power-driven vessel of less than 12 meters in length may, in lieu of the lights prescribed in paragraph (a) of this Rule, exhibit an all-round white light and sidelights.

(d) A power-driven vessel when operating on the Great Lakes may carry an all-round white light in lieu of the second masthead light and sternlight prescribed in paragraph (a) of this Rule. The light shall be carried in the position of the second

COMMENTS

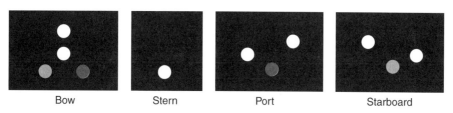

Bow Stern Port Starboard

Figure 14. Power-driven vessel ≥ 50 meters in length.

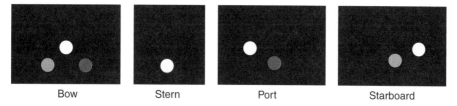

Bow Stern Port Starboard

Figure 15. Power-driven vessel < 50 meters in length.

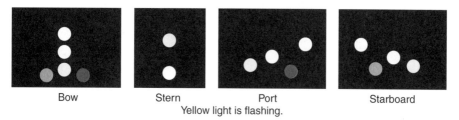

Bow Stern Port Starboard

Yellow light is flashing.

Figure 16. Air-cushion vessel in the nondisplacement mode > 50 meters in length.

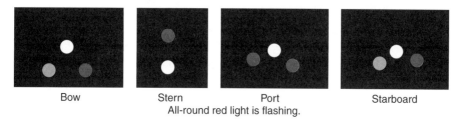

Bow Stern Port Starboard

All-round red light is flashing.

Figure 17. Wing-in-ground craft, taking off, landing, or in flight near the surface.

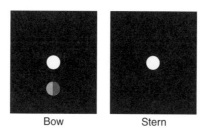

Bow Stern

Figure 18. Power-driven vessel < 12 meters in length.

Power-driven vessels less than 12 meters in length may show an all-round white light and sidelights. Sidelights may be combined into one lantern. If not practicable, power-driven vessels less than 7 meters in length don't need to show sidelights.

INTERNATIONAL	INLAND

masthead light and be visible at the same minimum range.

RULE 24. Towing and Pushing

(a) A power-driven vessel when towing shall exhibit:

(i) instead of the light prescribed in Rule 23(a)(i) or (a)(ii), two masthead lights in a vertical line. When the length of the tow, measuring from the stern of the towing vessel to the after end of the tow exceeds 200 meters, three such lights in a vertical line;

(ii) sidelights;

(iii) a sternlight;

(iv) a towing light in a vertical line above the sternlight; and

(v) when the length of the tow exceeds 200 meters, a diamond shape where it can best be seen.

RULE 24. Towing and Pushing

(a) A power-driven vessel when towing **astern** shall exhibit:

(i) instead of the light prescribed either in Rule 23(a)(i) or 23(a)(ii), two masthead lights in a vertical line. When the length of the tow, measuring from the stern of the towing vessel to the after end of the tow exceeds 200 meters, three such lights in a vertical line;

(ii) sidelights;

(iii) a sternlight;

(iv) a towing light in a vertical line above the sternlight; and

(v) when the length of the tow exceeds 200 meters, a diamond shape where it can best be seen.

COMMENTS

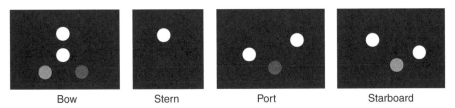

Figure 19. Power-driven vessel > 50 meters in length, on the Great Lakes.

Rule 24

Vessels towing or pushing don't get any special privileges in the Rule unless they are also restricted in ability to maneuver. But, the unique lights do communicate to approaching vessels that extra caution is due and that a barge may be present nearby.

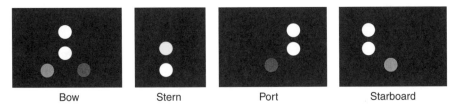

Figure 20. Vessel < 50 meters in length towing astern with tow ≤ 200 meters.

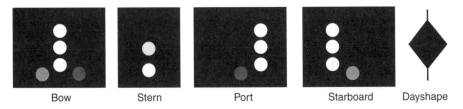

Figure 21. Vessel < 50 meters in length towing astern with tow > 200 meters.

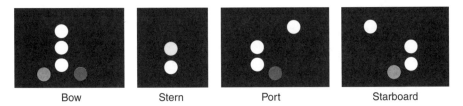

Figure 22. Vessel ≥ 50 meters in length towing astern with tow ≤ 200 meters.

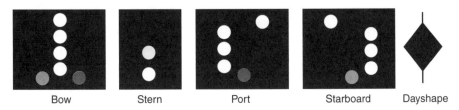

Figure 23. Vessel ≥ 50 meters in length towing astern with tow > 200 meters.

INTERNATIONAL	INLAND

(b) When a pushing vessel and a vessel being pushed ahead are rigidly connected in a composite unit they shall be regarded as a power-driven vessel and exhibit the lights prescribed in Rule 23.

(c) A power-driven vessel when pushing ahead or towing alongside, except **in the case of a composite unit,** shall exhibit:

(i) instead of the light prescribed in Rule 23(a)(i) or (a)(ii), two masthead lights in a vertical line;

(ii) sidelights; and

(iii) **a sternlight.**

(d) A power-driven vessel to which paragraph (a) or (c) of this Rule apply shall also comply with Rule 23(a)(ii).

(e) A vessel or object being **towed, other than those mentioned in paragraph (g) of this Rule,** shall exhibit:

(i) sidelights;

(ii) a sternlight;

(iii) when the length of the tow exceeds 200 meters, a diamond shape where it can best be seen.

(f) Provided that any number of vessels being towed alongside or pushed in a group shall be lighted as one vessel:

(i) a vessel being pushed ahead, not being part of a composite unit, shall exhibit at the forward end, sidelights;

(b) When a pushing vessel and a vessel being pushed ahead are rigidly connected in a composite unit they shall be regarded as a power-driven vessel and exhibit the lights prescribed in Rule 23.

(c) A power-driven vessel when pushing ahead or towing alongside, except **as required by paragraphs (b) and (i) of this Rule,** shall exhibit:

(i) instead of the light prescribed **either** in Rule 23(a)(i) or 23(a)(ii), two masthead lights in a vertical line;

(ii) sidelights; and

(iii) **two towing lights in a vertical line.**

(d) A power-driven vessel to which paragraphs (a) or (c) of this Rule apply shall also comply with Rule **23(a)(i)** and 23(a)(ii).

(e) A vessel or object **other than those referred to in paragraph (g) of this Rule being towed** shall exhibit:

(i) sidelights;

(ii) a sternlight; **and**

(iii) when the length of the tow exceeds 200 meters, a diamond shape where it can best be seen.

(f) Provided that any number of vessels being towed alongside or pushed in a group shall be lighted as one vessel, **except as provided in paragraph (iii):**

(i) a vessel being pushed ahead, not being part of a composite unit, shall exhibit at the forward end sidelights, and **a special flashing light;**

COMMENTS

(b) A vessel pushing ahead and a vessel being pushed are rigidly connected as a composite unit when they are connected by mechanical means so that they move as one vessel. According to 33 CFR 90, reproduced in the Interpretive Rules at the back of this book, "mechanical means does not include lines, wires, hawsers, or chains." An articulated tug and barge is a good example. A composite unit would display the same lights as a power-driven vessel of the same size.

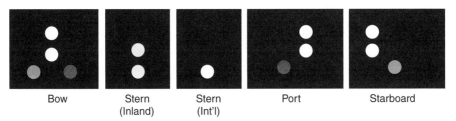

| Bow | Stern (Inland) | Stern (Int'l) | Port | Starboard |

Figure 24. Vessel < 50 meters in length pushing ahead or towing alongside.

(d) Inland. At first reading, it might appear that we are now being required to display additional masthead lights, after we just replaced them with the vertical identifying lights required by paragraphs (a) and (c). Such is not the case. This paragraph is merely telling us, in a confusing way, that if we carry our identifying lights in the position described in 23(a)(i) [forward], we must still comply with Rule 23(a)(ii), that is, we must carry an after masthead light if our vessel is over 50 meters in length. If we carry our identifying lights in the position described in 23(a)(ii) [aft], we must still comply with Rule 23(a)(i), that is, we must also carry a forward masthead light.

(d) International. Unlike the Inland Rules, this paragraph of the International Rules doesn't mention a requirement for a towing vessel to comply with Rule 23(a)(i). This raises the question as to whether a vessel engaged in towing, and exhibiting her identification lights in the after position is required to carry a forward light. This question may be answered by noting that the Rule provides for substitution of the identifying lights for the existing lights, as follows:

- Rule 24(c) states that a vessel can exhibit two or three lights in a vertical line "instead of the light prescribed in 23(a)(i) or 23(a)(ii)."
- The light prescribed in 23(a)(ii) is, by definition, a "second light, abaft of and higher than the forward one."
- Conclusion: If there is no forward light, there can't be a "second light, abaft of and higher than the forward one." Therefore, there must be a forward light.

(f) When a vessel is towing alongside or pushing ahead more than one vessel lashed together as a group, the vessels being towed or pushed shall be lighted as one vessel. The Rules don't specifically mention more than one vessel towed *astern*. If vessels being towed astern are lashed together, they should also be lighted as one vessel. But, if the barges towed aren't lashed together, each must display lights and shapes.

INTERNATIONAL	INLAND

(ii) a vessel being towed alongside shall exhibit a sternlight and at the forward end, sidelights.

(ii) a vessel being towed alongside shall exhibit a sternlight and at the forward end, sidelights **and a special flashing light; and**
(iii) when vessels are towed alongside on both sides of the towing vessels a sternlight shall be exhibited on the stern of the outboard vessel on each side of the towing vessel, and a single set of sidelights as far forward and as far outboard as is practicable, and a single special flashing light.

(g) An inconspicuous, partly submerged vessel or object, **or combination of such vessels or objects** being towed, shall exhibit:
(i) if it is less than 25 meters in breadth, one all-round white light **at or near the forward end and one at or near the after end except that dracones need not exhibit a light at or near the forward end;**
(ii) if it is 25 meters or more in breadth, **two additional all-round**

(g) An inconspicuous, partly submerged vessel or object being towed shall exhibit:

(i) if it is less than 25 meters in breadth, one all-round white light **at or near each end;**

(ii) if it is 25 meters or more in breadth, **four all-round white**

COMMENTS

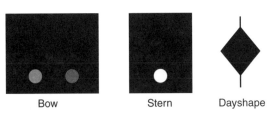

| Bow | Stern | Dayshape |

Figure 25. Vessel being towed astern, length of tow > 200 meters.

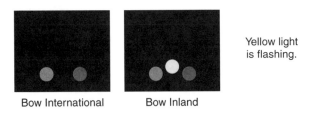

Yellow light is flashing.

| Bow International | Bow Inland |

Figure 26. Vessel being pushed ahead.

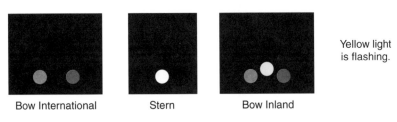

Yellow light is flashing.

| Bow International | Stern | Bow Inland |

Figure 27. Vessel being towed alongside.

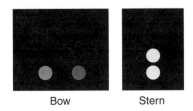

| Bow | Stern |

Figure 28. Vessel towing by pushing ahead or towing alongside on the Western Rivers (except below the Huey P. Long Bridge).

(g)(i) International. A dracone is a large flexible container for tranporting liquids by towing it on the surface of the water.

INTERNATIONAL	INLAND

white lights at or near the extremities of its breadth;

(iii) if it exceeds 100 meters in length, additional all-round white lights between the lights prescribed in subparagraphs (i) and (ii) so that the distance between the lights shall not exceed 100 meters;

(iv) a diamond shape at or near the aftermost extremity of the last vessel or object being towed **and if the length of the tow exceeds 200 meters an additional diamond shape where it can best be seen and located as far forward as is practicable.**

(h) Where from any sufficient cause it is impracticable for a vessel or object being towed to exhibit the lights **or shapes** prescribed in paragraph (e) or (g) of this Rule, all possible measures shall be taken to light the vessel or object towed or at least to indicate the presence of **such** vessel or object.

(i) Where from any sufficient cause it is impracticable for a vessel not normally engaged in towing operations to display the lights prescribed in paragraph (a) or (c) of this Rule, such vessel shall not be required to exhibit those lights when engaged in towing another

---

lights to mark its length and breadth;

(iii) if it exceeds 100 meters in length, additional all-round white lights between the lights prescribed in subparagraphs (i) and (ii) so that the distance between the lights shall not exceed 100 meters: **Provided, That any vessels or objects being towed alongside each other shall be lighted as one vessel or object;**

(iv) a diamond shape at or near the aftermost extremity of the last vessel or object being towed; **and**

(v) the towing vessel may direct a searchlight in the direction of the tow to indicate its presence to an approaching vessel.

(h) Where from any sufficient cause it is impracticable for a vessel or object being towed to exhibit the lights prescribed in paragraph (e) or (g) of this Rule, all possible measures shall be taken to light the vessel or object towed or at least to indicate the presence of **the unlighted** vessel or object.

(i) Notwithstanding paragraph (c), on the Western Rivers (except below the Huey P. Long Bridge on the Mississippi River) and on waters specified by the Secretary, a power-driven vessel when pushing ahead or towing alongside, except as paragraph (b) applies, shall exhibit:

(i) sidelights; and

(ii) two towing lights in a vertical line.

(j) Where from any sufficient cause it is impracticable for a vessel not normally engaged in towing operations to display the lights prescribed by paragraph (a), (c) **or (i)** of this Rule, such vessel shall not be required to exhibit those lights when engaged in towing another vessel in

COMMENTS

INTERNATIONAL	INLAND

vessel in distress or otherwise in need of assistance. All possible measures shall be taken to indicate the nature of the relationship between the towing vessel and the vessel being **towed as authorized by Rule 36, in particular by illuminating the towline.**

RULE 25. Sailing Vessels Underway and Vessels Under Oars

(a) A sailing vessel underway shall exhibit:
(i) sidelights;
(ii) a stern light.
(b) In a sailing vessel of less than 20 meters in length the lights prescribed in paragraph (a) of this Rule may be combined in one lantern carried at or near the top of the mast where it can best be seen.

(c) A sailing vessel underway may, in addition to the lights prescribed in paragraph (a) of this Rule, exhibit at or near the top of the mast, where they can best be seen, two all-round lights in a vertical line, the upper being red and the lower green, but these lights shall not be exhibited in conjunction with the combined lantern permitted by paragraph (b) of this Rule.

(d)(i) A sailing vessel of less than 7 meters in length shall, if practicable, exhibit the lights prescribed in paragraph (a) or (b) of this Rule, but if she does not, she shall have ready at hand an electric torch or lighted lantern showing a white light which shall be exhibited in sufficient time to prevent collision.

(ii) A vessel under oars may exhibit the lights prescribed in this Rule for sailing vessels, but if she does not, she shall have ready at hand an electric torch or lighted lantern showing a white light which shall be exhibited in sufficient time to prevent collision.

(e) A vessel proceeding under sail when also being propelled by machinery

---

distress or otherwise in need of assistance. All possible measures shall be taken to indicate the nature of the relationship between the towing vessel and the vessel being **assisted. The searchlight authorized by Rule 36 may be used to illuminate the tow.**

RULE 25. Sailing Vessels Underway and Vessels Under Oars

(a) A sailing vessel underway shall exhibit:
(i) sidelights; and
(ii) a stern light.
(b) In a sailing vessel of less than 20 meters in length the lights prescribed in paragraph (a) of this Rule may be combined in one lantern carried at or near the top of the mast where it can best be seen.

(c) A sailing vessel underway may, in addition to the lights prescribed in paragraph (a) of this Rule, exhibit at or near the top of the mast, where they can best be seen, two all-round lights in a vertical line, the upper being red and the lower green, but these lights shall not be exhibited in conjunction with the combined lantern permitted by paragraph (b) of this Rule.

(d)(i) A sailing vessel of less than 7 meters in length shall, if practicable, exhibit the lights prescribed in paragraph (a) or (b) of this Rule, but if she does not, she shall have ready at hand an electric torch or lighted lantern showing a white light which shall be exhibited in sufficient time to prevent collision.

(ii) A vessel under oars may exhibit the lights prescribed in this Rule for sailing vessels, but if she does not, she shall have ready at hand an electric torch or lighted lantern showing a white light which shall be exhibited in sufficient time to prevent collision.

(e) A vessel proceeding under sail when also being propelled by machinery

COMMENTS

Rule 25

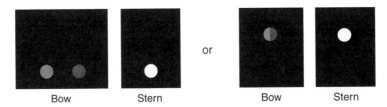

Figure 29. Sailing Vessel. If < 20 meters, sidelights and sternlight may be combined in a single lantern carried at the top of the mast.

(c) The age old memory aid for the lights of sailing vessels is "red over green, sailing machine." However, those lights, although easily memorized and recognized, are optional.

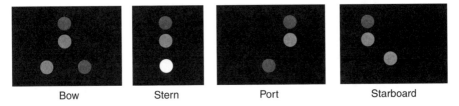

Figure 30. Sailing vessel with optional identification lights.

Figure 31. Dayshape for a vessel under sail and power.

INTERNATIONAL	INLAND
shall exhibit forward where it can best be seen a conical shape, apex downwards.	shall exhibit forward where it can best be seen a conical shape, apex downward. **A vessel of less than 12 meters in length is not required to exhibit this shape, but may do so.**

INTERNATIONAL	INLAND
RULE 26. Fishing Vessels	RULE 26. Fishing Vessels
(a) A vessel engaged in fishing, whether underway or at anchor, shall exhibit only the lights and shapes prescribed in this Rule.	(a) A vessel engaged in fishing, whether underway or at anchor, shall exhibit only the lights and shapes prescribed in this Rule.
(b) A vessel when engaged in trawling, by which is meant the dragging through the water of a dredge net or other apparatus used as a fishing appliance, shall exhibit:	(b) A vessel when engaged in trawling, by which is meant the dragging through the water of a dredge net or other apparatus used as a fishing appliance, shall exhibit:
(i) two all-round lights in a vertical line, the upper being green and the lower white, or a shape consisting of two cones with their apexes together in a vertical line one above the other;	(i) two all-round lights in a vertical line, the upper being green and the lower white, or a shape consisting of two cones with their apexes together in a vertical line one above the other;
(ii) a masthead light abaft of and higher than the all-round green light; a vessel of less than 50 meters in length shall not be obliged to exhibit such a light but may do so;	(ii) a masthead light abaft of and higher than the all-round green light; a vessel of less than 50 meters in length shall not be obliged to exhibit such a light but may do so; **and**
(iii) when making way through the water, in addition to the lights prescribed in this paragraph, sidelights and a sternlight.	(iii) when making way through the water, in addition to the lights prescribed in this paragraph, sidelights and a sternlight.
(c) A vessel engaged in fishing, other than trawling, shall exhibit:	(c) A vessel engaged in fishing, other than trawling, shall exhibit:
(i) two all-round lights in a vertical line, the upper being red and the lower white, or a shape consisting of two cones with apexes together in a vertical line one above the other;	(i) two all-round lights in a vertical line, the upper being red and the lower white, or a shape consisting of two cones with apexes together in a vertical line one above the other;
(ii) when there is outlying gear extending more than 150 meters horizontally from the vessel, an all-round white light or a cone apex upwards in the direction of the gear;	(ii) when there is outlying gear extending more than 150 meters horizontally from the vessel, an all-round white light or a cone apex upward in the direction of the gear; **and**
(iii) when making way through the water, in addition to the lights prescribed in this paragraph, sidelights and a sternlight.	(iii) when making way through the water, in addition to the lights prescribed in this paragraph, sidelights and a sternlight.

COMMENTS

Rule 26

(a) Vessels engaged in fishing show the same lights at anchor or underway.

(b) and (c) A fishing vessel that is making way through the water must display sidelights and a sternlight. When stopped, those light should be turned off. A vessel trawling greater than 50 meters in length shows a masthead light aft while other fishing vessels do not.

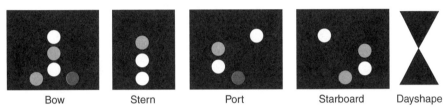

| Bow | Stern | Port | Starboard | Dayshape |

Figure 32. Vessel ≥ 50 meters in length fishing by trawling, making way.

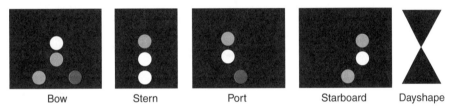

| Bow | Stern | Port | Starboard | Dayshape |

Figure 33. Vessel < 50 meters in length fishing by trawling, making way.

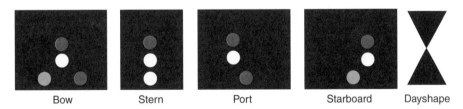

| Bow | Stern | Port | Starboard | Dayshape |

Figure 34. Vessel engaged in fishing, making way.

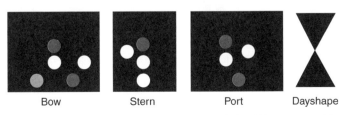

| Bow | Stern | Port | Dayshape |

Figure 35. Vessel engaged in fishing with gear extended > 150 meters, making way.

(d) The additional signals described in Annex II to these Rules apply to a vessel engaged in fishing in close proximity to other vessels engaged in fishing.

(e) A vessel when not engaged in fishing shall not exhibit the lights or shapes prescribed in this Rule, but only those prescribed for a vessel of her length.

RULE 27. Vessels Not Under Command or Restricted in Their Ability to Maneuver

(a) A vessel not under command shall exhibit:
(i) two all-round red lights in a vertical line where they can best be seen;
(ii) two balls or similar shapes in a vertical line where they can best be seen;
(iii) when making way through the water, in addition to the lights prescribed in this paragraph, sidelights and a sternlight.

(b) A vessel restricted in her ability to maneuver, except a vessel engaged in mineclearance operations, shall exhibit:
(i) three all-round lights in a vertical line where they can best be seen. The highest and lowest of these lights shall be red and the middle light shall be white;
(ii) three shapes in a vertical line where they can best be seen. The highest and lowest of these shapes shall be balls and the middle one a diamond;
(iii) when making way through the water, a masthead light or lights, sidelights and a sternlight, in addition to the lights prescribed in subparagraph **(i);**
(iv) when at anchor, in addition to the lights or shapes prescribed in subpara-

(d) The additional signals described in Annex II to these Rules apply to a vessel engaged in fishing in close proximity to other vessels engaged in fishing.

(e) A vessel when not engaged in fishing shall not exhibit the lights or shapes prescribed in this Rule, but only those prescribed for a vessel of her length.

RULE 27. Vessels Not Under Command or Restricted in Their Ability to Maneuver

(a) A vessel not under command shall exhibit:
(i) two all-round red lights in a vertical line where they can best be seen;
(ii) two balls or similar shapes in a vertical line where they can best be seen; **and**
(iii) when making way through the water, in addition to the lights prescribed in this paragraph, sidelights and a sternlight.

(b) A vessel restricted in her ability to maneuver, except a vessel engaged in mineclearance operations, shall exhibit:
(i) three all-round lights in a vertical line where they can best be seen. The highest and lowest of these lights shall be red and the middle light shall be white;
(ii) three shapes in a vertical line where they can best be seen. The highest and lowest of these shapes shall be balls and the middle one a diamond;
(iii) when making way through the water, masthead lights, sidelights and a sternlight, in addition to the lights prescribed in subparagraph **(b)(i); and**
(iv) when at anchor, in addition to the lights or shapes prescribed in subpara-

COMMENTS

A popular memory aid for the lights of a vessel trawling is "green over white, trawling at night." "Red over white, fishing at night" could be used for vessels fishing with other gear.

(d) Additional lights for vessels fishing in close proximity are specified in Annex II. In some cases those additional lights are required, but in most cases they are optional unless other local rules apply.

(e) When transiting to or from the fishing grounds or any other time she is not actually engaged in fishing, a vessel cannot display the lights listed in Rule 26 but only the lights appropriate for her category (power-driven or sailing) and size.

Rule 27

(a) Vessels not under command do not exhibit masthead lights. While making way through the water, the sidelights and sternlight must be on. Those lights are secured once all way is off. The memory aid, "red over red, the captain is dead" is often used, even though the captain's demise would not typically warrant a vessel claiming not under command status.

When a vessel is not under command anchors, she must secure her identity lights lest she be confused with a vessel aground. See Rule 30(d).

(b) A vessel restricted in ability to maneuver shows masthead lights, sidelights, and a sternlight only when making way. Otherwise they must be off. When at anchor she would display her red, white, red identity lights in addition to anchor lights (except for vessels dredging or involved in underwater operations. See 26(d)). This communicates to other vessels that they should pass with greater care and leave more room than they might otherwise because gear may be extended some distance from the vessel.

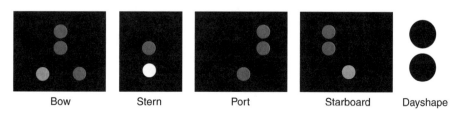

| Bow | Stern | Port | Starboard | Dayshape |

Figure 36. Vessel not under command, making way.

INTERNATIONAL	INLAND

graphs **(i) and (ii),** the light, lights or shape prescribed in Rule 30.

(c) A **power-driven** vessel engaged in a towing operation such as severely restricts the towing vessel and her tow in their ability to deviate from their course shall, in addition to the lights or shapes prescribed in **Rule 24(a), exhibit the lights or shapes prescribed in subparagraphs (b)(i) and (ii) of this Rule.**

(d) A vessel engaged in dredging or underwater operations, when restricted in her ability to maneuver, shall exhibit the lights and shapes prescribed in subparagraphs (b)(i), (ii) and (iii) of this Rule and shall in addition, when an obstruction exists, exhibit:

(i) two all-round red lights or two balls in a vertical line to indicate the side on which the obstruction exists;

(ii) two all-round green lights or two diamonds in a vertical line to indicate the side on which another vessel may pass;

(iii) when at anchor, the lights or shapes prescribed in this paragraph instead of the lights or shape prescribed in Rule 30.

(e) Whenever the size of a vessel engaged in diving operations makes it impracticable to exhibit all lights and shapes prescribed in paragraph (d) of this Rule, the following shall be exhibited:

(i) three all-round lights in a vertical line where they can best be seen. The highest and lowest of these

---

graphs **(b)(i) and (ii),** the light, lights or shapes prescribed in Rule 30.

(c) A vessel engaged in a towing operation **which** severely restricts the towing vessel and her tow in their ability to deviate from their course shall, in addition to the lights or shapes prescribed in **subparagraphs (b)(i) and (ii) of this Rule, exhibit the lights or shape prescribed in Rule 24.**

(d) A vessel engaged in dredging or underwater operations, when restricted in her ability to maneuver, shall exhibit the lights and shapes prescribed in subparagraphs (b)(i), (ii), and (iii) of this Rule and shall in addition, when an obstruction exists, exhibit:

(i) two all-round red lights or two balls in a vertical line to indicate the side on which the obstruction exists;

(ii) two all-round green lights or two diamonds in a vertical line to indicate the side on which another vessel may pass; **and**

(iii) when at anchor, the lights or shape prescribed by this paragraph, instead of the lights or shapes prescribed in Rule 30 **for anchored vessels.**

(e) Whenever the size of a vessel engaged in diving operations makes it impracticable to exhibit all lights and shapes prescribed in paragraph (d) of this Rule, the following shall **instead** be exhibited:

(i) Three all-round lights in a vertical line where they can best be seen. The highest and lowest of these

COMMENTS

(c) Rule 27(c) (International) refers to Rule 24(a) that lists lighting requirements for vessels towing astern. Although Rule 27 (International) doesn't refer to vessels towing alongside or pushing ahead, those vessels may also show these lights and shapes. The Inland Rules are more clear as they refer to all of the lights and shapes prescribed in Rule 24, not just those in Rule 24(a).

These lights cannot be displayed by every vessel engaged in towing, only those that are "severely restricted." See discussion of Rule 3(g)(vi).

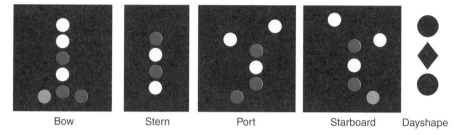

| Bow | Stern | Port | Starboard | Dayshape |

Figure 37. Vessel ≥ 50 m in length restricted in ability to maneuver, making way.

(d) Unlike other vessels restricted in their ability to maneuver, vessels restricted due to dredging or underwater operations do not exhibit anchor lights when at anchor.

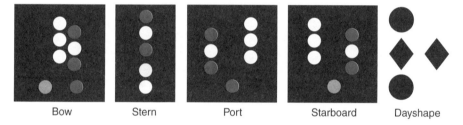

| Bow | Stern | Port | Starboard | Dayshape |

Figure 38. Vessel < 50 meters towing astern, unable to deviate from its course, tow > 200 meters.

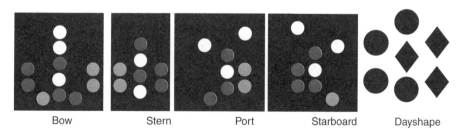

| Bow | Stern | Port | Starboard | Dayshape |

Figure 39. Vessel ≥ 50 meters engaged in dredging or underwater operations, obstruction to starboard.

INTERNATIONAL	INLAND

lights shall be red and the middle light shall be white;
(ii) a rigid replica of the International Code flag "A" not less than 1 meter in height. Measures shall be taken to ensure its all-round visibility.

(f) A vessel engaged in mineclearance operations shall, in addition to the lights prescribed for a power-driven vessel in Rule 23 or to the lights or shape prescribed for a vessel at anchor in Rule 30 as appropriate, exhibit three all-round green lights or three balls. One of these lights or shapes shall be exhibited near the foremast head and one at each end of the fore yard. These lights or shapes indicate that it is dangerous for another vessel to approach within 1000 meters of the mineclearance vessel.

(g) **Vessels** of less than 12 meters in length, except **those** engaged in diving operations, **shall** not be required to exhibit the lights and shapes prescribed in this Rule.

(h) The signals prescribed in this Rule are not signals of vessels in distress and requiring assistance. Such signals are contained in Annex IV to these **Regulations.**

---

lights shall be red and the middle light shall be white;
(ii) A rigid replica of the international Code flag "A" not less than 1 meter in height. Measures shall be taken to insure its all-round visibility.

(f) A vessel engaged in mineclearance operations shall, in addition to the lights prescribed for a power-driven vessel in Rule 23 or to the lights or shape prescribed for a vessel at anchor in Rule 30, as appropriate, exhibit three all-round green lights or three balls. One of these lights or shapes shall be exhibited near the foremast head and one at each end of the fore yard. These lights or shapes indicate that it is dangerous for another vessel to approach within 1000 meters of the mineclearance vessel.

(g) **A vessel** of less than 12 meters in length, except **when** engaged in diving operations, **is** not required to exhibit the lights or shapes prescribed in this Rule.

(h) The signals prescribed in this Rule are not signals of vessels in distress and requiring assistance. Such signals are contained in Annex IV to these **Rules.**

RULE 28. Vessels Constrained by Their Draft

A vessel constrained by her draft may, in addition to the lights prescribed for power-driven vessels in Rule 23, exhibit where they can best be seen three all-round red lights in a vertical line, or a cylinder.

RULE 28. [Reserved]

RULE 29. Pilot Vessels
(a) A vessel engaged on pilotage duty shall exhibit:

RULE 29. Pilot Vessels
(a) A vessel engaged on pilotage duty shall exhibit:

COMMENTS

Figure 40. Vessel engaged in dredging or underwater operations, not making way or anchored.

Figure 41. Small vessel engaged in diving operations—dayshape.

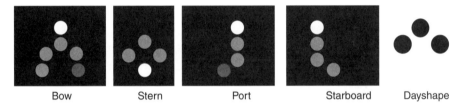

| Bow | Stern | Port | Starboard | Dayshape |

Figure 42. Vessel < 50 meters engaged in mineclearance operations.

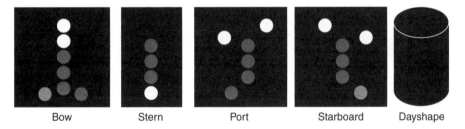

| Bow | Stern | Port | Starboard | Dayshape |

Figure 43. Vessel ≥ 50 meters, constrained by draft (International only).

Rule 28

This Rule applies only in International waters. There is no Inland Rule 28.

Rule 29

A vessel on pilotage duties will show all-round white over red lights instead of masthead lights. At anchor, she would show anchor lights appropriate to her size. When underway she would show sidelights and a sternlight. When not on duty, she

INTERNATIONAL	INLAND
(i) at or near the masthead, two all-round lights in a vertical line, the upper being white and the lower red; (ii) when underway, in addition, sidelights and a sternlight; (iii) when at anchor, in addition to the lights prescribed in subparagraph (i), the light, lights or shape prescribed in Rule 30 for vessels at anchor.	(i) at or near the masthead, two all-round lights in a vertical line, the upper being white and the lower red; (ii) when underway, in addition, sidelights and a sternlight; **and** (iii) when at anchor, in addition to the lights prescribed in subparagraph (i), the anchor light, lights, or shape prescribed in Rule 30 for anchored vessels.
(b) A pilot vessel when not engaged on pilotage duty shall exhibit the lights or shapes prescribed for a similar vessel of her length.	(b) A pilot vessel when not engaged on pilotage duty shall exhibit the lights or shapes prescribed for a vessel of her length.

RULE 30. Anchored Vessels and Vessels Aground

INTERNATIONAL	INLAND
(a) A vessel at anchor shall exhibit where it can best be seen: (i) in the fore part, an all-round white light or one ball; (ii) at or near the stern and at a lower level than the light prescribed in subparagraph (i), an all-round white light.	(a) A vessel at anchor shall exhibit where it can best be seen: (i) in the fore part, an all-round white light or one ball; **and** (ii) at or near the stern and at a lower level than the light prescribed in subparagraph (i), an all-round white light.
(b) A vessel of less than 50 meters in length may exhibit an all-round white light where it can best be seen instead of the lights prescribed in paragraph (a) of this Rule.	(b) A vessel of less than 50 meters in length may exhibit an all-round white light where it can best be seen instead of the lights prescribed in paragraph (a) of this Rule.
(c) A vessel at anchor may, and a vessel of 100 meters and more in length shall, also use the available working or equivalent lights to illuminate her decks.	(c) A vessel at anchor may, and a vessel of 100 meters or more in length shall, also use the available working or equivalent lights to illuminate her decks.
(d) A vessel aground shall exhibit the lights prescribed in paragraph (a) or (b) of this Rule and in addition, where they can best be seen: (i) two all-round red lights in a vertical line; (ii) three balls in a vertical line.	(d) A vessel aground shall exhibit the lights prescribed in paragraph (a) or (b) of this Rule and in addition, if practicable, where they can best be seen: (i) two all-round red lights in a vertical line; **and** (ii) three balls in a vertical line.
(e) A vessel of less than 7 meters in length, when at anchor, not in or near a narrow channel, fairway or anchorage, or where other vessels normally navigate, shall not be required to exhibit the lights or shape prescribed in paragraphs (a) and (b) of this Rule.	(e) A vessel of less than 7 meters in length, when at anchor, not in or near a narrow channel, fairway, anchorage, or where other vessels normally navigate, shall not be required to exhibit the lights or shape prescribed in paragraphs (a) and (b) of this Rule.

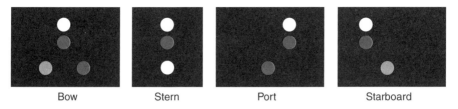

| Bow | Stern | Port | Starboard |

Figure 44. Pilot vessel, underway.

must not show the identity lights. Instead she must be lighted as a power-driven vessel (or, sailing vessel) of her size.

Rule 30

(a) The forward anchor light is higher than the aft anchor light. This enables vessels passing or anchoring near an anchored vessel to allow for the presence of the anchor and cable leading ahead.

As noted in previous Rules, vessels engaged in fishing and vessels restricted in ability to maneuver due to dredging or diving operations would not show anchor lights.

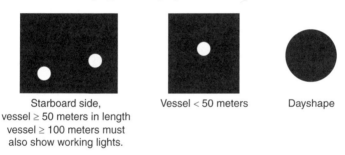

Starboard side,
vessel ≥ 50 meters in length
vessel ≥ 100 meters must
also show working lights.   Vessel < 50 meters   Dayshape

Figure 45. Vessels at anchor.

(d) A vessel aground at night would show the red over red lights of a vessel not under command plus anchor lights. These lights are to be displayed in the event of an accidental grounding. If you run aground on purpose and can get underway at will, you should display the light required if your vessel was underway but not making way.

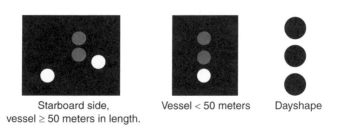

Starboard side,
vessel ≥ 50 meters in length.   Vessel < 50 meters   Dayshape

Figure 46. Vessels aground.

INTERNATIONAL	INLAND

(f) A vessel of less than 12 meters in length, when aground, shall not be required to exhibit the lights or shapes prescribed in subparagraphs (d)(i) and (ii) of this Rule.

(f) A vessel of less than 12 meters in length when aground shall not be required to exhibit the lights or shapes prescribed in subparagraphs (d)(i) and (ii) of this Rule.

(g) A vessel of less than 20 meters in length, when at anchor in a special anchorage area designated by the Secretary, shall not be required to exhibit the anchor lights and shapes required by this Rule.

RULE 31. Scaplanes

Where it is impracticable for a seaplane **or a WIG craft** to exhibit lights and shapes of the characteristics or in the positions prescribed in the Rules of this Part she shall exhibit lights and shapes as closely similar in characteristics and position as is possible.

RULE 31. Seaplanes

Where it is impracticable for a seaplane to exhibit lights and shapes of the characteristics or in the positions prescribed in the Rules of this Part she shall exhibit lights and shapes as closely similar in characteristics and position as is possible.

PART D
SOUND AND LIGHT SIGNALS

PART D
SOUND AND LIGHT SIGNALS

RULE 32. Definitions

(a) The word "whistle" means any sound signalling appliance capable of producing the prescribed blasts and which complies with the specifications in Annex III to these **Regulations.**

(b) The term "short blast" means a blast of about one second's duration.

(c) The term "prolonged blast" means a blast of from four to six seconds' duration.

RULE 32. Definitions

(a) The word "whistle" means any sound signalling appliance capable of producing the prescribed blasts and which complies with specifications in Annex III to these **Rules.**

(b) The term "short blast" means a blast of about 1 second's duration.

(c) The term "prolonged blast" means a blast of from 4 to 6 seconds' duration.

RULE 33. Equipment for Sound Signals

(a) A vessel of 12 meters or more in length shall be provided with a whistle, **a vessel of 20 meters or more in length shall be provided with a bell in addition to a whistle,** and a vessel of 100 meters or more in length shall, in addition, be provided with a gong, the tone and sound of which cannot be confused with that of the bell. The

RULE 33. Equipment for Sound Signals

(a) A vessel of 12 meters or more in length shall be provided with a whistle **and a bell** and a vessel of 100 meters or more in length shall, in addition, be provided with a gong, the tone and sound of which cannot be confused with that of the bell. The whistle, bell and gong shall comply with the specifications in Annex III to

COMMENTS

Rule 32

Rule 32 defines terms that will be used in Part D of the Rules. Part D, Sound and Light Signals, consists of Rules 32–37 and discusses definitions and carriage requirements for equipment, maneuvering and warning signals, signals in restricted visibility, and distress signals.

Previous sets of Rules included a "long blast." The only whistle signals now contained in the Rules are the short blast and the prolonged blast. No single blast of the whistle will be longer than six seconds in duration.

Rule 33

All vessels must have a means of making the required sound signals, and there are no exemptions from this requirement. Small vessel operators should make sure that they obtain a suitable device for this purpose, such as a compressed air, or aerosol, horn.

For sound signal specifications, the Rule refers to Annex III of the Rules where the frequencies of the whistles are given for various sizes of vessels. The lower the frequency, measured in Hertz (Hz), the deeper the tone of the whistle. If the vessels were singing in concert, the large vessels would sing bass (70–200 Hz), the medium-sized vessels would sing baritone (130–350 Hz), and the small vessels would sing tenor (250–700 Hz). For those not musically inclined, remember that, generally speaking, the deeper the tone of the whistle, the larger the vessel sounding it.

INTERNATIONAL	INLAND

whistle, bell and gong shall comply with the specifications in Annex III to these **Regulations.** The bell or gong or both may be replaced by other equipment having the same respective sound characteristics, provided that manual sounding of the prescribed signals shall always be possible.

(b) A vessel of less than 12 meters in length shall not be obliged to carry the sound signalling appliances prescribed in paragraph (a) of this Rule but if she does not, shc shall be provided with some other means of making an efficient sound signal.

RULE 34. Maneuvering and Warning Signals

(a) When vessels are in sight of one another, a power-driven vessel underway, when maneuvering as authorized or required by these Rules, shall indicate that maneuver by the following signals on her whistle:

- one short blast to mean "I am altering my course to starboard";
- two short blasts to mean "I am altering my course to port";
- three short blasts to mean "I am operating astern propulsion".

---

these **Rules.** The bell or gong or both may be replaced by other equipment having the same respective sound characteristics, provided that manual sounding of the prescribed signals shall always be possible.

(b) A vessel of less than 12 meters in length shall not be obliged to carry the sound signalling appliances prescribed in paragraph (a) of this Rule but if she does not, she shall be provided with some other means of making an efficient sound signal.

RULE 34. Maneuvering and Warning Signals

(a) When power-driven vessels are in sight of one another and meeting or crossing at a distance within half a mile of each other, each vessel underway, when maneuvering as authorized or required by these Rules:

(i) shall indicate that maneuver by the following signals on her whistle: one short blast to mean "I intend to leave you on my port side"; two short blasts to mean "I intend to leave you on my starboard side"; and three short blasts to mean "I am operating astern propulsion".

(ii) upon hearing the one or two blast signal of the other shall, if in agreement, sound the same whistle signal and take the steps necessary to effect a safe passing. If, however, from any cause, the vessel doubts the safety of the proposed maneuver, she shall sound the danger signal specified in paragraph (d) of this Rule and each vessel shall take appropriate precautionary action until a safe passing agreement is made.

COMMENTS

Annex III also gives the details of the bell and gong. These may be replaced by "other equipment," such as electronic devices, but they must have the same sound characteristics as those required by the Annex. Manual sounding of the signals must always be possible.

Rule 34

This Rule contains significant differences in requirements for signals, depending on whether the vessel is operating on inland or international waters. The differences are as follows:

- Maneuvering signals under International Rules are signals of execution and indicate that a power-driven vessel is making a maneuver. They need not be answered. Maneuvering signals under Inland Rules are signals of intent (a proposal of what a vessel intends to do), and they must be answered by the other vessel, as an indication of agreement.
- The International Rules require maneuvering signals by a power-driven vessel no matter the category of the second vessel. Under Inland Rules, both vessels in the situation must be power-driven. In other words, a power-driven vessel cannot exchange passing signals with a sailing vessel or vessel engaged in fishing in U.S. Inland waters.
- In the Inland Rules signals need to be sounded only if the vessels will pass within half a mile of each other. The International Rules do not specify a distance at which to sound the signals. There is normally no need to sound the whistle if vessels are at great distance and there is no risk of collision. If risk of collision does exist, the signals should be sounded even when the other vessel is further away than the minimum required distance of audibility of the whistle (2 nm for vessels 200 meters or longer). The sound might carry that far on a good day. If a collision does occur, you can honestly testify that you sounded the required signal even if the other vessel didn't hear them and your liability may be somewhat reduced.
- Under International Rules, the whistle light must be a white light with a 5-mile visibility range and may be "repeated as appropriate." Under Inland Rules, the light is a white or yellow light with a 2-mile visibility range and must be "synchronized with the whistle."
- Under International Rules, signals are provided for an overtaking situation in a narrow channel where the overtaken vessel has to take action to permit safe passage. There are no such special signals under Inland Rules.

INTERNATIONAL	INLAND

INTERNATIONAL

(b) **Any** vessel may supplement the whistle signals prescribed in paragraph (a) of this Rule by light signals, **repeated as appropriate, while the maneuver is being carried out:**
 (i) these light signals shall have the following significance:
 —one flash to mean "I am altering my course to starboard";
 —two flashes to mean "I am altering my course to port";
 —three flashes to mean "I am operating astern propulsion";
(ii) the duration of each flash shall be about one second, **the interval between flashes shall be about one second, and the interval between successive signals shall be not less than ten seconds;**
(iii) the light used for this signal shall, if fitted, be **an all-round white light, visible at a minimum range of 5 miles,** and shall comply with the provisions of Annex I to these **Regulations.**

(c) When in sight of one another in **a narrow channel or fairway:**
 (i) a vessel intending to overtake another shall in compliance with Rule 9(e)(i) indicate her intention by the following signals on her whistle:
 —two prolonged blasts followed by one short blast to mean "I intend to overtake you on your starboard side";
 —two prolonged blasts followed by two short blasts to mean "I intend to overtake you on your port side",
(ii) the vessel about to be overtaken when acting in accordance with Rule 9(e)(i) shall indicate her agreement by the following signal on her whistle:
 —one prolonged, one short, one prolonged and one short blast, in that order.

INLAND

(b) **A** vessel may supplement the whistle signals prescribed in paragraph (a) of this Rule by light signals:
 (i) These signals shall have the following significance: one flash to mean "I intend to leave you on my port side"; two flashes to mean "I intend to leave you on my starboard side"; three flashes to mean "I am operating astern propulsion";

 (ii) The duration of each flash shall be about 1 second; and

 (iii) The light used for this signal shall, if fitted, be **one all-round white or yellow light, visible at a minimum range of 2 miles, synchronized with the whistle,** and shall comply with the provisions of Annex I to these **Rules.**
(c) When in sight of one another:

 (i) a power-driven vessel intending to overtake another powerdriven vessel shall indicate her intention by the following signals on her whistle: one short blast to mean "I intend to overtake you on your starboard side"; two short blasts to mean "I intend to overtake you on your port side"; and

 (ii) the power-driven vessel about to be overtaken shall, if in agreement, sound a similar sound signal. If in doubt she shall sound the danger signal prescribed in paragraph (d).

COMMENTS

- The Inland Rules provide for a signal of a prolonged blast when leaving a dock or berth but this signal is not in International Rules.
- In international waters, the maneuvering signals are signals of execution, and they must be sounded when a maneuver is executed. In inland waters, the signals indicate to which side one vessel intends to leave the other and do not indicate maneuvers.
- The Inland Rules make provision for an agreement to be made by radiotelephone instead of sounding the whistle signals. However, with regard to agreements made by radiotelephone, the following should be noted:
  - Always be certain which vessel is making the agreement with you. There have been many instances of mistaken identity when using this handy device—the radiotelephone—some resulting in vehement disagreement.
  - Always be certain what was said on the radiotelephone. Voices are often garbled and unclear. "Going too fast" may be heard as "meet on two blasts," and "coming to starboard" could be mistaken for "leave you to starboard."
  - Always be certain that the other vessel is doing what he said he would do, or what you thought he said he would do. Keep a close eye on him. He may have told you he would "stop" when he only meant "stop engines."
  - Always be certain that you continue to monitor the radiotelephone after the agreement has been made. Something unexpected may develop and cause one or both of you to change your plans.
  - Remember that the Rule says if agreement is not reached, whistle signals "shall be exchanged in a timely manner and shall prevail."

(c) International. The requirements of this Rule are peculiar to the International Rules and provide for sound signals to be exchanged in narrow channels when one vessel is overtaking another. To provide these signals, the International Rules adopt the Inland Rules concept of "signals of intent." These signals are to be sounded "in compliance with Rule 9(e)(i)," so they are to be sounded when "overtaking can take place only if the vessel to be overtaken has to take action to permit safe passing." The decision as to whether the vessel being overtaken will have to take action evidently is made by the overtaking vessel, for it is she who initiates the signals. If the vessel being overtaken is in doubt that the action is safe, or is not willing to take action as would be required by the proposed signal, she may (and should) sound the danger signal. Since this signal is optional, however, she may choose not to sound any signal, in which case the overtaking vessel should not attempt to pass. If the vessel being overtaken agrees to the maneuver, she will sound "a prolonged, a short, a prolonged, and a short blast, in that order." If the vessel being overtaken must change course to facilitate the other vessel's passage, she must sound the maneuvering signals given in Rule 34 (a), because these signals are to be sounded "when maneuvering as authorized or required by these Rules." It would be advisable to have frequent and open communication by radiotelephone during a maneuver such as this.

INTERNATIONAL	INLAND

(d) When vessels in sight of one another are approaching each other and from any cause either vessel fails to understand the intentions or actions of the other, or is in doubt whether sufficient action is being taken by the other to avoid collision, the vessel in doubt shall immediately indicate such doubt by giving at least five short and rapid blasts on the whistle. Such signal may be supplemented by a light signal of at least five short and rapid flashes.

(e) A vessel nearing a bend or an area of a channel or fairway where other vessels may be obscured by an intervening obstruction shall sound one prolonged blast. Such signal shall be answered with a prolonged blast by any approaching vessel that may be within hearing around the bend or behind the intervening obstruction.

(f) If whistles are fitted on a vessel at a distance apart of more than 100 meters, one whistle only shall be used for giving maneuvering and warning signals.

(d) When vessels in sight of one another are approaching each other and from any cause either vessel fails to understand the intentions or actions of the other, or is in doubt whether sufficient action is being taken by the other to avoid collision, the vessel in doubt shall immediately indicate such doubt by giving at least five short and rapid blasts on the whistle. This signal may be supplemented by a light signal of at least five short and rapid flashes.

(e) A vessel nearing a bend or an area of a channel or fairway where other vessels may be obscured by an intervening obstruction shall sound one prolonged blast. This signal shall be answered with a prolonged blast by any approaching vessel that may be within hearing around the bend or behind the intervening obstruction.

(f) If whistles are fitted on a vessel at a distance apart of more than 100 meters, one whistle only shall be used for giving maneuvering and warning signals.

(g) When a power-driven vessel is leaving a dock or berth, she shall sound one prolonged blast.

(h) A vessel that reaches agreement with another vessel in a head-on, crossing, or overtaking situation, as for example, by using the radiotelephone as prescribed by the Vessel Bridge-to-Bridge Radiotelephone Act (85 Stat. 164; 33 U.S.C. 1201 et seq.), is not obliged to sound the whistle signals prescribed by this Rule, but may do so. If agreement is not reached, then whistle signals shall be exchanged in a timely manner and shall prevail.

COMMENTS

(d) The danger (or doubt) signal is the same under International and Inland Rules—at least five short and rapid blasts on the whistle. Its sounding is mandatory for any vessel approaching another when failing to understand the intentions of that vessel, or thinking that the vessel's action is not sufficient or appropriate.

The danger signal may also be sounded by a vessel at anchor. The only requirement for the signal is that the vessels be "in sight of one another". Therefore, vessels should not sound the danger signal in fog. If a watch officer knowledgeable in the rules heard a danger signal in fog, the assumption would be that there were two other vessels in the area that were in sight of one another. The vessel sounding the signal in fog would potentially be creating a very confusing and dangerous situation. He might well be held at fault if collision resulted.

Officers would be well advised to use only proper fog signals in restricted visibility. Such signals will accomplish the desired effect of letting others know they are present, without introducing complications.

(g) The Inland Rules state that a vessel leaving a dock or berth shall sound one prolonged blast. The International Rules do not state the same thing. However, a case may be made for giving this signal when moving from a dock, as it can be argued that the dock presents an "intervening obstruction" and the signal would be allowed under Rules 9 (f) and 34 (e). It does appear, however, that the intent of the International Rule is not to require the signal simply because a vessel is leaving a dock.

(h) 33 CFR 26.04 (b) requires an operator to use the radiotelephone when necessary, to "transmit and confirm, on the designated frequency, the intentions of his vessel and any other information necessary for the safe navigation of vessels."

INTERNATIONAL	INLAND

RULE 35. Sound Signals in Restricted Visibility

In or near an area of restricted visibility, whether by day or night, the signals prescribed in this Rule shall be used as follows:

(a) A power-driven vessel making way through the water shall sound at intervals of not more than 2 minutes one prolonged blast.

(b) A power-driven vessel underway but stopped and making no way through the water shall sound at intervals of not more than 2 minutes two prolonged blasts in succession with an interval of about 2 seconds between them.

(c) A vessel not under command, a vessel restricted in her ability to maneuver, **a vessel constrained by her draft,** a sailing vessel, a vessel engaged in fishing and a vessel engaged in towing or pushing another vessel shall, instead of the signals prescribed in paragraphs (a) or (b) of this Rule, sound at intervals of not more than 2 minutes three blasts in succession, namely one prolonged followed by two short blasts.

(d) A vessel engaged in fishing, when at anchor, and a vessel restricted in her ability to maneuver when carrying out her work at anchor, shall instead of the signals prescribed in paragraph (g) of this Rule sound the signal prescribed in paragraph (c) of this Rule.

(e) A vessel towed or if more than one vessel is towed the last vessel of the tow, if manned, shall at intervals of not more than 2 minutes sound four blasts in succession, namely one prolonged followed by three short blasts. When practicable, this signal shall be made immediately after the signal made by the towing vessel.

RULE 35. Sound Signals in Restricted Visibility

In or near an area of restricted visibility, whether by day or night, the signals prescribed in this Rule shall be used as follows:

(a) A power-driven vessel making way through the water shall sound at intervals of not more than 2 minutes one prolonged blast.

(b) A power-driven vessel underway but stopped and making no way through the water shall sound at intervals of not more than 2 minutes two prolonged blasts in succession with an interval of about 2 seconds between them.

(c) A vessel not under command; a vessel restricted in her ability to maneuver, whether underway or at anchor; a sailing vessel; a vessel engaged in fishing, **whether underway or at anchor;** and a vessel engaged in towing or pushing another vessel shall, instead of the signals prescribed in paragraphs (a) or (b) of this Rule, sound at intervals of not more than 2 minutes, three blasts in succession; namely, one prolonged followed by two short blasts.

(d) A vessel towed or if more than one vessel is towed the last vessel of the tow, if manned, shall at intervals of not more than 2 minutes sound four blasts in succession; namely, one prolonged followed by three short blasts. When practicable, this signal shall be made immediately after the signal made by the towing vessel.

COMMENTS

Rule 35

Fog signals are to be used when operating "in or near an area of restricted visibility." Since this phrase is used in Rule 19 of the Steering and Sailing Rules, you may wish to review the discussion of that Rule.

The question might come to mind as to how restricted the visibility must be for fog signals to be required. In other words, "How foggy is too foggy?" Note from the audibility table in Annex III of the International Rules that the range at which you can expect to hear the fog signal of a large vessel is about two miles. This might be increased slightly by existing meteorological conditions. If the prevailing visibility is two and a half miles or more, then you can probably be safe in assuming that sounding the fog signals will accomplish little more than the aggravation of the crew. If the range of visibility is less than the range of your whistle, you should certainly be sounding fog signals.

Although worded differently, both sets of Rules require that vessels engaged in fishing, and vessels restricted in their ability to maneuver, do not sound the regular anchor signals that apply to other vessels. These vessels sound the same signal (one prolonged and two short blasts) whether underway or at anchor.

The Rule specifies the maximum interval at which the signals shall be sounded. The signals can be sounded more often if desired.

As you read paragraph (f) (Inland) or (g) (International) of the Rule, you might be tempted to think that any vessel at anchor would sound these signals, but this is not the case. A fishing vessel or a vessel restricted in her ability to maneuver sounds the same signal underway or at anchor, but the other vessels listed in paragraph (c) (sailing vessel, towing vessel, etc.) presumably sound the anchor signal given here. Of course this means that some anchored vessels sound their fog signals at two-minute intervals (paragraph (c)) and some at one-minute intervals (paragraph (f)(g)).

As already mentioned small vessels must carry a means of making the required sound signals. This is reinforced in paragraph (h) (Inland) or (j) (International) that requires vessels even less than twelve meters in length to make the required signals or "some other efficient sound signal."

INTERNATIONAL	INLAND

(f) When a pushing vessel and a vessel being pushed ahead are rigidly connected in a composite unit they shall be regarded as a power-driven vessel and shall give the signals prescribed in paragraphs (a) or (b) of this Rule.

(g) A vessel at anchor shall at intervals of not more than one minute ring the bell rapidly for about 5 seconds. In a vessel of 100 meters or more in length the bell shall be sounded in the forepart of the vessel and immediately after the ringing of the bell, the gong shall be sounded rapidly for about 5 seconds in the after part of the vessel. A vessel at anchor may in addition sound three blasts in succession, namely one short, one prolonged and one short blast, to give warning of her position and of the possibility of collision to an approaching vessel.

(h) A vessel aground shall give the bell signal and if required the gong signal prescribed in paragraph **(g)** of this Rule and shall, in addition, give three separate and distinct strokes on the bell immediately before and after the rapid ringing of the bell. A vessel aground may in addition sound an appropriate whistle signal.

(i) A vessel of 12 meters or more but less than 20 meters in length shall not be obliged to give the bell signals prescribed in paragraphs (g) and (h) of this Rule. However, if she does not, she shall make some other efficient sound signal at intervals of not more than 2 minutes.

(j) A vessel of less than 12 meters in length shall not be obliged to give the above-mentioned signals but, if she does not, shall make some other efficient sound signal at intervals of not more than 2 minutes.

(e) When a pushing vessel and a vessel being pushed ahead are rigidly connected in a composite unit they shall be regarded as a power-driven vessel and shall give the signals prescribed in paragraphs (a) or (b) of this Rule.

(f) A vessel at anchor shall at intervals of not more than 1 minute ring the bell rapidly for about 5 seconds. In a vessel of 100 meters or more in length the bell shall be sounded in the forepart of the vessel and immediately after the ringing of the bell, the gong shall be sounded rapidly for about 5 seconds in the after part of the vessel. A vessel at anchor may in addition sound three blasts in succession; namely, one short, one prolonged and one short blast, to give warning of her position and of the possibility of collision to an approaching vessel.

(g) A vessel aground shall give the bell signal and if required the gong signal prescribed in paragraph **(f)** of this Rule and shall, in addition, give three separate and distinct strokes on the bell immediately before and after the rapid ringing of the bell. A vessel aground may in addition sound an appropriate whistle signal.

(h) A vessel of less than 12 meters in length shall not be obliged to give the above-mentioned signals but, if she does not, shall make some other efficient sound signal at intervals of not more than 2 minutes.

COMMENTS

INTERNATIONAL	INLAND

(k) A pilot vessel when engaged on pilotage duty may in addition to the signals prescribed in paragraphs (a), (b) or (**g**) of this Rule sound an identity signal consisting of four short blasts.

(i) A pilot vessel when engaged on pilotage duty may in addition to the signals prescribed in paragraphs (a), (b) or (**f**) of this Rule sound an identity signal consisting of four short blasts.

(**j**) **The following vessels shall not be required to sound signals as prescribed in paragraph (f) of this Rule when anchored in a special anchorage area designated by the Secretary:**

(**i**) **a vessel of less than 20 meters in length; and**

(**ii**) **a barge, canal boat, scow, or other nondescript craft.**

RULE 36. Signals to Attract Attention

If necessary to attract the attention of another vessel, any vessel may make light or sound signals that cannot be mistaken for any signal authorized elsewhere in these Rules, or may direct the beam of her searchlight in the direction of the danger, in such a way as not to embarrass any vessel. **Any light to attract the attention of another vessel shall be such that it cannot be mistaken for any aid to navigation. For the purpose of this Rule the use of high intensity intermittent or revolving lights, such as strobe lights, shall be avoided.**

RULE 36. Signals to Attract Attention

If necessary to attract the attention of another vessel, any vessel may make light or sound signals that cannot be mistaken for any signal authorized elsewhere in these Rules, or may direct the beam of her searchlight in the direction of the danger, in such a way as not to embarrass any vessel.

RULE 37. Distress Signals

When a vessel is in distress and requires assistance she shall use or exhibit the signals described in Annex IV to these **Regulations.**

RULE 37. Distress Signals

When a vessel is in distress and requires assistance she shall use or exhibit the signals described in Annex IV to these **Rules.**

PART E—EXEMPTIONS

PART E—EXEMPTIONS

RULE 38. Exemptions

Any vessel (or class of vessels) provided that she complies with the requirements of the International Regulations for Preventing Collisions at Sea, 1960, the keel of which

RULE 38. Exemptions

Any vessel or class of vessels, the keel of which is laid or which is at a corresponding stage of construction before December 24, 1980, provided

Rule 36

According to this Rule if you must attract the attention of another vessel, you may use light or sound signals, as long as these signals cannot be confused with required signals. You may also direct the beam of a searchlight in the direction of danger, "in such a way as not to embarrass any vessel." The word embarrass can mean any of the following:

- To beset with difficulties
- To impede
- To complicate

If a vessel has to cross the path of your searchlight, the chances are good that the light will cause vision "difficulties" for the lookouts and bridge watches of other vessels, thereby "impeding" the safe passage of such vessels and "complicating" their navigation. You should be sure, then, that the beam of any light employed in such a situation will not have such adverse effects.

Rule 37

The distress signals, pictured, below, are listed in Annex IV.

INTERNATIONAL	INLAND

is laid or which is at a corresponding stage of construction before the entry into force of these Regulations may be exempted from compliance therewith as follows:

that she complies with the requirements of—

(a) The Act of June 7, 1897 (30 Stat. 96), as amended (33 U.S.C. 154–232) for vessels navigating the waters subject to that statute;

(b) Section 4233 of the Revised Statutes (33 U.S.C. 301–356) for vessels navigating the waters subject to that statute;

(c) The Act of February 8, 1895 (28 Stat. 645), as amended (33 U.S.C. 241–295) for vessels navigating the waters subject to that statute; or

(d) Sections 3, 4, and 5 of the Act of April 25, 1940 (54 Stat. 163), as amended (46 U.S.C. 526 b, c, and d) for motorboats navigating the waters subject to that statute; shall be exempted from compliance with the technical Annexes to these Rules as follows:

(a) The installation of lights with ranges prescribed in Rule 22, until four years after the **date of entry into force of these Regulations.**

(i) the installation of lights with ranges prescribed in Rule 22, until 4 years after the **effective date of these Rules, except that vessels of less than 20 meters in length are permanently exempt;**

(b) The installation of lights with color specifications as prescribed in **Section 7** of Annex I to these **Regulations,** until four years after the date of entry into force of these **Regulations.**

(ii) the installation of lights with color specifications as prescribed in Annex I to these **Rules,** until 4 years after the effective date of these **Rules, except that vessels of less than 20 meters in length are permanently exempt;**

(c) The repositioning of lights as a result of conversion **from Imperial** to metric units and rounding off measurement figures, **permanent exemption.**

(iii) the repositioning of lights as a result of conversion to metric units and rounding off measurement figures, **are permanently exempt; and**

(d)(i) The repositioning of masthead lights on vessels of less than 150 meters in length, resulting from the prescriptions of Section 3(a) of Annex I to these Regulations, permanent exemption.
(ii) The repositioning of masthead lights on vessels of 150 meters or

(iv) the horizontal repositioning of masthead lights prescribed by Annex I to these Rules:
(1) on vessels of less than 150 meters in length, permanent exemption.
(2) on vessels of 150 meters or more in length, until 9 years

COMMENTS

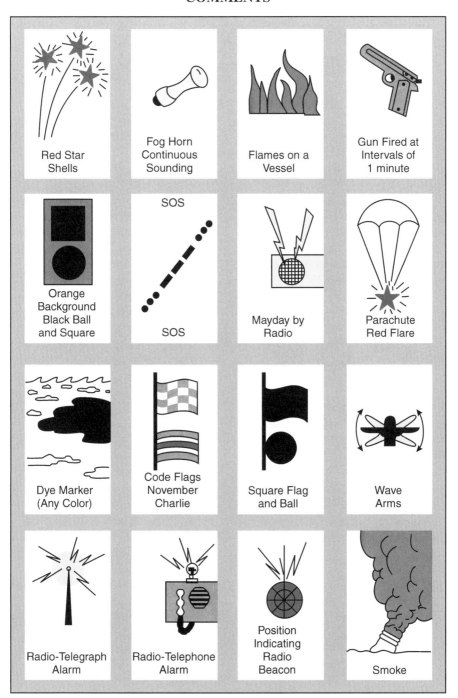

Figure 47. Distress signals.

more in length, resulting from the prescriptions of Section 3(a) of Annex I to these Regulations, until 9 years after the date of entry into force of these Regulations.

(e) The repositioning of masthead lights resulting from the prescriptions of Section 2(b) of Annex I to these Regulations, until 9 years after the date of entry into force of these Regulations.

(f) The repositioning of sidelights resulting from the prescriptions of Sections 2(g) and 3(b) of Annex I to these Regulations, until 9 years after the date of entry into force of these Regulations.

(g) The requirements for sound signal appliances prescribed in Annex III to these Regulations, until 9 years after the date of entry into force of these Regulations.

(h) The repositioning of all-round lights resulting from the prescription of Section 9(b) of Annex I to these Regulations, permanent exemption.

after the effective date of these Rules.

(v) the restructuring or repositioning of all lights to meet the prescriptions of Annex I to these Rules, until 9 years after the effective date of these Rules;

(vi) power-driven vessels of 12 meters or more but less than 20 meters in length are permanently exempt from the provisions of Rule 23(a)(i) and 23(a)(iv) provided that, in place of these lights, the vessel exhibits a white light aft visible all round the horizon; and

(vii) the requirements for sound signal appliances prescribed in Annex III to these Rules, until 9 years after the effective date of these Rules.

COMMENTS

Positioning and Technical Details
of Lights and Shapes

1. Definition

The term "height above the hull" means height above the uppermost continuous deck. This height shall be measured from the position vertically beneath the location of the light.

2. Vertical positioning and spacing of lights

(a) On a power-driven vessel of 20 meters or more in length the masthead lights shall be placed as follows:

(i) the forward masthead light, or if only one masthead light is carried, then that light, at a height above the hull of not less than 6 meters, and, if the breadth of the vessel exceeds 6 meters, then at a height above the hull not less than such breadth, so however that the light need not be placed at a greater height above the hull than 12 meters;

(ii) when two masthead lights are carried the after one shall be at least 4.5 meters vertically higher than the forward one.

(b) The vertical separation of masthead lights of power-driven vessels shall be such that in all normal conditions of trim the after light will be seen over and separate from the forward light at a distance of 1000 meters from the stem when viewed from sea level.

(c) The masthead light of a power-driven vessel of 12 meters but less than 20 meters in length shall be placed at a height above the gunwale of not less than 2.5 meters.

33 CFR 84
Positioning and Technical Details
of Lights and Shapes

§ 84.01 Definitions

(a) The term "height above the hull" means height above the uppermost continuous deck. This height shall be measured from the position vertically beneath the location of the light.

(b) High-speed craft means a craft capable of maximum speed in meters per second (m/s) equal to or exceeding: $3.7\nabla0.1667$; where ∇ = displacement corresponding to the design waterline (meters^3).

(c) The term "practical cut-off" means, for vessels 20 meters or more in length, 12.5 percent of the minimum luminous intensity (Table 84.15(b)) corresponding to the greatest range of visibility for which the requirements of Annex I are met.

(d) The term "Rule" or "Rules" means the Inland Navigation Rules contained in Sec. 2 of the Inland Navigational Rules Act of 1980 (Pub. L. 96-591, 94 Stat. 3415, 33 U.S.C. 2001, December 24, 1980) as amended.

Note to paragraph (b): The same formula expressed in pounds and knots is maximum speed in knots (kts) equal to or exceeding 1.98 (lbs) $3.7\nabla0.1667$; where ∇ = displacement corresponding to design waterline in pounds.

§ 84.03 Vertical positioning and spacing of lights

(a) On a power-driven vessel of 20 meters or more in length, the masthead lights shall be placed as follows:

(1) The forward masthead light, or if only one masthead light is carried, then that light, at a height above the hull of not less than 5 meters, and, if the breadth of the vessel exceeds 5 meters, then at a height above the hull not less than such breadth, so however that the light need not be placed at a greater height above the hull than 8 meters;

(2) When two masthead lights are carried, the after one shall be at least 2 meters vertically higher than the forward one.

(b) The vertical separation of the masthead lights of power-driven vessels shall be such that in all normal conditions of trim, the after light will be seen over and separate from the forward light at a distance of 1000 meters from the stem when viewed from water level.

(c) The masthead light of a power-driven vessel of 12 meters but less than 20 meters in length shall be placed at a height above the gunwale of not less than 2.5 meters.

(d) A power-driven vessel of less than 12 meters in length may carry the uppermost light at a height of less than 2.5 meters above the gunwale. When, however, a masthead light is carried in addition to sidelights and a sternlight or the all-round light prescribed in Rule 23(c)(i) is carried in addition to sidelights, then such masthead light or all-round light shall be carried at least 1 meter higher than the sidelights.

(e) One of the two or three masthead lights prescribed for a power-driven vessel when engaged in towing or pushing another vessel shall be placed in the same position as either the forward masthead light or the after masthead light; provided that, if carried on the aftermast, the lowest after masthead light shall be at least 4.5 meters vertically higher than the forward masthead light.

(f)(i) The masthead light or lights prescribed in Rule 23(a) shall be so placed as to be above and clear of all other lights and obstructions except as described in subparagraph (ii).

(ii) When it is impracticable to carry the all-round lights prescribed by Rule 27(b)(i) or Rule 28 below the masthead lights, they may be carried above the after masthead light(s) or vertically in between the forward masthead light(s) and after masthead light(s), provided that in the latter case the requirement of Section 3(c) of this Annex shall be complied with.

(g) The sidelights of a power-driven vessel shall be placed at a height above the hull not greater than three quarters of that of the forward masthead light. They shall not be so low as to be interfered with by deck lights.

(h) The sidelights, if in a combined lantern and carried on a power-driven vessel of less than 20 meters in length, shall be placed not less than 1 meter below the masthead light.

(i) When the Rules prescribe two or three lights to be carried in a vertical line, they shall be spaced as follows:

(i) on a vessel of 20 meters in length or more, such lights shall be spaced not less than 2 meters apart, and the lowest of these lights shall, except where a towing light is required, be placed at a height of not less than 4 meters above the hull;

(ii) on a vessel of less than 20 meters in length such lights shall be spaced not less than 1 meter apart and the lowest of these lights shall, except where a towing light is required, be placed at a height of not less than 2 meters above the gunwale;

(iii) when three lights are carried they shall be equally spaced.

(j) The lower of the two all-round lights prescribed for a vessel when engaged in fishing shall be at a height above the sidelights not less than twice the distance between the two vertical lights.

(k) The forward anchor light prescribed in Rule 30(a)(i), when two are carried, shall not be less than 4.5 meters above the after one. On a vessel of 50 meters or more in length, this forward anchor light shall be placed at a height of not less than 6 meters above the hull.

3. Horizontal positioning and spacing of lights

(a) When two masthead lights are prescribed for a power-driven vessel, the horizontal distance between them shall not be less than one half of the length of the vessel but need not be more than 100 meters. The forward light shall be placed not more than one quarter of the length of the vessel from the stem.

(d) The masthead light, or the all-round light described in Rule 23(c), of a power-driven vessel of less than 12 meters in length shall be carried at least one meter higher than the sidelights.

(e) One of the two or three masthead lights prescribed for a power-driven vessel when engaged in towing or pushing another vessel shall be placed in the same position as either the forward masthead light or the after masthead light, provided that the lowest after masthead light shall be at least 2 meters vertically higher than the highest forward masthead light.

(f)(1) The masthead light or lights prescribed in Rule 23(a) shall be so placed as to be above and clear of all other lights and obstructions except as described in paragraph (f)(2) of this section.

(2) When it is impracticable to carry the all-round lights prescribed in Rule 27(b)(i) below the masthead lights, they may be carried above the after masthead light(s) or vertically in between the forward masthead light(s) and after masthead light(s), provided that in the latter case the requirement of 84.05(d) shall be complied with.

(g) The sidelights of a power-driven vessel shall be placed at least one meter lower than the forward masthead light. They shall not be so low as to be interfered with by deck lights.

(h) [Reserved]

(i) When the Rules prescribe two or three lights to be carried in a vertical line, they shall be spaced as follows:

(1) On a vessel of 20 meters in length or more such lights shall be spaced not less than 1 meter apart, and the lowest of these lights shall, except where a towing light is required, be placed at a height of not less than 4 meters above the hull;

(2) On a vessel of less than 20 meters in length such lights shall be spaced not less than 1 meter apart and the lowest of these lights shall, except where a towing light is required, be placed at a height of not less than 2 meters above the gunwale;

(3) When three lights are carried they shall be equally spaced.

(j) The lower of the two all-round lights prescribed for a vessel when engaged in fishing shall be at a height above the sidelights not less than twice the distance between the two vertical lights.

(k) The forward anchor light prescribed in Rule 30(a)(i), when two are carried, shall not be less than 4.5 meters above the after one. On a vessel of 50 meters or more in length, this forward anchor light shall be placed at a height of not less than 6 meters above the hull.

§ 84.05 Horizontal positioning and spacing of lights

(a) Except as specified in paragraph (e) of this section, when two masthead lights are prescribed for a power-driven vessel, the horizontal distance between them must not be less than one quarter of the length of the vessel but need not be more than 50

(b) On a power-driven vessel of 20 meters or more in length the sidelights shall not be placed in front of the forward masthead lights. They shall be placed at or near the side of the vessel.

(c) When the lights prescribed in Rule 27(b)(i) or Rule 28 are placed vertically between the forward masthead light(s) and the after masthead light(s) these all-round lights shall be placed at a horizontal distance of not less than 2 meters from the fore and aft centerline of the vessel in the athwartship direction.

(d) When only one masthead light is prescribed for a power-driven vessel, this light shall be exhibited forward of amidships; except that a vessel of less than 20 meters in length need not exhibit this light forward of amidships but shall exhibit it as far forward as is practicable.

4. Details of location of direction-indicating lights for fishing vessels, dredgers, and vessels engaged in underwater operations

(a) The light indicating the direction of the outlying gear from a vessel engaged in fishing as prescribed in Rule 26(c)(ii) shall be placed at a horizontal distance of not less than 2 meters and not more than 6 meters away from the two all-round red and white lights. This light shall be placed not higher than the all-round white light prescribed in Rule 26(c)(i) and not lower than the sidelights.

(b) The lights and shapes on a vessel engaged in dredging or underwater operations to indicate the obstructed side and/or the side on which it is safe to pass, as prescribed in Rule 27(d)(i) and (ii), shall be placed at the maximum practical horizontal distance, but in no case less than 2 meters, from the lights or shapes prescribed in Rule 27(b)(i) and (ii). In no case shall the upper of these lights or shapes be at a greater height than the lower of the three lights or shapes prescribed in Rule 27(b)(i) and (ii).

5. Screens for sidelights

The sidelights of vessels of 20 meters or more in length shall be fitted with inboard screens painted matt black and meeting the requirements of Section 9 of this Annex. On vessels of less than 20 meters in length the sidelights, if necessary to meet the requirements of Section 9 of this Annex, shall be fitted with inboard matt black screens. With a combined lantern, using a single vertical filament and a very narrow division between the green and red sections, external screens need not be fitted.

6. Shapes

(a) Shapes shall be black and of the following sizes:
(i) a ball shall have a diameter of not less than 0.6 meter;
(ii) a cone shall have a base diameter of not less than 0.6 meter and a height equal to its diameter;
(iii) a cylinder shall have a diameter of at least 0.6 meter and a height of twice its diameter;

meters. The forward light shall be placed not more than one half of the length of the vessel from the stem.

(b) On a power-driven vessel of 20 meters or more in length, the sidelights shall not be placed in front of the forward masthead lights. They shall be placed at or near the side of the vessel.

(c) When the lights prescribed in Rule 27(b)(i) are placed vertically between the forward masthead light(s) and the after masthead light(s), these all-round lights shall be placed at a horizontal distance of not less than 2 meters from the fore and aft centerline of the vessel in the athwartship direction.

(d) When only one masthead light is prescribed for a power-driven vessel, this light must be exhibited forward of amidships. For a vessel of less than 20 meters in length, the vessel shall exhibit one masthead light as far forward as is practicable.

(e) On power-driven vessels 50 meters but less than 60 meters in length operated on the Western Rivers, and those waters specified in § 89.25, the horizontal distance between masthead lights shall not be less than 10 meters.

§ 84.07 Details of location of direction-indicating lights for fishing vessels, dredgers, and vessels engaged in underwater operations

(a) The light indicating the direction of the outlying gear from a vessel engaged in fishing as prescribed in Rule 26(c)(ii) shall be placed at a horizontal distance of not less than 2 meters and not more than 6 meters away from the two all-round red and white lights. This light shall be placed not higher than the all-round white light prescribed in Rule 26(c)(i) and not lower than the sidelights.

(b) The lights and shapes on a vessel engaged in dredging or underwater operations to indicate the obstructed side and/or the side on which it is safe to pass, as prescribed in Rule 27(d)(i) and (ii), shall be placed at the maximum practical horizontal distance, but in no case less than 2 meters, from the lights or shapes prescribed in Rule 27(b)(i) and (ii). In no case shall the upper of these lights or shapes be at a greater height than the lower of the three lights or shapes prescribed in Rule 27(b)(i) and (ii).

§ 84.09 Screens

(a) The sidelights of vessels of 20 meters or more in length shall be fitted with mat black inboard screens and meet the requirements of § 84.17. On vessels of less than 20 meters in length, the sidelights, if necessary to meet the requirements of § 84.17, shall be fitted with mat black inboard screens. With a combined lantern, using a single vertical filament and a very narrow division between the green and red sections, external screens need not be fitted.

(b) On power-driven vessels less than 12 meters in length constructed after July 31, 1983, the masthead light, or the all-round light described in Rule 23(c) shall be screened to prevent direct illumination of the vessel forward of the operator's position.

§ 84.11 Shapes

(a) Shapes shall be black and of the following sizes:
(1) A ball shall have a diameter of not less than 0.6 meter;
(2) A cone shall have a base diameter of not less than 0.6 meter and a height equal to its diameter;
(3) A diamond shape shall consist of two cones (as defined in paragraph (a)(2) of this section) having a common base.

119

(iv) a diamond shape shall consist of two cones as defined in (ii) above having a common base.

(b) The vertical distance between shapes shall be at least 1.5 meter.

(c) In a vessel of less than 20 meters in length, shapes of lesser dimensions but commensurate with the size of the vessel may be used and the distance apart may be correspondingly reduced.

7. Color specification of lights

The chromaticity of all navigation lights shall conform to the following standards, which lie within the boundaries of the area of the diagram specified for each color by the International Commission on Illumination (CIE).

The boundaries of the area for each color are given by indicating the corner coordinates, which are as follows:

(i) White:

x	0.525	0.525	0.452	0.310	0.310	0.443
y	0.382	0.440	0.440	0.348	0.283	0.382

(ii) Green:

x	0.028	0.009	0.300	0.203
y	0.385	0.723	0.511	0.356

(iii) Red:

x	0.680	0.660	0.735	0.721
y	0.320	0.320	0.265	0.259

(iv) Yellow:

x	0.612	0.618	0.575	0.575
y	0.382	0.382	0.425	0.406

8. Intensity of lights

(a) The minimum luminous intensity of lights shall be calculated by using the formula:

$$I = 3.43 \times 10^6 \times T \times D^2 \times K^{-D}$$

where:

I is luminous intensity in candelas under service conditions,

T is threshold factor 2×10^{-7} lux,

D is range of visibility (luminous range) of the light in nautical miles,

K is atmospheric transmissivity. For prescribed lights, the value of K shall be 0.8, corresponding to a meteorological visibility of approximately 13 nautical miles.

(b) A selection of figures derived from the formula is given in the following table:

(b) The vertical distance between shapes shall be at least 1.5 meter.

(c) In a vessel of less than 20 meters in length shapes of lesser dimensions but commensurate with the size of the vessel may be used and the distance apart may be correspondingly reduced.

§ 84.13 Color specification of lights

(a) The chromaticity of all navigation lights shall conform to the following standards, which lie within the boundaries of the area of the diagram specified for each color by the International Commission on Illumination (CIE), in the "Colors of Light Signals", which is incorporated by reference. It is Publication CIE No. 2.2. (TC-1.6), 1975, and is available from the Illumination Engineering Society, 345 East 47th Street, New York, NY 10017. It is also available for inspection at the Office of the Federal Register, Room 8401, 1100 L Street N.W., Washington, D.C. 20408. This incorporation by reference was approved by the Director of the Federal Register.

(b) The boundaries of the area for each color are given by indicating the corner coordinates, which are as follows:

(i) White:

x	0.525	0.525	0.452	0.310	0.310	0.443
y	0.382	0.440	0.440	0.348	0.283	0.382

(ii) Green:

x	0.028	0.009	0.300	0.203
y	0.385	0.723	0.511	0.356

(iii) Red:

x	0.680	0.660	0.735	0.721
y	0.320	0.320	0.265	0.259

(iv) Yellow:

x	0.612	0.618	0.575	0.575
y	0.382	0.382	0.425	0.406

§ 84.15 Intensity of lights

(a) The minimum luminous intensity of lights shall be calculated by using the formula:

$$I = 3.43 \times 10^6 \times T \times D^2 \times K^{-D}$$

where:

I is luminous intensity in candelas under service conditions,

T is threshold factor 2×10^{-7} lux,

D is range of visibility (luminous range) of the light in nautical miles,

K is atmospheric transmissivity. For prescribed lights, the value of K shall be 0.8, corresponding to a meteorological visibility of approximately 13 nautical miles.

(b) A selection of figures derived from the formula is given in Table 84.15(b).

Table 84.15(b)

Range of Visibility (Luminous Range) of Light in Nautical Miles D	Luminous Intensity of Light in Candelas for K = 0.9 I
1	0.9
2	1.3
3	12
4	27
5	52
6	94

Note: The maximum luminous intensity of navigation lights should be limited to avoid undue glare. This shall not be achieved by a variable control of the luminous intensity.

9. Horizontal sectors

(a)(i) In the forward direction, sidelights as fitted on the vessel shall show the minimum required intensities. The intensities shall decrease to reach practical cut-off between 1 degree and 3 degrees outside the prescribed sectors.

(ii) For sternlights and masthead lights and at 22.5 degrees abaft the beam for sidelights, the minimum required intensities shall be maintained over the arc of the horizon up to 5 degrees within the limits of the sectors prescribed in Rule 21. From 5 degrees within the prescribed sectors the intensity may decrease by 50 percent up to the prescribed limits; it shall decrease steadily to reach practical cut-off at not more than 5 degrees outside the prescribed sectors.

(b)(i) All-round lights shall be so located as not to be obscured by masts, topmasts, or structures within angular sectors of more than 6 degrees, except anchor lights prescribed in Rule 30, which need not be placed at an impracticable height above the hull.

(ii) If it is impracticable to comply with paragraph (b)(i) of this section by exhibiting only one all-round light, two all-round lights shall be used suitably positioned or screened so that they appear, as far as practicable, as one light at a distance of one mile."

10. Vertical sectors

(a) The vertical sectors of electric lights as fitted, with the exception of lights on sailing vessels underway shall ensure that:

(i) at least the required minimum intensity is maintained at all angles from 5 degrees above to 5 degrees below the horizontal;

(ii) at least 60 percent of the required minimum intensity is maintained from 7.5 degrees above to 7.5 degrees below the horizontal.

(b) In the case of sailing vessels underway, the vertical sectors of electric lights as fitted shall ensure that:

(i) at least the required minimum intensity is maintained at all angles from 5 degrees above to 5 degrees below the horizontal;

(ii) at least 50 percent of the required minimum intensity is maintained from 25 degrees above to 25 degrees below the horizontal.

Range of Visibility (Luminous Range) of Light in Nautical Miles *D*	Luminous Intensity of Light in Candelas for K = 0.9 *I*
1	0.9
2	1.3
3	12
4	27
5	52
6	94

§ 84.17 Horizontal sectors

(a)(1) In the forward direction, sidelights as fitted on the vessel shall show the minimum required intensities. The intensities shall decrease to reach practical cut-off between 1 degree and 3 degrees outside the prescribed sectors.

(2) For sternlights and masthead lights and at 22.5 degrees abaft the beam for sidelights, the minimum required intensities shall be maintained over the arc of the horizon up to 5 degrees within the limits of the sectors prescribed in Rule 21. From 5 degrees within the prescribed sectors, the intensity may decrease by 50 percent up to the prescribed limits; it shall decrease steadily to reach practical cutoff at not more than 5 degrees outside the prescribed sectors.

(b) All-round lights shall be so located as not to be obscured by masts, topmasts or structures within angular sectors of more than 6 degrees, except anchor lights prescribed in Rule 30, which need not be placed at an impracticable height above the hull, and the all-round white light described in Rule 23(d), which may not be obscured at all.

(c) If it is impracticable to comply with paragraph (b) of this section by exhibiting only one all-round light, two all-round lights shall be used suitably positioned or screened to appear, as far as practicable, as one light at a minimum distance of one nautical mile.

Note to paragraph (c): Two unscreened all-round lights that are 1.28 meters apart or less will appear as one light to the naked eye at a distance of one nautical mile.

§ 84.19 Vertical sectors

(a) The vertical sectors of electric lights as fitted, with the exception of lights on sailing vessels underway and on unmanned barges, shall ensure that:

(1) At least the required minimum intensity is maintained at all angles from 5 degrees above to 5 degrees below the horizontal;

(2) At least 60 percent of the required minimum intensity is maintained from 7.5 degrees above to 7.5 degrees below the horizontal.

(b) In the case of sailing vessels underway, the vertical sectors of electric lights as fitted shall ensure that:

(1) At least the required minimum intensity is maintained at all angles from 5 degrees above to 5 degrees below the horizontal;

(2) At least 50 percent of the required minimum intensity is maintained from 25 degrees above to 25 degrees below the horizontal.

(c) In the case of lights other than electric, these specifications shall be met as closely as possible.

11. Intensity of nonelectric lights

Nonelectric lights shall so far as practicable comply with the minimum intensities, as specified in the Table given in Section 8 of this Annex.

12. Maneuvering light

Notwithstanding the provisions of paragraph 2(f) of this Annex, the maneuvering light described in Rule 34(b) shall be placed in the same fore and aft vertical plane as the masthead light or lights and, where practicable, at a minimum height of 2 meters vertically above the forward masthead light, provided that it shall be carried not less than 2 meters vertically above or below the after masthead light. On a vessel where only one masthead light is carried, the maneuvering light, if fitted, shall be carried where it can best be seen, not less than 2 meters vertically apart from the masthead light.

13. High-Speed Craft[*]

(a) The masthead light of high-speed craft may be placed at a height related to the breadth of the craft lower than that prescribed in paragraph 2(a)(i) of this annex, provided that the base angle of the isosceles triangles formed by the sidelights and masthead light, when seen in end elevation, is not less than 27°.

(b) On high-speed craft of 50 meters or more in length, the vertical separation between foremast and mainmast light of 4.5 meters required by paragraph 29(a)(ii) of this annex may be modified provided that such distance shall not be less than the value determined by the following formula:

$$y = \frac{(a + 17\Psi)C + 2}{1,000}$$

where:

y is the height of the mainmast light above the foremast light in meters;
a is the height of the foremast light above the water surface in service condition in meters;
Ψ is the trim in service condition in degrees;
C is the horizontal separation of masthead lights in meters.

14. Approval

The construction of lights and shapes and the installation of lights onboard the vessel shall be to the satisfaction of the appropriate authority of the State whose flag the vessel is entitled to fly.

---

[*] Refer to the International Code of Safety for High-Speed Craft, 1994 and the International Code of Safety for High-Speed Craft, 2000.

(c) In the case of unmanned barges, the minimum required intensity of electric lights as fitted shall be maintained on the horizontal.

(d) In the case of lights other than electric lights, these specifications shall be met as closely as possible.

§ 84.21 Intensity of nonelectric lights

Nonelectric lights shall so far as practicable comply with the minimum intensities, as specified in the Table given in § 84.15.

§ 84.23 Maneuvering light

Notwithstanding the provisions of § 84.03(f), the maneuvering light described in Rule 34(b) shall be placed approximately in the same fore and aft vertical plane as the masthead light or lights and, where practicable, at a minimum height of one-half meter vertically above the forward masthead light, provided that it shall be carried not less than one-half meter vertically above or below the after masthead light. On a vessel where only one masthead light is carried the maneuvering light, if fitted, shall be carried where it can best be seen, not less than one-half meter vertically apart from the masthead light.

§ 84.24 High-Speed Craft

The masthead light of high-speed craft with a length to breadth ratio of less than 3.0 may be placed at a height related to the breadth lower than that prescribed in Sec. 84.03(a)(1), provided that the base angle of the isosceles triangle formed by the sidelights and masthead light when seen in end elevation is not less than 27° as determined by the formula in paragraph (b) of this section.

(b) The minimum height of masthead light above sidelights is to be determined by the following formula:

$$\text{Tan } 27° = x/y$$

where:

y is the horizontal distance between the sidelights and
x is the height of the forward masthead light.

§ 84.25 Approval [Reserved]

Additional Signals for Fishing Vessels Fishing in Close Proximity

1. General

The lights mentioned herein shall, if exhibited in pursuance of Rule 26(d), be placed where they can best be seen. They shall be at least 0.9 meter apart but at a lower level than lights prescribed in Rule 26(b)(i) and (c)(i). The lights shall be visible all around the horizon at a distance of at least 1 mile but at a lesser distance than the lights prescribed by these rules for fishing vessels.

2. Signals for trawlers

(a) Vessels of 20 meters or more in length when engaged in trawling, whether using demersal or pelagic gear, shall exhibit:
   (i) when shooting their nets: two white lights in a vertical line;
   (ii) when hauling their nets: one white light over one red light in a vertical line;
   (iii) when the net has come fast upon an obstruction: two red lights in a vertical line.

(b) Each vessel of 20 meters or more in length engaged in pair trawling shall exhibit:
   (i) by night, a searchlight directed forward and in the direction of the other vessel of the pair;
   (ii) when shooting or hauling their nets or when their nets have come fast upon an obstruction, the lights prescribed in 2(a) above.

(c) A vessel of less than 20 meters in length engaged in trawling, whether using demersal or pelagic gear, or engaged in pair trawling, may exhibit the lights prescribed in paragraphs (a) or (b) of this section, as appropriate.

3. Signals for purse seiners

Vessels engaged in fishing with purse seine gear may exhibit two yellow lights in a vertical line. These lights shall flash alternately every second and with equal light and occultation duration. These lights may be exhibited only when the vessel is hampered by its fishing gear.

33 CFR 85
Additional Signals for Fishing Vessels Fishing in Close Proximity

§ 85.1 General

The lights mentioned herein shall, if exhibited in pursuance of Rule 26(d), be placed where they can best be seen. They shall be at least 0.9 meter apart but at a lower level than lights prescribed in Rule 26(b)(i) and (c)(i) contained in the Inland Navigational Rules Act of 1980. The lights shall be visible all around the horizon at a distance of at least 1 mile but at a lesser distance from the lights prescribed by these Rules for fishing vessels.

§ 85.3 Signals for trawlers

(a) Vessels when engaged in trawling, whether using demersal or pelagic gear, may exhibit:

(1) When shooting their nets: two white lights in a vertical line;

(2) When hauling their nets: one white light over one red light in a vertical line;

(3) When the net has come fast upon an obstruction: two red lights in a vertical line.

(b) Each vessel engaged in pair trawling may exhibit:

(1) By night, a searchlight directed forward and in the direction of the other vessel of the pair;

(2) When shooting or hauling their nets or when their nets have come fast upon an obstruction, the lights prescribed in paragraph (a) of this section.

§ 85.5 Signals for purse seiners

Vessels engaged in fishing with purse seine gear may exhibit two yellow lights in a vertical line. These lights shall flash alternately every second and with equal light and occultation duration. These lights may be exhibited only when the vessel is hampered by its fishing gear.

Technical Details of Sound Signal Appliances

1. WHISTLES

(a) Frequencies and range of audibility

The fundamental frequency of the signal shall lie within the range 70–700 Hz. The range of audibility of the signal from a whistle shall be determined by those frequencies, which may include the fundamental and/or one or more higher frequencies, which lie within the range 180–700Hz (± 1 percent) for a vessel of 20 meters or more in length, or 180–2100Hz (± 1 percent) for a vessel of less than 20 meters in length and which provide the sound pressure levels specified in paragraph 1(c) below.

(b) Limits of fundamental frequencies

To ensure a wide variety of whistle characteristics, the fundamental frequency of a whistle shall be between the following limits:

(i) 70–200 Hz, for a vessel 200 meters or more in length;

(ii) 130–350 Hz, for a vessel 75 meters but less than 200 meters in length;

(iii) 250–700 Hz, for a vessel less than 75 meters in length.

(c) Sound signal intensity and range of audibility

A whistle fitted in a vessel shall provide, in the direction of maximum intensity of the whistle and at a distance of 1 meter from it, a sound pressure level in at least one 1/3-octave band within the range of frequencies 180–700Hz (± 1 percent) for a vessel of 20 meters or more in length, or 180–2100Hz (± 1 percent) for a vessel of less than 20 meters in length, of not less than the appropriate figure given in the table below.

33 CFR 86
Technical Details of Sound Signal Appliances

SUBPART A—WHISTLES

§ 86.01 Frequencies and range of audibility

The fundamental frequency of the signal shall lie within the range 70–525 Hz. The range of audibility of the signal from a whistle shall be determined by those frequencies, which may include the fundamental and/or one or more higher frequencies that lie within the frequency ranges and provide the sound pressure levels specified in § 86.05.

§ 86.03 Limits of fundamental frequencies

To ensure a wide variety of whistle characteristics, the fundamental frequency of a whistle shall be between the following limits:

(a) 70–200 Hz, for a vessel 200 meters or more in length;

(b) 130–350 Hz, for a vessel 75 meters but less than 200 meters in length;

(c) 250–525 Hz, for a vessel less than 75 meters in length.

§ 86.05 Sound signal intensity and range of audibility

A whistle on a vessel shall provide, in the direction of the forward axis of the whistle and at a distance of 1 meter from it, a sound pressure level in at least one 1/3-octave band of not less than the appropriate figure given in Table 86.05 within the following frequency ranges (± 1 percent):

(a) 130–1,200 Hz, for a vessel 75 meters or more in length;

(b) 250–1,600 Hz, for a vessel 20 meters but less than 75 meters in length;

(c) 250–2,100 Hz, for a vessel 12 meters but less than 20 meters in length.

Length of Vessel in Meters	$\frac{1}{3}$-octave band level at 1 meter in dB referred to 2×10^{-5} N/m²	Audibility Range in Nautical Miles
200 or more	143	2
75 but less than 200	138	1.5
20 but less than 75	130	1
Less than 20	120[1] 115[2] 111[3]	0.5

[1] When the measured frequencies lie within the range 180–450Hz
[2] When the measured frequencies lie within the range 450–800Hz
[3] When the measured frequencies lie within the range 800–2100Hz

Note: The range of audibility in the table above is for information and is approximately the range at which a whistle may be heard on its forward axis with 90 percent probability in conditions of still air onboard a vessel having average background noise level at the listening posts (taken to be 68 dB in the octave band centered on 250 Hz and 63 dB in the octave band centered on 500 Hz). In practice the range at which a whistle may be heard is extremely variable and depends critically on weather conditions; the values given can be regarded as typical but under conditions of strong wind or high ambient noise level at the listening post the range may be much reduced.

(d) Directional properties

The sound pressure level of a directional whistle shall be not more than 4 dB below the prescribed sound pressure level on the axis at any direction in the horizontal plane within ± 45 degrees of the axis. The sound pressure level at any other direction in the horizontal plane shall be not more than 10 dB below the prescribed sound pressure level on the axis, so that the range in any direction will be at least half the range on the forward axis. The sound pressure level shall be measured in that one-third octave band that determines the audibility range.

(e) Positioning of whistles

When a directional whistle is to be used as the only whistle on a vessel, it shall be installed with its maximum intensity directed straight ahead. A whistle shall be placed as high as practicable on a vessel, in order to reduce interception of the emitted sound by obstructions and also to minimize hearing damage risk to personnel. The sound pressure level of the vessel's own signal at listening posts shall not exceed 110 dB(A) and so far as practicable should not exceed 100 dB(A).

(f) Fitting of more than one whistle

If whistles are fitted at a distance apart of more than 100 meters, it shall be so arranged that they are not sounded simultaneously.

Table 86.05

Length of Vessel in Meters	Fundamental Frequency Range (Hz)	For Measured Frequencies (Hz)	$\frac{1}{3}$-octave band level at 1 meter in dB referred to $2 \times 10^{-5} \, N/m^2$	Audibility Range in Nautical Miles
200 or more	70–200	130–180	145	2
		180–250	143	
		250–1,200	140	
75 but less than 200	130–350	130–180	140	1.5
		180–250	138	
		250–1,200	134	
20 but less than 75	250–525	250–450	130	1.0
		450–800	125	
		800–1,600	121	
12 but less than 20	250–525	250–450	120	0.5
		450–800	115	
		800–2100	111	

Note: The range of audibility in the table above is for information and is approximately the range at which a whistle may usually be heard on its forward axis in conditions of still air onboard a vessel having average background noise level at the listening posts (taken to be 68 dB in the octave band centered on 250 Hz and 63 dB in the octave band centered on 500 Hz). In practice the range at which a whistle may be heard is extremely variable and depends critically on weather conditions; the values given can be regarded as typical but under conditions of strong wind or high ambient noise level at the listening post the range may be much reduced.

§ 86.07 Directional properties

The sound pressure level of a directional whistle shall be not more than 4 dB below the sound pressure level specified in § 86.05 in any direction in the horizontal plane within + 45° of the forward axis. The sound pressure level of the whistle in any other direction in the horizontal plane shall not be more than 10 dB less than the sound pressure level specified for the forward axis, so that the range of audibility in any direction will be at least half the range required on the forward axis. The sound pressure level shall be measured in that one-third octave band that determines the audibility range.

§ 86.09 Positioning of whistles

(a) When a directional whistle is to be used as the only whistle on the vessel and is permanently installed, it shall be installed with its forward axis directed forward.

(b) A whistle shall be placed as high as practicable on a vessel, in order to reduce interception of the emitted sound by obstructions and also to minimize hearing damage risk to personnel. The sound pressure level of the vessel's own signal at listening posts shall not exceed 110 dB(A) and so far as practicable should not exceed 100 dB(A).

§ 86.11 Fitting of more than one whistle

If whistles are fitted at a distance apart of more than 100 meters, they shall not be sounded simultaneously.

(g) Combined whistle systems

If due to the presence of obstructions, the sound field of a single whistle or of one of the whistles referred to in paragraph 1(f) above is likely to have a zone of greatly reduced signal level, it is recommended that a combined whistle system be fitted so as to overcome this reduction. For the purposes of the Rules, a combined whistle system is to be regarded as a single whistle. The whistles of a combined system shall be located at a distance apart of not more than 100 meters and arranged to be sounded simultaneously. The frequency of any one whistle shall differ from those of the others by at least 10 Hz.

2. BELL OR GONG

(a) Intensity of signal

A bell or gong, or other device having similar sound characteristics shall produce a sound pressure level of not less than 110 dB at a distance of 1 meter from it.

(b) Construction

Bells and gongs shall be made of corrosion-resistant material and designed to give a clear tone. The diameter of the mouth of the bell shall be not less than 300 mm for vessels of 20 meters or more in length. Where practicable, a power-driven bell striker is recommended to ensure constant force but manual operation shall be possible. The mass of the striker shall be not less than 3 percent of the mass of the bell.

3. APPROVAL

The construction of sound signal appliances, their performance and their installation on board the vessel shall be to the satisfaction of the appropriate authority of the State whose flag the vessel is entitled to fly.

§ 86.13 Combined whistle systems

(a) A combined whistle system is a number of whistles (sound emitting sources) operated together. For the purposes of the Rules a combined whistle system is to be regarded as a single whistle.

(b) The whistles of a combined system shall:

(1) Be located at a distance apart of not more than 100 meters,

(2) Be sounded simultaneously,

(3) Each have a fundamental frequency different from those of the others by at least 10 Hz, and

(4) Have a tonal characteristic appropriate for the length of vessel that shall be evidenced by at least two-thirds of the whistles in the combined system having fundamental frequencies falling within the limits prescribed in § 86.03, or if there are only two whistles in the combined system, by the higher fundamental frequency falling within the limits prescribed § 86.03.

Note: If due to the presence of obstructions, the sound field of a single whistle or of one of the whistles referred to in § 86.11 is likely to have a zone of greatly reduced signal level a combined whistle system should be fitted so as to overcome this reduction.

§ 86.15 Towing vessel whistles

A power-driven vessel normally engaged in pushing ahead or towing alongside may, at all times, use a whistle whose characteristic falls within the limits prescribed by § 86.03 for the longest customary composite length of the vessel and its tow.

SUBPART B—BELL OR GONG

§ 86.21 Intensity of signal

A bell or gong, or other device having similar sound characteristics shall produce a sound pressure level of not less than 110 dB at 1 meter.

§ 86.23 Construction

Bells and gongs shall be made of corrosion-resistant material and designed to give a clear tone. The diameter of the mouth of the bell shall be not less than 300 mm for vessels of more than 20 meters in length, and shall be not less than 200 mm for vessels of 12 to 20 meters in length. The mass of the striker shall be not less than 3 percent of the mass of the bell. The striker shall be capable of manual operation.

Note: When practicable, a power-driven bell striker is recommended to ensure constant force.

SUBPART C—APPROVAL

§ 86.31 Approval [Reserved]

Distress Signals

1. The following signals, used or exhibited either together or separately, indicate distress and need of assistance:

(a) a gun or other explosive signal fired at intervals of about a minute;

(b) a continuous sounding with any fog-signalling apparatus;

(c) rockets or shells, throwing red stars fired one at a time at short intervals;

(d) a signal made by radiotelegraphy or by any other signaling method consisting of the group . . . – – – . . . (SOS) in the Morse Code;

(e) a signal sent by radiotelephony consisting of the spoken word "Mayday";

(f) the International Code Signal of distress indicated by N.C.;

(g) a signal consisting of a square flag having above or below it a ball or anything resembling a ball;

(h) flames on the vessel (as from a burning tar barrel, oil barrel, etc.);

(i) a rocket parachute flare or a hand flare showing a red light;

(j) a smoke signal giving off orange-colored smoke;

(k) slowly and repeatedly raising and lowering arms outstretched to each side;

(l) the radiotelegraph alarm signal;

(m) the radiotelephone alarm signal;

(n) signals transmitted by emergency position-indicating radio beacons;

(o) approved signals transmitted by radiocommunication systems, including survival craft radar transponders.

2. The use or exhibition of any of the foregoing signals except for the purpose of indicating distress and need of assistance and the use of other signals that may be confused with any of the above signals is prohibited.

3. Attention is drawn to the relevant sections of the International Code of Signals, the Merchant Ship Search and Rescue Manual, and the following signals:

(a) a piece of orange-colored canvas with either a black square and circle or other appropriate symbol (for identification from the air);

(b) a dye marker.

33 CFR 87
Distress Signals

§ 87.1 Need of assistance

The following signals, used or exhibited either together or separately, indicate distress and need of assistance:

(a) A gun or other explosive signal fired at intervals of about a minute;

(b) A continuous sounding with any fog-signalling apparatus;

(c) Rockets or shells, throwing red stars fired one at a time at short intervals;

(d) A signal made by radiotelegraphy or by any other signaling method consisting of the group . . . − − − . . . (SOS) in the Morse Code;

(e) A signal sent by radiotelephony consisting of the spoken word "Mayday";

(f) The International Code Signal of distress indicated by N.C.;

(g) A signal consisting of a square flag having above or below it a ball or anything resembling a ball;

(h) Flames on the vessel (as from a burning tar barrel, oil barrel, etc.);

(i) A rocket parachute flare or a hand flare showing a red light;

(j) A smoke signal giving off orange-colored smoke;

(k) Slowly and repeatedly raising and lowering arms outstretched to each side;

(l) The radiotelegraph alarm signal;

(m) The radiotelephone alarm signal;

(n) Signals transmitted by emergency position-indicating radio beacons;

(o) Signals transmitted by radiocommunication systems, including survival craft radar transponders meeting the requirements of 47 CFR 80.1095.

(p) A high-intensity white light flashing at regular intervals from 50 to 70 times per minute.

§ 87.3 Exclusive use

The use or exhibition of any of the foregoing signals except for the purpose of indicating distress and need of assistance and the use of other signals that may be confused with any of the above signals is prohibited.

§ 87.5 Supplemental signals

Attention is drawn to the relevant sections of the International Code of Signals, the Merchant Ship Search and Rescue Manual, the International Telecommunication Union Radio Regulations, and the following signals:

(a) A piece of orange-colored canvas with either a black square and circle or other appropriate symbol (for identification from the air);

(b) A dye marker.

33 CFR 88
Pilot Rules

§ 88.01 Purpose and applicability

This part applies to all vessels operating on United States inland waters and to United States vessels operating on the Canadian waters of the Great Lakes to the extent there is no conflict with Canadian law.

§ 88.03 Definitions

The terms used in this part have the same meaning as defined in the Inland Navigational Rules Act of 1980.

§ 88.05 Copy of Rules

After January 1, 1983, the operator of each self-propelled vessel 12 meters or more in length shall carry onboard and maintain for ready reference a copy of the Inland Navigation Rules.

§ 88.09 Temporary exemption from light and shape requirements when operating under bridges

A vessel's navigation lights and shapes may be lowered if necessary to pass under a bridge.

§ 88.11 Law enforcement vessels

(a) Law enforcement vessels may display a flashing blue light when engaged in direct law enforcement or public safety activities. This light must be located so that it does not interfere with the visibility of the vessel's navigation lights.

(b) The blue light described in this section may be displayed by law enforcement vessels of the United States and the States and their political subdivisions.

§ 88.12 Public Safety Activities

(a) Vessels engaged in government sanctioned public safety activities, and commercial vessels performing similar functions, may display an alternately flashing red and yellow light signal. This identification light signal must be located so that it does not interfere with the visibility of the vessel's navigation lights. The identification light signal may be used only as an identification signal and conveys no special privilege. Vessels using the identification light signal during public safety activities must abide by the Inland Navigation Rules and must not presume that the light or the exigency gives them precedence or right of way.

(b) Public safety activities include but are not limited to patrolling marine parades, regattas, or special water celebrations; traffic control; salvage; firefighting; medical assistance; assisting disabled vessels; and search and rescue.

§ 88.13 Lights on moored barges

(a) The following barges shall display at night and if practicable in periods of restricted visibility the lights described in paragraph (b) of this section:

(1) Every barge projecting into a buoyed or restricted channel.

(2) Every barge so moored that it reduces the available navigable width of any channel to less than 80 meters.

(3) Barges moored in groups more than two barges wide or to a maximum width of over 25 meters.

(4) Every barge not moored parallel to the bank or dock.

(b) Barges described in paragraph (a) of this section shall carry two unobstructed all-round white lights of an intensity to be visible for at least one nautical mile and meeting the technical requirements as prescribed in § 84.15 of this chapter.

(c) A barge or a group of barges at anchor or made fast to one or more mooring bouys or other similar device, in lieu of the provisions of Inland Navigation Rule 30, may carry unobstructed all-round white lights of an intensity to be visible for at least one nautical mile that meet the requirements of § 84.15 of this chapter and shall be arranged as follows:

(1) Any barge that projects from a group formation shall be lighted on its outboard corners.

(2) On a single barge moored in water where other vessels normally navigate on both sides of the barge, lights shall be placed to mark the corner extremities of the barge.

(3) On barges moored in group formation, moored in water where other vessels normally navigate on both sides of the group, lights shall be placed to mark the corner extremities of the group.

(d) The following are exempt from the requirements of this section:

(1) A barge or group of barges moored in a slip or slough used primarily for mooring purposes.

(2) A barge or group of barges moored behind a pierhead.

(3) A barge less than 20 meters in length when moored in a special anchorage area designated in accordance with § 109.10 of this chapter.

(e) Barges moored in well-illuminated areas are exempt from the lighting requirements of this section. These areas are as follows:

Chicago Sanitary Ship Canal	Calumet Sag Channel
(1) Mile 293.2 to 293.9	(61) Mile 316.5
(3) Mile 295.2 to 296.1	
(5) Mile 297.5 to 297.8	
(7) Mile 298 to 298.2	
(9) Mile 298.6 to 298.8	*Little Calumet River*
(11) Mile 299.3 to 299.4	(71) Mile 321.2
(13) Mile 299.8 to 300.5	(73) Mile 322.3
(15) Mile 303 to 303.2	
(17) Mile 303.7 to 303.9	
(19) Mile 305.7 to 305.8	
(21) Mile 310.7 to 310.9	*Calumet River*
(23) Mile 311 to 311.2	(81) Mile 328.5 to 328.7
(25) Mile 312.5 to 312.6	(83) Mile 329.2 to 329.4
(27) Mile 313.8 to 314.2	(85) Mile 330 west bank to 330.2
(29) Mile 314.6	(87) Mile 331.4 to 331.6
(31) Mile 314.8 to 315.3	(89) Mile 332.2 to 332.4
(33) Mile 315.7 to 316	(91) Mile 332.6 to 332.8
(35) Mile 316.8	
(37) Mile 316.85 to 317.05	
(39) Mile 317.5	
(41) Mile 318.4 to 318.9	*Cumberland River*
(43) Mile 318.7 to 318.8	(101) Mile 126.8
(45) Mile 320 to 320.3	(103) Mile 191
(47) Mile 320.6	
(49) Mile 322.3 to 322.4	
(51) Mile 322.8	
(53) Mile 322.9 to 327.2	

§ 88.15 Lights on dredge pipelines

Dredge pipelines that are floating or supported on trestles shall display the following lights at night and in periods of restricted visibility.

(a) One row of yellow lights. The lights must be:

(1) Flashing 50 to 70 times per minute,

(2) Visible all around the horizon,

(3) Visible for at least 2 miles on a clear dark night,

(4) Not less than 1 and not more than 3.5 meters above the water,

(5) Approximately equally spaced, and

(6) Not more than 10 meters apart where the pipeline crosses a navigable channel. Where the pipeline does not cross a navigable channel, the lights must be sufficient in number to clearly show the pipeline's length and course.

(b) Two red lights at each end of the pipeline, including the ends in a channel where the pipeline is separated to allow vessels to pass (whether open or closed). The lights must be:

(1) Visible all around the horizon, and

(2) Visible for at least 2 miles on a clear dark night, and

(3) One meter apart in a vertical line with the lower light at the same height above the water as the flashing yellow light.

RELATED GOVERNMENT REGULATIONS

International Interpretative Rules (33 CFR 82)

§ 82.1 Purpose

This part contains the interpretative rules concerning the 72 COLREGS that are adopted by the Coast Guard for the guidance of the public.

§ 82.3 Pushing vessel and vessel being pushed: Composite unit

Rule 24(b) of the 72 COLREGS states that when a pushing vessel and a vessel being pushed ahead are rigidly connected in a composite unit, they are regarded as a power-driven vessel and must exhibit the lights under Rule 23. A "composite unit" is interpreted to be a pushing vessel that is rigidly connected by mechanical means to a vessel being pushed so they react to sea and swell as one vessel. "Mechanical means" does not include the following:

(a) Lines.
(b) Hawsers.
(c) Wires.
(d) Chains.

§ 82.5 Lights for moored vessels

For the purposes of Rule 30 of the 72 COLREGS, a vessel at anchor includes a barge made fast to one or more mooring buoys or other similar device attached to the sea or river floor. Such a barge may be lighted as a vessel at anchor in accordance with Rule 30, or may be lighted on the corners in accordance with 33 CFR 88.13.

§ 82.7 Sidelights for unmanned barges

An unmanned barge being towed may use the exception of COLREG Rule 24(h). However, this exception only applies to the vertical sector requirements.

Inland Interpretative Rules (33 CFR 90)

§ 90.1 Purpose

This part contains the interpretative rules for the Inland Rules. These interpretative rules are intended as a guide to assist the public and promote compliance with the Inland Rules.

§ 90.3 Pushing vessel and vessel being pushed: Composite unit

Rule 24(b) of the Inland Rules states that when a pushing vessel and a vessel being pushed ahead are rigidly connected in a composite unit, they are regarded as a power-driven vessel and must exhibit the lights prescribed in Rule 23. A "composite unit" is interpreted to be the combination of a pushing vessel and a vessel being pushed ahead that are rigidly connected by mechanical means so they react to sea and swell as one vessel. Mechanical means does not include lines, wires, hawsers, or chains.

§ 90.5 Lights for moored vessels

A vessel at anchor includes a vessel made fast to one or more mooring buoys or other similar device attached to the ocean floor. Such vessels may be lighted as a vessel at anchor in accordance with Rule 30, or may be lighted on the corners in accordance with 33 CFR 88.13.

§ 90.7 Sidelights for unmanned barges

An unmanned barge being towed may use the exception of COLREG Rule 24(h). However, this exception only applies to the vertical sector requirements.

COLREGS Demarcation Lines (33 CFR 80)

GENERAL

Sec.

80.01 General basis and purpose of demarcation lines.

ATLANTIC COAST
FIRST DISTRICT

80.105 Calais, ME to Cape Small, ME.
80.110 Casco Bay, ME.
80.115 Portland Head, ME to Cape Ann, MA.
80.120 Cape Ann, MA to Marblehead Neck, MA.
80.125 Marblehead Neck, MA to Nahant, MA.
80.130 Boston Harbor entrance.
80.135 Hull, MA to Race Point, MA.
80.145 Race Point, MA to Watch Hill, RI.
80.150 Block Island, RI.
80.155 Watch Hill, RI to Montauk Point, NY.
80.160 Montauk Point, NY to Atlantic Beach, NY.
80.165 New York Harbor.
80.170 Sandy Hook, NJ to Tom's River, NJ.

FIFTH DISTRICT

80.501 Tom's River NJ to Cape May, NJ.
80.503 Delaware Bay.

80.505 Cape Henlopen, DE to Cape Charles, VA.
80.510 Chesapeake Bay Entrance, VA.

Sec.

80.515 Cape Henry, VA to Cape Hatteras, NC.
80.520 Cape Hatteras, NC to Cape Lookout, NC.
80.525 Cape Lookout, NC to Cape Fear, NC.
80.530 Cape Fear, NC to New River Inlet, NC.

SEVENTH DISTRICT

80.703 Little River Inlet, SC to Cape Romain, SC.
80.707 Cape Romain, SC to Sullivans Island, SC.
80.710 Charleston Harbor, SC.
80.712 Morris Island, SC to Hilton Head Island, SC.
80.715 Savannah River.
80.717 Tybee Island, GA to St. Simons Island, GA.
80.720 St. Simons Island, GA to Amelia Island, FL.
80.723 Amelia Island, FL to Cape Canaveral, FL.
80.727 Cape Canaveral, FL to Miami Beach, FL.
80.730 Miami Harbor, FL.
80.735 Miami, FL to Long Key, FL.

PUERTO RICO AND VIRGIN ISLANDS
SEVENTH DISTRICT

80.738 Puerto Rico and Virgin Islands

GULF COAST
SEVENTH DISTRICT
Sec.

80.740 Long Key, FL to Cape Sable, FL.
80.745 Cape Sable, FL to Cape Romano, FL.
80.748 Cape Romano, FL to Sanibel Island, FL.
80.750 Sanibel Island, FL to St. Petersburg, FL.
80.753 St. Petersburg, FL to Anclote, FL.
80.755 Anclote, FL to the Suncoast Keys, FL.
80.757 Suncoast Keys, FL to Horseshoe Point, FL.
80.760 Horseshoe Point, FL to Rock Island, FL.

EIGHTH DISTRICT

80.805 Rock Island, FL to Cape San Blas, FL.
80.810 Cape San Blas, FL to Perdido Bay, FL.
80.815 Mobile Bay, AL to the Chandeleur Islands, LA.
80.825 Mississippi Passes, LA.
80.830 Mississippi Passes, LA to Point Au Fer, LA.
80.835 Point Au Fer, LA to Calcasieu Pass, LA.
80.840 Sabine Pass, TX to Galveston, TX.
80.845 Galveston, TX to Freeport, TX.
80.850 Brazos River, TX to Rio Grande, TX.

PACIFIC COAST
ELEVENTH DISTRICT
Sec.

80.1102 Santa Catalina Island, CA.
80.1104 San Diego Harbor, CA.
80.1106 Mission Bay, CA.
80.1108 Oceanside Harbor, CA.
80.1110 Dana Point Harbor, CA.
80.1112 Newport Bay, CA.
80.1114 San Pedro Bay-Anaheim Bay, CA.
80.1116 Redondo Harbor, CA.
80.1118 Marina Del Rey, CA.
80.1120 Port Hueneme, CA.
80.1122 Channel Islands Harbor, CA.
80.1124 Ventura Marina, CA.
80.1126 Santa Barbara Harbor, CA.
80.1130 San Luis Obispo Bay, CA.
80.1132 Estero-Morro Bay, CA.
80.1134 Monterey Harbor, CA.
80.1136 Moss Landing Harbor, CA.
80.1138 Santa Cruz Harbor, CA.
80.1140 Pillar Point Harbor, CA.
80.1142 San Francisco Harbor, CA.
80.1144 Bodega and Tomales Bay, CA.
80.1146 Albion River, CA.
80.1148 Noyo River, CA.
80.1150 Arcata-Humboldt Bay, CA.
80.1152 Crescent City Harbor, CA.

THIRTEENTH DISTRICT
Sec.

80.1305 Chetco River, OR.
80.1310 Rogue River, OR.
80.1315 Coquille River, OR.
80.1320 Coos Bay, OR.
80.1325 Umpqua River, OR.
80.1330 Siuslaw River, OR.
80.1335 Alsea Bay, OR.
80.1340 Yaquina Bay, OR.
80.1345 Depoe Bay, OR.
80.1350 Netarts Bay, OR.
80.1355 Tillamook Bay, OR.
80.1360 Nehalem River, OR.
80.1365 Columbia River Entrance, OR/WA.
80.1370 Willapa Bay, WA.
80.1375 Grays Harbor, WA.
80.1380 Quillayute River, WA.

80.1385 Strait of Juan de Fuca.
80.1390 Haro Strait and Strait of Georgia.
80.1395 Puget Sound and adjacent waters.

PACIFIC ISLANDS
FOURTEENTH DISTRICT
80.1410 Hawaiian Island Exemption from General Rule.
80.1420 Mamala Bay, Oahu, HI.
80.1430 Kaneohe Bay, Oahu, HI.
80.1440 Port Allen, Kauai, HI.
80.1450 Nawiliwili Harbor, Kauai, HI.
80.1460 Kahului Harbor, Maui, HI.
80.1470 Kawaihae Harbor, Hawaii, HI.
80.1480 Hilo Harbor, Hawaii, HI.
80.1490 Apra Harbor, U.S. Territory of Guam.
80.1495 U.S. Pacific Island Possessions.

ALASKA
SEVENTEENTH DISTRICT
80.1705 Alaska.

GENERAL

§ 80.01 General basis and purpose of demarcation lines.

(a) The regulations in this part establish the lines of demarcation delineating those waters upon which mariners shall comply with the International Regulations for Preventing Collisions at Sea, 1972 (72 COLREGS) and those waters upon which mariners shall comply with the Inland Navigation Rules.

(b) The waters inside of the lines are Inland Rules Waters. The waters outside the lines are COLREGS Waters.

ATLANTIC COAST
FIRST DISTRICT
§ 80.105 Calais, ME to Cape Small, ME.

The 72 COLREGS shall apply on the harbors, bays, and inlets on the east coast of Maine from International Bridge at Calais, ME to the southwesternmost extremity of Bald Head at Cape Small.

§ 80.110 Casco Bay, ME.

(a) A line drawn from the southwesternmost extremity of Bald Head at Cape Small to the southeasternmost extremity of Ragged Island; thence to the southern tangent of Jaquish Island thence to Little Mark Island Monument Light; thence to the northernmost extremity of Jewell Island.

(b) A line drawn from the tower on Jewell Island charted in approximate position latitude 43°40.6'N. longitude 70°05.9'W. to the northeasternmost extremity of Outer Green Island.

(c) A line drawn from the southwesternmost extremity of Outer Green Island to Ram Island Ledge Light; thence to Portland Head Light.

§ 80.115 Portland Head, ME to Cape Ann, MA.

(a) Except inside lines specifically described in this section, the 72 COLREGS shall apply on the harbors, bays, and inlets on the east coast of Maine, New Hampshire, and Massachusetts from Portland Head to Halibut Point at Cape Ann.

(b) A line drawn from the southernmost tower on Gerrish Island charted in approximate position latitude 43°04.0'N. longitude 70°41.2'W. to Whaleback Light; thence to Jeffrey Point Light 2A; thence to the northeasternmost extremity of Frost Point.

(c) A line drawn from the northernmost extremity of Farm Point to Annisquam Harbor Light.

§ 80.120 Cape Ann, MA to Marblehead Neck, MA.

(a) Except inside lines specifically described in this section, the 72 COLREGS shall apply on the harbors, bays and inlets on the east coast of Massachusetts from Halibut Point at Cape Ann to Marblehead Neck.

(b) A line drawn from Gloucester Harbor Breakwater Light to the twin towers charted in approximate position latitude 42°35.1'N. longitude 70°41.6'W.

(c) A line drawn from the westernmost extremity of Gales Point to the easternmost extremity of House Island; thence to Bakers Island Light; thence to Marblehead Light.

§ 80.125 Marblehead Neck, MA to Nahant, MA.

The 72 COLREGS apply on the harbors, bays, and inlets on the east coast of Massachusetts from Marblehead Neck to the easternmost tower at Nahant, charted in approximate position latitude 42°25.4'N., longitude 70°54.6'W.

§ 80.130 Boston Harbor entrance.

A line drawn from the easternmost tower at Nahant, charted in approximate position latitude 42°25.4'N., longitude 70°54.6'W., to Boston Lighted Horn Buoy "B"; thence to the easternmost radio tower at Hull, charted in approximate position latitude 42°16.7'N., longitude 70°52.6'W.

§ 80.135 Hull, MA to Race Point, MA.

(a) Except inside lines described in this section, the 72 COLREGS apply on the harbors, bays, and inlets on the east coast of Massachusetts from the easternmost radio tower at Hull, charted in approximate position latitude 42°16.7'N., longitude 70°52.6'W., to Race Point on Cape Cod.

(b) A line drawn from Canal Breakwater Light 4 south to the shoreline.

§ 80.145 Race Point, MA to Watch Hill, RI.

(a) Except inside lines specifically described in this section, the 72 COLREGS shall apply on the sounds, bays, harbors and inlets along the coast of Cape Cod and the southern coasts of Massachusetts and Rhode Island from Race Point to Watch Hill.

(b) A line drawn from Nobska Point Light to Tarpaulin Cove Light on the southeastern side of Naushon Island; thence from the southernmost tangent of Naushon Island to the easternmost extremity of Nashawena Island; thence from the southwestern most extremity of Nashawena Island to the easternmost extremity of Cuttyhunk Island; thence from the southwestern tangent of Cuttyhunk Island to the tower on Gooseberry Neck charted in approximate position latitude 41°29.1'N. longitude 71°02.3'W.

(c) A line drawn from Sakonnet Breakwater Light 2 tangent to the southernmost part of Sachuest Point charted in approximate position latitude 41°28.5'N. longitude 71°14.8'W.

(d) An east-west line drawn through Beavertail Light between Brenton Point and the Boston Neck shoreline.

§ 80.150 Block Island, RI.

The 72 COLREGS shall apply on the harbors of Block Island.

§ 80.155 Watch Hill, RI to Montauk Point, NY.

(a) A line drawn from Watch Hill Light to East Point on Fishers Island.

(b) A line drawn from Race Point to Race Rock Light; thence to Little Gull Island Light thence to East Point on Plum Island.

(c) A line drawn from Plum Island Harbor East Dolphin Light to Plum Island Harbor West Dolphin Light.

(d) A line drawn from Plum Island Light to Orient Point Light; thence to Orient Point.

(e) A line drawn from the lighthouse ruins at the southwestern end of Long Beach Point to Cornelius Point.

(f) A line drawn from Coecles Harbor Entrance Light to Sungic Point.

(g) A line drawn from Nicoll Point to Cedar Island Light.

(h) A line drawn from Threemile Harbor West Breakwater Light to Threemile Harbor East Breakwater Light.

(i) A line drawn from Montauk West Jetty Light 1 to Montauk East Jetty Light 2.

§ 80.160 Montauk Point, NY to Atlantic Beach, NY.

(a) A line drawn from Shinnecock Inlet East Breakwater Light to Shinnecock Inlet West Breakwater Light 1.

(b) A line drawn from Moriches Inlet East Breakwater Light to Moriches Inlet West Breakwater Light.

(c) A line drawn from Fire Island Inlet Breakwater Light 348° true to the southernmost extremity of the spit of land at the western end of Oak Beach.

(d) A line drawn from Jones Inlet Light 322° true across the southwest tangent of the island on the north side of Jones Inlet to the shoreline.

§ 80.165 New York Harbor.

A line drawn from East Rockaway Inlet Breakwater Light to Sandy Hook Light.

§ 80.170 Sandy Hook, NJ to Tom's River, NJ.

(a) A line drawn from Shark River Inlet North Breakwater Light 2 to Shark River Inlet South Breakwater Light 1.

(b) A line drawn from Manasquan Inlet North Breakwater Light 4 to Manasquan Inlet South Breakwater Light 3.

(c) A line drawn from Barnegat Inlet North Breakwater Light 4A to the seaward extremity of the submerged Barnegat Inlet South Breakwater; thence along the submerged breakwater to the shoreline.

FIFTH DISTRICT

§ 80.501 Tom's River, NJ to Cape May, NJ.

(a) A line drawn from the seaward tangent of Long Beach Island to the seaward tangent to Pullen Island across Beach Haven and Little Egg Inlets.

(b) A line drawn from the seaward tangent of Pullen Island to the seaward tangent of Brigantine Island across Brigantine Inlet.

(c) A line drawn from the seaward extremity of Absecon Inlet North Jetty to Atlantic City Light.

(d) A line drawn from the southernmost point of Longport at latitude 39°18.2'N. longitude 74°33.1'W. to the northeasternmost point of Ocean City at latitude 39°17.6'N. longitude 74°33.1'W. across Great Egg Harbor Inlet.

(e) A line drawn parallel with the general trend of highwater shoreline across Corson Inlet.

(f) A line formed by the centerline of the Townsend Inlet Highway Bridge.

(g) A line formed by the shoreline of Seven Mile Beach and Hereford Inlet Light.

(h) A line drawn from Cape May Inlet East Jetty Light to Cape May Inlet West Jetty Light.

§ 80.503 Delaware Bay.

A line drawn from Cape May Light to Harbor of Refuge Light; thence to the northernmost extremity of Cape Henlopen.

§ 80.505 Cape Henlopen, DE to Cape Charles, VA.

(a) A line drawn from the seaward extremity of Indian River Inlet North Jetty to Indian River Inlet South Jetty Light.

(b) A line drawn from Ocean City Inlet Light 6 225° true across Ocean City Inlet to the submerged south breakwater.

(c) A line drawn from Assateague Beach Tower Light to the tower charted at latitude 37°52.6'N. longitude 75°26.7'W.

(d) A line formed by the range of Wachapreague Inlet Light 3 and Parramore Beach Lookout Tower drawn across Wachapreague Inlet.

(e) A line drawn from the lookout tower charted on the northern end of Hog Island to the seaward tangent of Parramore Beach.

(f) A line drawn 207° true from the lookout tower charted on the southern end of Hog Island across Great Machipongo Inlet.

(g) A line formed by the range of the two cupolas charted on the southern end of Cobb Island drawn across Sand Shoal Inlet.

(h) Except as provided elsewhere in this section from Cape Henlopen to Cape Charles, lines drawn parallel with the general trend of the highwater shoreline across the entrances to small bays and inlets.

§ 80.510 Chesapeake Bay Entrance, VA.

A line drawn from Cape Charles Light to Cape Henry Light.

§ 80.515 Cape Henry, VA to Cape Hatteras, NC.

(a) A line drawn from Rudee Inlet Jetty Light 2 to Rudee Inlet Jetty Light 1.

(b) A line formed by the centerline of the highway bridge across Oregon Inlet.

§ 80.520 Cape Hatteras, NC to Cape Lookout, NC.

(a) A line drawn from Hatteras Inlet Lookout Tower at latitude 35°11.8'N. 75°44.9'W. 255° true to the eastern end of Ocracoke Island.

(b) A line drawn from the westernmost extremity of Ocracoke Island at latitude 35°04.0'N. longitude 76°00.8'W. to the northeastern extremity of Portsmouth Island at latitude 35°03.7'N. longitude 76°02.3'W.

(c) A line drawn across Drum Inlet parallel with the general trend of the highwater shoreline.

§ 80.525 Cape Lookout, NC to Cape Fear, NC.

(a) A line drawn from Cape Lookout Light to the seaward tangent of the southeastern end of Shackleford Banks.

(b) A line drawn from Morehead City Channel Range Front Light to the seaward extremity of the Beaufort Inlet West Jetty.

(c) A line drawn from the southernmost extremity of Bogue Banks at latitude 34°38.7'N. longitude 77°06.0'W. across Bogue Inlet to the northernmost extremity of Bear Beach at latitude 34°38.5'N. longitude 77°07.1'W.

(d) A line drawn from the tower charted in approximate position latitude 34°31.5'N. longitude 77°20.8'W. to the seaward tangent of the shoreline on the northeast side of New River Inlet.

(e) A line drawn across New Topsail Inlet between the closest extremities of the shore on either side of the inlet from latitude 34°20.8'N. longitude 77°39.2'W. to latitude 34°20.6'N. longitude 77°39.6'W.

(f) A line drawn from the seaward extremity of the jetty on the northeast side of Masonboro Inlet to the seaward extremity of the jetty on the southeast side of the Inlet.

(g) Except as provided elsewhere in this section from Cape Lookout to Cape Fear, lines drawn parallel with the general trend of the highwater shoreline across the entrance of small bays and inlets.

§ 80.530 Cape Fear, NC to Little River Inlet, NC.

(a) A line drawn from the abandoned lighthouse charted in approximate position latitude 33°52.4'N. longitude 78°00.1'W. across the Cape Fear River Entrance to Oak Island Light.

(b) Except as provided elsewhere in this section from Cape Fear to Little River Inlet, lines drawn parallel with the general trend of the highwater shoreline across the entrance to small inlets.

SEVENTH DISTRICT

§ 80.703 Little River Inlet, SC to Cape Romain, SC.

(a) A line drawn from the westernmost extremity of the sand spit on Bird Island to the Easternmost extremity of Waties Island across Little River Inlet.

(b) From Little River Inlet, a line drawn parallel with the general trend of the highwater shoreline across Hog Inlet; thence a line drawn from Murrels Inlet Light 2 to Murrels Inlet Light 1; thence a line drawn parallel with the general trend of the highwater shoreline across Midway Inlet, Pawleys Inlet and North Inlet.

(c) A line drawn from the charted position of Winyah Bay North Jetty End Buoy 2N south to the Winyah Bay South Jetty.

(d) A line drawn from Santee Point to the seaward tangent of Cedar Island.

(e) A line drawn from Cedar Island Point west to Murphy Island.

(f) A north-south line (longitude 79°20.3'W.) drawn from Murphy Island to the northernmost extremity of Cape Island Point.

§ 80.707 Cape Romain, SC to Sullivans Island, SC.

(a) A line drawn from the western extremity of Cape Romain 292° true to Racoon Key on the west side of Racoon Creek.

(b) A line drawn from the westernmost extremity of Sandy Point across Bull Bay to the northernmost extremity of Northeast Point.

(c) A line drawn from the southernmost extremity of Bull Island to the easternmost extremity of Capers Island.

(d) A line formed by the overhead power cable from Capers Island to Dewees Island.

(e) A line formed by the overhead power cable from Dewees Island to Isle of Palms.

(f) A line formed by the centerline of the highway bridge between Isle of Palms and Sullivans Island over Breach Inlet.

§ 80.710 Charleston Harbor, SC.

(a) A line formed by the submerged north jetty from the shore to the west end of the north jetty.

(b) A line drawn from across the seaward extremity of the Charleston Harbor Jetties.

(c) A line drawn from the west end of the South Jetty across the South Entrance to Charleston Harbor to shore on a line formed by the submerged south jetty.

§ 80.712 Morris Island, SC to Hilton Head Island, SC.

(a) A line drawn from the easternmost tip of Folly Island to the abandoned light-house tower on the northside of Lighthouse Inlet; thence west to the shoreline of Morris Island.

(b) A straight line drawn from the seaward tangent of Folly Island through Folly River Daybeacon 10 across Stono River to the shoreline of Sandy Point.

(c) A line drawn from the southernmost extremity of Seabrook Island 257° true across the North Edisto River Entrance to the shore of Botany Bay Island.

(d) A line drawn from the microwave antenna tower on Edisto Beach charted in approximate position latitude 32°29.3'N. longitude 80°19.2'W. across St. Helena Sound to the abandoned lighthouse tower on Hunting Island.

(e) A line formed by the centerline of the highway bridge between Hunting Island and Fripp Island.

(f) A line drawn from the westernmost extremity of Bull Point on Capers Island to Port Royal Sound Channel Range Rear Light, latitude 32°13.7'N. longitude 80°36.0'W.; thence 259° true to the easternmost extremity of Hilton Head at latitude 32°13.7'N. longitude 80°40.1'W.

§ 80.715 Savannah River.

A line drawn from the southernmost tank on Hilton Head Island charted in approximate position latitude 32°06.7'N. longitude 80°49.3'W. to Bloody Point Range Rear Light; thence to Tybee (Range Rear) Light.

§ 80.717 Tybee Island, GA to St. Simons Island, GA.

(a) A line drawn from the southernmost extremity of Savannah Beach on Tybee Island 255° true across Tybee Inlet to the shore of Little Tybee Island south of the entrance to Buck Hammock Creek.

(b) A straight line drawn from the northeasternmost extremity of Wassaw Island 031° true through Tybee River Daybeacon 1 to the shore of Little Tybee Island.

(c) A line drawn approximately parallel with the general trend of the highwater shorelines from the seaward tangent of Wassau Island to the seaward tangent of Bradley Point on Ossabaw Island.

(d) A north-south line (longitude 81°08.4'W.) drawn from the southernmost extremity of Ossabaw Island to St. Catherines Island.

(e) A north-south line (longitude 81°10.6'W.) drawn from the southernmost extremity of St. Catherines Island to North-east Point on Blackbeard Island.

(f) A line following the general trend of the seaward highwater shoreline across Cabretta Inlet.

(g) A north-south line (longitude 81°16.9'W.) drawn from the southwesternmost point on Sapelo Island to Wolf Island.

(h) A north-south line (longitude 81°17.1'W.) drawn from the southeasternmost point of Wolf Island to the northeasternmost point on Little St. Simons Island.

(i) A line drawn from the northeasternmost extremity of Sea Island 045° true to Little St. Simons Island.

(j) An east-west line from the southernmost extremity of Sea Island across Goulds Inlet to St. Simons Island.

§ 80.720 St. Simons Island, GA to Amelia Island, FL.

(a) A line drawn from St. Simons Light to the northernmost tank on Jekyll Island charted in approximate position latitude 31°05.9'N. longitude 81°24.5'W.

(b) A line drawn from the southernmost tank on Jekyll Island charted in approximate position latitude 31°01.6'N. longitude 81°25.2'W. to coordinate latitude 30°59.4'N. longitude 81°23.7'W. (0.5 nautical mile east of the charted position of St. Andrew Sound Lighted Buoy 32); thence to the abandoned lighthouse tower on the north end of Little Cumberland Island charted in approximate position latitude 30°58.5'N. longitude 81°24.8'W.

(c) A line drawn across the seaward extremity of the St. Marys Entrance Jetties.

§80.723 Amelia Island, FL to Cape Canaveral, FL.

(a) A line drawn from the southernmost extremity of Amelia Island to the northeasternmost extremity of Little Talbot Island.

(b) A line formed by the centerline of the highway bridge from Little Talbot Island to Fort George Island.

(c) A line drawn across the seaward extremity of the St. Johns River Entrance Jetties.

(d) A line drawn across the seaward extremity of the St. Augustine Inlet Jetties.

(e) A line formed by the centerline of the highway bridge over Matanzas Inlet.

(f) A line drawn across the seaward extremity of the Ponce de Leon Inlet Jetties.

§ 80.727 Cape Canaveral, FL to Miami Beach, FL.

(a) A line drawn across the seaward extremity of the Port Canaveral Entrance Channel Jetties.

(b) A line drawn across the seaward extremity of the Sebastian Inlet Jetties.

(c) A line drawn across the seaward extremity of the Fort Pierce Inlet Jetties.

(d) A north-south line (longitude 80°09.7'W.) drawn across St. Lucie Inlet.

(e) A line drawn from the seaward extremity of Jupiter Inlet North Jetty to the northeast extremity of the concrete apron on the south side of Jupiter inlet.

(f) A line drawn across the seaward extremity of the Lake Worth Inlet Jetties.

(g) A line drawn across the seaward extremity of the Boynton Inlet Jetties.

(h) A line drawn from Boca Raton Inlet North Jetty Light 2 to Boca Raton Inlet South Jetty Light 1.

(i) A line drawn from Hillsboro Inlet Light to Hillsboro Inlet Entrance Light 2; thence to Hillsboro Inlet Entrance Light 1; thence west to the shoreline.

(j) A line drawn across the seaward extremity of the Port Everglades Entrance Jetties.

(k) A line formed by the centerline of the highway bridge over Bakers Haulover Inlet.

§ 80.730 Miami Harbor, FL.

A line drawn across the seaward extremity of the Miami Harbor Government Cut Jetties.

§ 80.735 Miami, FL to Long Key, FL.

(a) A line drawn from the southernmost extremity of Fisher Island 212° truc to the point latitude 25°45.0'N. longitude 80°08.6'W. on Virginia Key.

(b) A line formed by the centerline of the highway bridge between Virginia Key and Key Biscayne.

(c) A line drawn from Cape Florida Light to the northern most extremity on Soldier Key.

(d) A line drawn from the southernmost extremity on Soldier Key to the northernmost extremity of the Ragged Keys.

(e) A line drawn from the Ragged Keys to the southernmost extremity of Angelfish Key following the general trend of the seaward shoreline.

(f) A line drawn on the centerline of the Overseas Highway (U.S. 1) and bridges from latitude 25°19.3'N. longitude 80°16.0'W. at Little Angelfish Creek to the radar dome charted on Long Key at approximate position latitude 24°49.3'N. longitude 80°49.2'W.

PUERTO RICO AND VIRGIN ISLANDS
SEVENTH DISTRICT
§ 80.738 Puerto Rico and Virgin Islands.

(a) Except inside lines specifically described in this section, the 72 COLREGS shall apply on all other bays, harbors and lagoons of Puerto Rico and the U.S. Virgin Islands.

(b) A line drawn from Puerto San Juan Light to Cabras Light across the entrance of San Juan Harbor.

GULF COAST
SEVENTH DISTRICT
§80.740 Long Key, FL to Cape Sable, FL.

A line drawn from the microwave tower charted on Long Key at approximate position latitude 24°48.8'N. longitude 80°49.6'W. to Long Key Light 1; thence to Arsenic Bank Light 2; thence to Sprigger Bank Light 5; thence to Schooner Bank Light 6; thence to Oxfoot Bank Light 10; thence to East Cape Light 2; thence through East Cape Daybeacon 1A to the shoreline at East Cape.

§ 80.745 Cape Sable, FL to Cape Romano, FL.

(a) A line drawn following the general trend of the mainland, highwater shoreline from Cape Sable at East Cape to Little Shark River Light 1; thence to westernmost extremity of Shark Point; thence following the general trend of the mainland, highwater shoreline crossing the entrances of Harney River, Broad Creek, Broad River, Rodgers River First Bay, Chatham River, Huston River, to the shoreline at coordinate latitude 25°41.8'N. longitude 81°17.9'W.

(b) The 72 COLREGS shall apply to the waters surrounding the Ten Thousand Islands and the bays, creeks, inlets, and rivers between Chatham Bend and Marco Island except inside lines specifically described in this part.

(c) A north-south line drawn at longitude 81°20.2'W. across the entrance to Lopez River.

(d) A line drawn across the entrance to Turner River parallel to the general trend of the shoreline.

(e) A line formed by the centerline of Highway 92 Bridge at Goodland.

§ 80.748 Cape Romano, FL to Sanibel Island, FL.

(a) A line drawn across Big Marco Pass parallel to the general trend of the seaward, highwater shoreline.

(b) A line drawn from the northwesternmost extremity of Coconut Island 000°T across Capri Pass.

(c) Lines drawn across Hurricane and Little Marco Passes parallel to the general trend of the seaward, highwater shoreline.

(d) A line from the seaward extremity of Gordon Pass South Jetty 014° true to the shoreline at approximate coordinate latitude 26°05.7'N. longitude 81°48.1'W.

(e) A line drawn across the seaward extremity of Doctors Pass Jetties.

(f) Lines drawn across Wiggins, Big Hickory, New, and Big Carlos Passes parallel to the general trend of the seaward highwater shoreland.

(g) A straight line drawn from Sanibel Island Light through Matanzas Pass Channel Light 2 to the shore of Estero Island.

§ 80.750 Sanibel Island, FL to St. Petersburg, FL.

(a) A line formed by the centerline of the highway bridge over Blind Pass, between Captiva Island and Sanibel Island, and lines drawn across Redfish and Captiva Passes parallel to the general trend of the seaward, highwater shorelines.

(b) A line drawn from La Costa Test Pile North Light to Port Boca Grande Light.

(c) Lines drawn across Gasparilla and Stump Passes parallel to the general trend of the seaward, highwater shorelines.

(d) A line across the seaward extremity of Venice Inlet Jetties.

(e) A line drawn across Midnight Pass parallel to the general trend of the seaward, highwater shoreline.

(f) A line drawn from Big Sarasota Pass Light 14 to the southernmost extremity of Lido Key.

(g) A line drawn across New Pass tangent to the seaward, highwater shoreline of Longboat Key.

(h) A line drawn across Longboat Pass parallel to the seaward, highwater shoreline.

(i) A line drawn from the northwesternmost extremity of Bean Point to the southeasternmost extremity of Egmont Key.

(j) A straight line drawn from Egmont Key Light through Egmont Channel Range Rear Light to the shoreline on Mullet Key.

(k) A line drawn from the northernmost extremity of Mullet Key across Bunces Pass and South Channel to Pass-a-Grille Channel Light 8; thence to Pass-a-Grille Channel Daybeacon 9; thence to the southwesternmost extremity of Long Key.

§ 80.753 St. Petersburg, FL to Anclote, FL.

(a) A line drawn across Blind Pass, between Treasure Island and Long Key, parallel with the general trend of the seaward, highwater shoreline.

(b) Lines formed by the centerline of the highway bridges over Johns and Clearwater Passes.

(c) A line drawn across Dunedin and Hurricane Passes parallel with the general trend of the seaward, highwater shoreline.

(d) A line drawn from the northernmost extremity of Honeymoon Island to Anclote Anchorage South Entrance Light 7; thence to Anclote Key 28°10.0'N. 82°50.6'W.; thence a straight line through Anclote River Cut B Range Rear Light to the shoreline.

§ 80.755 Anclote, FL to the Suncoast Keys, FL.

(a) Except inside lines specifically described in this section, the 72 COLREGS shall apply on the bays, bayous, creeks, marinas, and rivers from Anclote to the Suncoast Keys.

(b) A north-south line drawn at longitude 82°38.3'W. across the Chassahowitzka River Entrance.

§ 80.757 Suncoast Keys, FL to Horseshoe Point, FL.

(a) Except inside lines specifically described in this section, the 72 COLREGS shall apply on the bays, bayous, creeks, and marinas from the Suncoast Keys to Horseshoe Point.

(b) A line formed by the centerline of Highway 44 Bridge over the Salt River.

(c) A north-south line drawn through Crystal River Entrance Daybeacon 25 across the river entrance.

(d) A north-south line drawn through the Cross Florida Barge Canal Daybeacon 48 across the canal.

(e) A north-south line drawn through Withlacoochee River Daybeacon 40 across the river.

(f) A line drawn from the westernmost extremity of South Point north to the shoreline across the Waccasassa River Entrance.

(g) A line drawn from position latitude 29°16.6'N. longitude 83°06.7'W. 300° true to the shoreline of Hog Island.

(h) A north-south line drawn through Suwannee River Wadley Pass Channel Daybeacons 30 and 31 across the Suwannee River.

§ 80.760 Horseshoe Point, FL to Rock Island, FL.

(a) Except inside lines specifically described provided in this section, the 72 COLREGS shall apply on the bays, bayous, creeks, marinas, and rivers from Horseshoe Point to the Rock Islands.

(b) A north-south line drawn through Steinhatchee River Light 21.

(c) A line drawn from Fenholloway River Approach Light FR east across the entrance to Fenholloway River.

EIGHTH DISTRICT
§ 80.805 Rock Island, FL to Cape San Blas, FL.

(a) A north-south line drawn from the Econfina River Light to the opposite shore.

(b) A line drawn from Gamble Point Light to the southernmost extremity of Cabell Point.

(c) A line drawn from St. Marks (Range Rear) Light to St. Marks Channel Light 11; thence to the southernmost extremity of Live Oak Point; thence in a straight line through Shell Point Light to the southernmost extremity of Ochlockonee Point; thence to Bald Point along longitude 84°20.5'W.

(d) A line drawn from the south shore of Southwest Cape at longitude 84°22.7'W. to Dog Island Reef East Light 1; thence to Turkey Point Light 2; thence to the eastern-most extremity of Dog Island.

(e) A line drawn from the westernmost extremity of Dog Island to the easternmost extremity of St. George Island.

(f) A line drawn across the seaward extremity of the St. George Island Channel Jetties.

(g) A line drawn from the northwesternmost extremity of Sand Island to West Pass Light 7.

(h) A line drawn from the westernmost extremity of St. Vincent Island to the southeast, highwater shoreline of Indian Peninsula at longitude 85°13.5'W.

§ 80.810 Cape San Blas, FL to Perdido Bay, FL.

(a) A line drawn from St. Joseph Bay Entrance Range A Rear Light through St. Joseph Bay Entrance Range B Front Light to St. Joseph Point.

(b) A line drawn across the mouth of Salt Creek as an extension of the general trend of the shoreline to continue across the inlet to St. Andrews Sound in the middle of Crooked Island.

(c) A line drawn from the northernmost extremity of Crooked Island 000°T to the mainland.

(d) A line drawn from the easternmost extremity of Shell Island 120° true to the shoreline across the east entrance to St. Andrews Bay.

(e) A line drawn between the seaward end of the St. Andrews Bay Entrance Jetties.

(f) A line drawn between the seaward end of the Choctawatchee Bay Entrance Jetties.

(g) A east-west line drawn from Fort McRee Leading Light across the Pensacola Bay Entrance along latitude 30°19.5'N.

(h) A line drawn between the seaward end of the Perdido Pass Jetties.

§ 80.815 Mobile Bay, AL to the Chandeleur Islands, LA.

(a) A line drawn across the inlets to Little Lagoon as an extension of the general trend of the shoreline.

(b) A line drawn from Mobile Point Light to Dauphin Island Channel Light No. 1 to the eastern corner of Fort Gaines at Pelican Point.

(c) A line drawn from the westernmost extremity of Dauphin Island to the eastern-most extremity of Petit Bois Island.

(d) A line drawn from Horn Island Pass Entrance Range Front Light on Petit Bois Island to the easternmost extremity of Horn Island.

(e) An east-west line (latitude 30°14.7'N.) drawn between the westernmost extremity of Horn Island to the easternmost extremity of Ship Island.

(f) A curved line drawn following the general trend of the seaward, highwater shoreline of Ship Island.

(g) A line drawn from Ship Island Light to Chandeleur Light; thence in a curved line following the general trend of the seaward, highwater shorelines of the Chandeleur

Islands to the island at latitude 29°44.1'N. longitude 88°53.0'W.; thence to latitude 29°26.5'N. longitude 88°55.6'W.

§ 80.825 Mississippi Passes, LA.

(a) A line drawn from latitude 29°26.5'N., longitude 88°55.6'W., to latidude 29°10.6'N., longitude 88°59.8'W.; thence to latitude 29°03.5'N., longitude 89°03.7'W.; thence to latitude 28°58.8'N., longitude 89°04.3'W.

(b) A line drawn from latitude 28°58.8'N., longitude 89°04.3'W.; to latitude 28°57.3'N., longitude 89°05.3'W.; thence to latitude 28°56.95'N., longitude 89°05.6'W.; thence to latitude 29°00.4'N., longitude 89°09.8'W.; thence following the general trend of the seaward highwater shoreline in a northwesterly direction to latitude 29°03.4'N., longitude 89°13.0'W.; thence west to latitude 9°03.5'N., longitude 89°15.5'W.; thence following the general trend of the seaward highwater shoreline in a southwesterly direction to latitude 28°57.7'N., longitude 89°22.3'W.

(c) A line drawn from latitude 28°57.7'N., longitude 89°22.3'W.; to latitude 28°51.4'N., longitude 89°24.5'W.; thence to latitude 28°52.65'N., longitude 89°27.1'W.; thence to the seaward extremity of the Southwest Pass West Jetty located at latitude 28°54.5'N., longitude 89°26.1'W.

(d) A line drawn from Mississippi River South Pass East Jetty Light 4 to Mississippi River South Pass West Jetty Light; thence following the general trend of the seaward highwater shoreline in a northwesterly direction to coordinate latitude 29°03.4'N., longitude 89°13.0'W.; thence west to coordinate latitude 29°03.5'N., longitude 89°15.5'W., thence following the general trend of the seaward, highwater shoreline in a southwesterly direction to Mississippi River Southwest Pass Entrance Light.

(e) A line drawn from Mississippi River Southwest Pass Entrance Light; thence to the seaward extremity of the Southwest Pass West Jetty located at coordinate latitude 28°54.5'N., longitude 89°26.1'W.

§ 80.830 Mississippi Passes, LA to Point Au Fer, LA.

(a) A line drawn from the seaward extremity of the Southwest Pass West Jetty located at coordinate latitude 28°54.5'N. longitude 89°26.1'W.; thence following the general trend of the seaward, highwater jetty and shoreline in a north, northeasterly direction to Old Tower latitude 28°58.8'N. longitude 89°23.3'W.; thence to West Bay Light; thence to coordinate latitude 29°05.2'N. longitude 89°24.3'W.; thence a curved line following the general trend of the highwater shoreline to Point Au Fer Island except as otherwise described in this section.

(b) A line drawn across the seaward extremity of the Empire Waterway (Bayou Fontanelle) entrance jetties.

(c) An east-west line drawn from the westernmost extremity of Grand Terre Islands in the direction of 194° true to the Grand Isle Fishing Jetty Light.

(d) A line drawn between the seaward extremity of the Belle Pass Jetties.

(e) A line drawn from the westernmost extremity of the Timbalier Island to the easternmost extremity of Isles Dernieres.

(f) A north-south line drawn from Caillou Bay Light 13 across Caillou Boca.

(g) A line drawn 107° true from Caillou Bay Boat Landing Light across the entrances to Grand Bayou du Large and Bayou Grand Caillou.

(h) A line drawn on an axis of 103° true through Taylors Bayou Entrance Light 2 across the entrances to Jack Stout Bayou, Taylors Bayou, Pelican Pass, and Bayou de West.

§ 80.835 Point Au Fer, LA to Calcasieu Pass, LA.

(a) A line drawn from Point Au Fer to Atchafalaya Channel Light 34; thence to Point Au Fer Reef Light 33; thence to Atchafalaya Bay Pipeline Light D latitude 29°25.0'N. longitude 91°31.7'W.; thence to Atchafalaya Bay Light 1 latitude 29°25.3'N. longitude 91°35.8'W.; thence to South Point.

(b) Lines following the general trend of the highwater shoreline drawn across the bayou and canal inlets from the Gulf of Mexico between South Point and Calcasieu Pass except as otherwise described in this section.

(c) A line drawn on an axis of 140° true through Southwest Pass Vermillion Bay Light 4 across Southwest Pass.

(d) A line drawn across the seaward extremity of the Freshwater Bayou Canal Entrance Jetties.

(e) A line drawn from Mermentau Channel East Jetty Light 6 to Mermentau Channel West Jetty Light 7.

(f) A line drawn from the radio tower charted in approximate position latitude 29°45.7'N. longitude 93°06.3'W. 115° true across Mermentau Pass.

(g) A line drawn across the seaward extremity of the Calcasieu Pass Jetties.

§ 80.840 Sabine Pass, TX to Galveston, TX.

(a) A line drawn from the Sabine Pass East Jetty Light to the seaward end of the Sabine Pass West Jetty.

(b) A line drawn across the small boat passes through the Sabine Pass East and West Jetties.

(c) A line formed by the centerline of the highway bridge over Rollover Pass at Gilchrist.

§ 80.845 Galveston, TX to Freeport, TX.

(a) A line drawn from Galveston North Jetty Light 6A to Galveston South Jetty Light 5A.

(b) A line formed by the centerline of the highway bridge over San Luis Pass.

(c) Lines formed by the centerlines of the highway bridges over the inlets to Christmas Bay (Cedar Cut) and Drum Bay.

(d) A line drawn from the seaward extremity of the Freeport North Jetty to Freeport Entrance Light 6; thence to Freeport Entrance Light 7; thence to the seaward extremity of Freeport South Jetty.

§ 80.850 Brazos River, TX to Rio Grande, TX.

(a) Except as otherwise described in this section lines drawn continuing the general trend of the seaward, highwater shorelines across the inlets to Brazos River Diversion Channel, San Bernard River, Cedar Lakes, Brown Cedar Cut, Colorado River, Matagorda Bay, Cedar Bayou, Corpus Christi Bay, and Laguna Madre.

(b) A line drawn across the seaward extremity of Matagorda Ship Channel North Jetties.

(c) A line drawn from the seaward tangent of Matagorda Peninsula at Decros Point to Matagorda Light.

(d) A line drawn across the seaward extremity of the Aransas Pass Jetties.

(e) A line drawn across the seaward extremity of the Port Mansfield Entrance Jetties.

(f) A line drawn across the seaward extremity of the Brazos Santiago Pass Jetties.

PACIFIC COAST
ELEVENTH DISTRICT
§ 80.1102 Santa Catalina Island, CA.

The 72 COLREGS shall apply to the harbors on Santa Catalina Island.

§ 80.1104 San Diego Harbor, CA.

A line drawn from Zuniga Jetty Light "V" to Zuniga Jetty Light "Z"; thence to Point Loma Light.

§ 80.1106 Mission Bay, CA.

A line drawn from Mission Bay South Jetty Light 2 to Mission Bay North Jetty Light 1.

§ 80.1108 Oceanside Harbor, CA.

A line drawn from Oceanside South Jetty Light 4 to Oceanside Breakwater Light 3.

§ 80.1110 Dana Point Harbor, CA.

A line drawn from Dana Point Jetty Light 6 to Dana Point Breakwater Light 5.

§ 80.1112 Newport Bay, CA.

A line drawn from Newport Bay East Jetty Light 4 to Newport Bay West Jetty Light 3.

§ 80.1114 San Pedro Bay-Anaheim Bay, CA.

(a) A line drawn across the seaward extremities of the Anaheim Bay Entrance East Jetties; thence to Long Beach Breakwater East End Light 1.

(b) A line drawn from Long Beach Channel Entrance Light 2 to Long Beach Light.

(c) A line drawn from Los Angeles Main Entrance Channel Light 2 to Los Angeles Light.

§ 80.1116 Redondo Harbor, CA.

A line drawn from Redondo Beach East Jetty Light 2 to Redondo Beach West Jetty Light 3.

§ 80.1118 Marina Del Rey, CA.

(a) A line drawn from Marina Del Rey Breakwater South Light 1 to Marina Del Rey Light 4.

(b) A line drawn from Marina Del Rey Breakwater North Light 2 to Marina Del Rey Light 3.

(c) A line drawn from Marina Del Rey Light 4 to the seaward extremity of the Ballona Creek South Jetty.

§ 80.1120 Port Hueneme, CA.

A line drawn from Port Hueneme East Jetty Light 4 to Port Hueneme West Jetty Light 3.

§ 80.1122 Channel Islands Harbor, CA.

(a) A line drawn from Channel Islands Harbor South Jetty Light 2 to Channel Islands Harbor Breakwater South Light 1.

(b) A line drawn from Channel Islands Harbor Breakwater North Light to Channel Islands Harbor North Jetty Light 5.

§ 80.1124 Ventura Marina, CA.

A line drawn from Ventura Marina South Jetty Light 6 to Ventura Marina Breakwater South Light 3; thence to Ventura Marina North Jetty Light 7.

§ 80.1126 Santa Barbara Harbor, CA.

A line drawn from Santa Barbara Harbor Light 4 to Santa Barbara Harbor Breakwater Light.

§ 80.1130 San Luis Obispo Bay, CA.

A line drawn from the southernmost extremity of Fossil Point to the seaward extremity of Whaler Island Breakwater.

§ 80.1132 Estero-Morro Bay, CA.

A line drawn from the seaward extremity of the Morro Bay East Breakwater to the Morro Bay West Breakwater Light.

§ 80.1134 Monterey Harbor, CA.

A line drawn from Monterey Harbor Light 6 to the northern extremity of Monterey Municipal Wharf 2.

§ 80.1136 Moss Landing Harbor, CA.

A line drawn from the seaward extremity of the pier located 0.3 mile south of Moss Landing Harbor Entrance to the seaward extremity of the Moss Landing Harbor North Breakwater.

§ 80.1138 Santa Cruz Harbor, CA.

A line drawn from the seaward extremity of the Santa Cruz Harbor East Breakwater to Santa Cruz Harbor West Breakwater Light; thence to Santa Cruz Light.

§ 80.1140 Pillar Point Harbor, CA.

A line drawn from Pillar Point Harbor Light 6 to Pillar Point Harbor Entrance Light.

§ 80.1142 San Francisco Harbor, CA.

A straight line drawn from Point Bonita Light through Mile Rocks Light to the shore.

§ 80.1144 Bodega and Tomales Bay, CA.

(a) An east-west line drawn from Sand Point to Avalis Beach.

(b) A line drawn from the seaward extremity of Bodega Harbor North Breakwater to Bodega Harbor Entrance Light 1.

§ 80.1146 Albion River, CA.

A line drawn on an axis of 030° true through Albion River Light 1 across Albion Cove.

§ 80.1148 Noyo River, CA.

A line drawn from Noyo River Entrance Daybeacon 4 to Noyo River Entrance Light 5.

§ 80.1150 Arcata-Humboldt Bay, CA.

A line drawn from Humboldt Bay Entrance Light 4 to Humboldt Bay Entrance Light 3.

§ 80.1152 Crescent City Harbor, CA.

A line drawn from Crescent City Entrance Light to the southeasternmost extremity of Whaler Island.

THIRTEENTH DISTRICT
§ 80.1305 Chetco River, OR.

A line drawn across the seaward extremities of the Chetco River Entrance Jetties.

§ 80.1310 Rogue River, OR.

A line drawn across the seaward extremities of the Rogue River Entrance Jetties.

§ 80.1315 Coquille River, OR.

A line drawn across the seaward extremities of the Coquille River Entrance Jetties.

§ 80.1320 Coos Bay, OR.

A line drawn across the seaward extremities of the Coos Bay Entrance Jetties.

§ 80.1325 Umpqua River, OR.

A line drawn across the seaward extremities of the Umpqua Entrance Jetties.

§ 80.1330 Siuslaw River, OR.

A line drawn across the seaward extremities of the Siuslaw River Entrance Jetties.

§ 80.1335 Alsea Bay, OR.

A line drawn from the seaward shoreline on the north of the Alsea Bay Entrance 165° true across the channel entrance.

§ 80.1340 Yaquina Bay, OR.

A line drawn across the seaward extremities of Yaquina Bay Entrance Jetties.

§ 80.1345 Depoe Bay, OR.

A line drawn across the Depoe Bay Channel entrance parallel with the general trend of the highwater shoreline.

§ 80.1350 Netarts Bay, OR.

A line drawn from the northernmost extremity of the shore on the south side of Netarts Bay north to the opposite shoreline.

§ 80.1355 Tillamook Bay, OR.

A line drawn across the seaward extremities of the Tillamook Bay Entrance Jetties.

§ 80.1360 Nehalem River, OR.

A line drawn approximately parallel with the general trend of the highwater shoreline across the Nehalem River Entrance.

§ 80.1365 Columbia River Entrance, OR/WA.

A line drawn from the seaward extremity of the Columbia River North Jetty (above water) 155° true to the seaward extremity of the Columbia River South Jetty (above water).

§ 80.1370 Willapa Bay, WA.

A line drawn from Willapa Bay Light 169.8° true to the westernmost tripod charted 1.6 miles south of Leadbetter Point.

§ 80.1375 Grays Harbor, WA.

A line drawn across the seaward extremities (above water) of the Grays Harbor Entrance Jetties.

§ 80.1380 Quillayute River, WA.

A line drawn from the seaward extremity of the Quillayute River Entrance East Jetty to the overhead power cable tower charted on James Island; thence a straight line through Quillayute River Entrance Light 3 to the shoreline.

§ 80.1385 Strait of Juan de Fuca.

The 72 COLREGS shall apply on all waters of the Strait of Juan de Fuca.

§ 80.1390 Haro Strait and Strait of Georgia.

The 72 COLREGS shall apply on all waters of the Haro Strait and the Strait of Georgia.

§ 80.1395 Puget Sound and Adjacent Waters.

The 72 COLREGS shall apply on all waters of Puget Sound and adjacent waters, including Lake Union, Lake Washington, Hood Canal, and all tributaries.

PACIFIC ISLANDS
FOURTEENTH DISTRICT
§ 80.1410 Hawaiian Island Exemption from General Rule.

Except as provided elsewhere in this part for Mamala Bay and Kaneohe Bay on Oahu; Port Allen and Nawiliwili Bay on Kauai; Kahului Harbor on Maui; and Kawailae and Hilo Harbors on Hawaii, the 72 COLREGS shall apply on all other bays, harbors, and lagoons of the Hawaiian Island including Midway).

§ 80.1420 Mamala Bay, Oahu, HI.

A line drawn from Barbers Point Light to Diamond Head Light.

§ 80.1430 Kaneohe Bay, Oahu, HI.

A straight line drawn from Pyramid Rock Light across Kaneohe Bay through the center of Mokolii Island to the shoreline.

§ 80.1440 Port Allen, Kauai, HI.

A line drawn from Hanapepe Light to Hanapepe Bay Breakwater Light.

§ 80.1450 Nawiliwili Harbor, Kauai, HI.

A line drawn from Nawiliwili Harbor Breakwater Light to Kukii Point Light.

§ 80.1460 Kahului Harbor, Maui, HI.

A line drawn from Kahului Harbor Entrance East Breakwater Light to Kahului Harbor Entrance West Breakwater Light.

§ 80.1470 Kawaihae Harbor, Hawaii, HI.

A line drawn from Kawaihae Light to the seaward extremity of the Kawaihae South Breakwater.

§ 80.1480 Hilo Harbor, Hawaii, HI.

A line drawn from the seaward extremity of the Hilo Breakwater 265° true (as an extension of the seaward side of the breakwater) to the shoreline 0.2 nautical mile north of Alealea Point.

§ 80.1490 Apra Harbor, U.S. Territory of Guam.

A line drawn from the westernmost extremity of Orote Island to the westernmost extremity of Glass Breakwater.

§ 80.1495 U.S. Pacific Island Possessions.

The 72 COLREGS shall apply on the bays, harbors, lagoons, and waters surrounding the U.S. Pacific Island Possessions of American Samoa, Baker, Howland, Jarvis, Johnson, Palmyra, Swains and Wake Island.

ALASKA
SEVENTEENTH DISTRICT
§ 80.1705 Alaska.

The 72 COLREGS shall apply on all the sounds, bays, harbors, and inlets of Alaska.

Penalty Provisions

VIOLATIONS OF INTERNATIONAL
NAVIGATION RULES AND REGULATIONS (33 U.S.C. 1608)

(a) Whoever operates a vessel, subject to the provisions of this Chapter, in violation of this Chapter or of any regulation promulgated pursuant to section 1607 of this title, shall be liable to a civil penalty of not more than $5,000 for each such violation.

(b) Every vessel subject to the provisions of this Chapter, other than a public vessel being used for noncommercial purposes, which is operated in violation of this Chapter or of any regulation promulgated pursuant to section 1607 of this title, shall be liable to a civil penalty of not more than $5,000 for each such violation, for which penalty the vessel may be seized and proceeded against in the district court of the United States of any district within which such vessel may be found.

(c) The Secretary of the department in which the Coast Guard is operating may assess any civil penalty authorized by this section. No such penalty may be assessed until the person charged, or the owner of the vessel charged, as appropriate, shall have been given notice of the violation involved and an opportunity for a hearing. For good cause shown, the Secretary may remit, mitigate, or compromise any penalty assessed. Upon the failure of the person charged, or the owner of the vessel charged, to pay an assessed penalty, as it may have been mitigated or compromised, the Secretary may request the Attorney General to commence an action in the appropriate district court of the United States for collection of the penalty as assessed, without regard to the amount involved, together with such other relief as may be appropriate.

VIOLATIONS OF INLAND NAVIGATION RULES AND REGULATIONS (33 U.S.C. 2072)

(a) Whoever operates a vessel in violation of this Chapter, or of any regulation issued thereunder, or in violation of a certificate of alternative compliance issued under Rule 1 is liable to a civil penalty of not more than $5,000 for each violation.

(b) Every vessel subject to this Chapter, other than a public vessel being used for noncommercial purposes, that is operated in violation of this Chapter, or of any regulation issued thereunder, or in violation of a certificate of alternative compliance issued under Rule 1 is liable to a civil penalty of not more than $5,000 for each violation, for which penalty the vessel may be seized and proceeded against in the district court of the United States of any district within which the vessel may be found.

(c) The Secretary may assess any civil penalty authorized by this section. No such penalty may be assessed until the person charged, or the owner of the vessel charged, as appropriate, shall have been given notice of the violation involved and an opportunity for a hearing. For good cause shown, the Secretary may remit, mitigate, or compromise any penalty assessed. Upon the failure of the person charged, or the owner of the vessel charged, to pay an assessed penalty, as it may have been mitigated or compromised, the Secretary may request the Attorney General to commence an action in the appropriate district court of the United States for collection of the penalty as assessed, without regard to the amount involved, together with such other relief as may be appropriate.

(d)(1) If any owner, operator, or individual in charge of a vessel is liable for a penalty under this section, or if reasonable cause exists to believe that the owner, operator, or individual in charge may be subject to a penalty under this section, the Secretary of the Treasury, upon the request of the Secretary, shall with respect to such vessel refuse or revoke any clearance required by section 4197 of the Revised Statutes of the United States (46 App. U.S.C. 91).

(2) Clearance or a permit refused or revoked under this subsection may be granted upon filing of a bond or other surety satisfactory to the Secretary.

PENALTIES FOR NEGLIGENT OPERATIONS; DUTIES RELATED TO MARINE CASUALTY ASSISTANCE AND INFORMATION; DUTY TO PROVIDE ASSISTANCE AT SEA; INJUNCTIONS (46 U.S.C. 2301-2305) EXCERPT FROM TITLE 46 OF THE UNITED STATES CODE

CHAPTER 23—OPERATIONS OF VESSELS GENERALLY [ENACTED ON AUGUST 26,1983]

Sec.

2301 Application.
2302 Penalties for negligent operations.
2303 Duties related to marine casualty assistance.
2304 Duty to provide assistance at sea.
2305 Injunctions.
2306 Vessel reporting requirements.

§ 2301 Application

This chapter applies to a vessel operated on waters subject to the jurisdiction of the United States and, for a vessel owned in the United States, on the high seas.

§ 2302 Penalties for negligent operations

(a) A person operating a vessel in a negligent manner that endangers the life, limb, or property of a person is liable to the United States Government for a civil penalty of not more than $1,000.

(b) A person operating a vessel in a grossly negligent manner that endangers the life, limb, or property of a person shall be fined not more than $5,000, imprisoned for not more than one year, or both.

(c) An individual who is under the influence of alcohol, or a dangerous drug in violation of a law of the United States when operating a vessel, as determined under standards prescribed by the Secretary by regulation—

(1) is liable to the United States Government for a civil penalty of not more than $1,000 for a first violation and not more than $5,000 for a subsequent violation; or

(2) commits a class A misdemeanor.

(d) For a penalty imposed under this section, the vessel also is liable in rem unless the vessel is—

(1) owned by a State or a political subdivision of a State;

(2) operated principally for governmental purposes; and

(3) identified clearly as a vessel of that State or subdivision.

§ 2303 Duties related to marine casualty assistance and information

(a) The master or individual in charge of a vessel involved in a marine casualty shall—

(1) render necessary assistance to each individual affected to save that affected individual from danger caused by the marine casualty, so far as the master or individual in charge can do so without serious danger to the master's or individual's vessel or to individuals on board; and

(2) give the master's or individual's name and address and identification of the vessel to the master or individual in charge of any other vessel involved in the casualty, to any individual injured, and to the owner of any property damaged.

(b) An individual violating this section or a regulation prescribed under this section shall be fined not more than $1,000 or imprisoned for not more than 2 years. The vessel also is liable in rem to the United States Government for the fine.

(c) An individual complying with subsection (a) of this section or gratuitously and in good faith rendering assistance at the scene of a marine casualty without objection by an individual assisted, is not liable for damages as a result of rendering assistance or for an act or omission in providing or arranging salvage, towage, medical treatment, or other assistance when the individual acts as an ordinary, reasonable, and prudent individual would have acted under the circumstances.

§ 2304 Duty to provide assistance at sea

(a) A master or individual in charge of a vessel shall render assistance to any individual found at sea in danger of being lost, so far as the master or individual in charge can do so without serious danger to the master's or individual's vessel or individuals on board.

(b) A master or individual violating this section shall be fined not more than $1,000, imprisoned for not more than 2 years, or both.

§ 2305 Injunctions

(a) The district courts of the United States have jurisdiction to enjoin the negligent operation of vessels prohibited by this chapter on the petition of the Attorney General for the United States Government.

(b) When practicable, the Secretary shall—

(1) give notice to any person against whom an action for injunctive relief is considered under this section an opportunity to present that person's views; and

(2) except for a knowing and willful violation, give the person a reasonable opportunity to achieve compliance.

(c) The failure to give notice and opportunity to present views under subsection (b) of this section does not preclude the court from granting appropriate relief.

§ 2306 Vessel Reporting Requirements

(a)(1) An owner, charterer, managing operator, or agent of a vessel of the United States, having reason to believe (because of lack of communication with or nonappearance of a vessel or any other incident) that the vessel may have been lost or imperiled, immediately shall—

(A) notify the Coast Guard; and

(B) use all available means to determine the status of the vessel.

(2) When more than 48 hours have passed since the owner, charterer, managing operator, or agent of a vessel required to report to the United States Flag Merchant Vessel Location Filing System under authority of section 212 (A) of the Merchant Marine Act, 1936 (46 App. U. S. C. 1122a), has received a communication from the vessel, the owner, charterer, managing operator, or agent immediately shall—

(A) notify the Coast Guard; and

(B) use all available means to determine the status of the vessel.

(3) A person notifying the Coast Guard under paragraph (1) or (2) of this subsection shall provide the name and identification number of the vessel, the names of individuals on board, and other information that may be requested by the Coast Guard. The owner, charterer, managing operator, or agent also shall submit written confirmation to the Coast Guard 24 hours after nonwritten notification to the Coast Guard under those paragraphs.

(4) An owner, charterer, managing operator, or agent violating this subsection is liable to the United States Government for a civil penalty of not more than $5,000 for each day during which the violation occurs.

(b)(1) The master of a vessel of the United States required to report to the System shall report to the owner, charterer, managing operator, or agent at least once every 48 hours.

(2) A master violating this subsection is liable to the Government for a civil penalty of not more than $1,000 for each day during which the violation occurs.

(c) The Secretary may prescribe regulations to carry out this section.

Alternative Compliance

The alternative compliance procedures for the International Rules and the Inland Rules are the same, although they appear both in the International Rules section of the Code of Federal Regulations (33 CFR Part 81) and in the Inland Rules section (33 CFR Part 89).

SEC

1. Definitions.
2. General.
3. Application for a Certificate.
4. Certificate of Alternative Compliance: Contents.
5. Certificate of Alternative Compliance: Termination.
6. Record of certification of vessels of special of construction or purpose.

1. Definitions.

As used in this part:

"72 COLREGS" refers to the International Regulations for Preventing Collisions at Sea, 1972, done at London, October 20, 1972, as rectified by the Proces-Verbal of December 1, 1973, as amended.

"Inland Rules" refers to the Inland Navigation Rules contained in the Inland Navigational Rules Act of 1980 (Pub. L. 96-591) and the technical annexes established under that Act.

"A vessel of special construction or purpose" means a vessel designed or modified to perform a special function and whose arrangement is thereby made relatively inflexible.

"Interference with the special function of the vessel" occurs when installation or use of lights, shapes, or sound-signalling appliances under the 72 COLREGS/Inland Rules prevents or significantly hinders the operation in which the vessel is usually engaged.

2. General.

Vessels of special construction or purpose which cannot fully comply with the light, shape, and sound signal provisions of the 72 COLREGS/ Inland Rules without interfering with their special function may instead meet alternative requirements. The Chief of the Marine Safety Division in each Coast Guard District Office makes this determination and requires that alternative compliance be as close as possible with the 72 COLREGS/Inland Rules. These regulations set out the procedure by which a vessel may be certified for alternative compliance.

3. Application for a Certificate of Alternative Compliance.

(a) The owner, builder, operator, or agent of a vessel of special construction or purpose who believes the vessel cannot fully comply with the 72 COLREGS/Inland Rules light, shape, or sound signal provisions without interference with its special function may apply for a determination that alternative compliance is justified. The application must be in writing, submitted to the Chief of the Marine Safety Division of the Coast Guard District in which the vessel is being built or operated, and include the following information:

(1) The name, address, and telephone number of the applicant.

(2) The identification of the vessel by its:

(i) Official number;

(ii) Shipyard hull number;

(iii) Hull identification number; or

(iv) State number, if the vessel does not have an official number or hull identification number.

(3) Vessel name and home port, if known.

(4) A description of the vessel's area of operation.

(5) A description of the provision for which the Certificate of Alternative Compliance is sought, including:

(i) The 72 COLREGS/Inland Rules Rule or Annex section number for which the Certificate of Alternative Compliance is sought;

(ii) A description of the special function of the vessel that would be interfered with by full compliance with the provision of that Rule or Annex section; and

(iii) A statement of how full compliance would interfere with the special function of the vessel.

(6) A description of the alternative installation that is in closest possible compliance with the applicable 72 COLREGS/Inland Rules Rule or Annex section.

(7) A copy of the vessel's plans or an accurate scale drawing that clearly shows—

(i) The required installation of the equipment under the 72 COLREGS/Inland Rules,

(ii) The proposed installation of the equipment for which certification is being sought, and

(iii) Any obstructions that may interfere with the equipment when installed in:

(A) The required location; and

(B) The proposed location.

(b) The Coast Guard may request from the applicant additional information concerning the application.

4. Certificate of Alternative Compliance: Contents.

The Chief of the Marine Safety Division issues the Certificate of Alternative Compliance to the vessel based on a determination that it cannot comply fully with 72 COLREGS/Inland Rules light, shape, and sound signal provisions without interference with its special function.

This certificate includes:

(a) Identification of the vessel as supplied in the application;

(b) The provision of the 72 COLREGS/Inland Rules for which the Certificate authorizes alternative compliance;

(c) A certification that the vessel is unable to comply fully with the 72 COLREGS/Inland Rules light, shape, and sound signal requirements without interference with its special function;

(d) A statement of why full compliance would interfere with the special function of the vessel;

(e) The required alternative installation;

(f) A statement that the required alternative installation is in the closest possible compliance with the 72 COLREGS/Inland Rules without interfering with the special function of the vessel;

(g) The date of issuance;

(h) A statement that the Certificate of Alternative Compliance terminates when the vessel ceases to be usually engaged in the operation for which the certificate is issued.

5. Certificate of Alterative Compliance: Termination.

The Certificate of Alternative Compliance terminates if the information supplied under 3(a) or the Certificate issued under 4 is no longer applicable to the vessel.

6. Record of certification of vessels of special construction or purpose.

(a) Copies of Certificates of Alternative Compliance and documentation concerning Coast Guard vessels are available for inspection at the offices of Assistant Commandant for Marine Safety and Environmental Protection, U.S. Coast Guard Headquarters, 2100 Second Street, S.W., Washington, D.C. 20593-0001.

(b) The owner or operator of a vessel issued a certificate shall ensure that the vessel does not operate unless the Certificate of Alternative Compliance or a certified copy of that certificate is on board the vessel and available for inspection by Coast Guard personnel.

Waters Specified by the Secretary

33 CFR § 89.25 Waters upon which Inland Rules 9(a)(ii), 14(d), and 15(b) apply.

Inland Rules 9(a)(ii), 14(d), and 15(b) apply on the Great Lakes, the Western Rivers, and the following specified waters:

(a) Tennessee-Tombigbee Waterway;

(b) Tombigbee River;

(c) Black Warrior River;

(d) Alabama River;

(e) Coosa River

(f) Mobile River above the Cochrane Bridge at St Louis Point;

(g) Flint River;

(h) Chattahoochee River, and

(i) The Apalachicola River above its confluence with the Jackson River.

33 CFR § 89.27 Waters upon which Inland Rule 24(i) applies.

(a) Inland Rule 24(i) applies on the Western Rivers and the specified waters listed in § 89.25 (a) through (i).

(b) Inland Rule 24(i) applies on the Gulf Intracoastal Waterway from St. Marks, Florida, to the Rio Grande, Texas, including the Morgan City-Port Allen Alternate Route and the Galveston-Freeport Cutoff, except that a power-driven vessel pushing ahead or towing alongside shall exhibit the lights required by Inland Rule 24(c), while transiting within the following areas:

(1) St. Andrews Bay from the Hathaway Fixed Bridge at Mile 284.6 East of Harvey Locks (EHL) to the DuPont Fixed Bridge at Mile 295.4 EHL.

(2) Pensacola Bay, Santa Rosa Sound and Big Lagoon from the Light "10" off of Trout Point at Mile 176.9 EHL to the Pensacola Fixed Bridge at Mile 189.1 EHL.

(3) Mobile Bay and Bon Secour Bay from the Dauphin Island Causeway Fixed Bridge at Mile 127.7 EHL to Little Point Clear at Mile 140 EHL.

(4) Mississippi Sound from Grand Island Waterway Light "1" at Mile 53.8 EHL to Light "40" off the West Point of Dauphin Island at Mile 118.7 EHL.

(5) The Mississippi River at New Orleans, Mississippi River-Gulf Outlet Canal and the Inner Harbor Navigation Canal from the junction of the Harvey Canal and the Algiers Alternate Route at Mile 6.5 West of Harvey Locks (WHL) to the Michoud Canal at Mile 18 EHL.

(6) The Calcasieu River from the Calcasieu Lock at Mile 238.6 WHL to the Ellender Lift Bridge at Mile 243.6 WHL.

(7) The Sabine Neches Canal from Mile 262.5 WHL to Mile 291.5 WHL.

(8) Bolivar Roads from the Bolivar Assembling Basin at Mile 346 WHL to the Galveston Causeway Bridge at Mile 357.3 WHL.

(9) Freeport Harbor from Surfside Beach Fixed Bridge at Mile 393.8 WHL to the Bryan Beach Pontoon Bridge at Mile 397.6 WHL.

(10) Matagorda Ship Channel area of Matagorda Bay from Range "K" Front Light at Mile 468.7 WHL to the Port O'Connor Jetty at Mile 472.2 WHL.

(11) Corpus Christi Bay from Redfish Bay Day Beacon "55" at Mile 537.4 WHL when in the Gulf Intracoastal Waterway main route or from the north end of Lydia Ann Island Mile 531.1A when in the Gulf Intracoastal Waterway Alternate Route to Corpus Christi Bay LT 76 at Mile 543.7 WHL.

(12) Port Isabel and Brownsville Ship Channel south of the Padre Island Causeway Fixed Bridge at Mile 665.1 WHL.

Vessel Bridge-to-Bridge Radiotelephone Regulations (33 CFR 26)

The Vessel Bridge-to-Bridge Radiotelephone Act is applicable on navigable waters of the United States inside the boundary lines established in 46 CFR 7. In all cases, the Act applies on waters subject to the Inland Rules. The Act applies out to the three mile limit. In no instance does the Act apply beyond the three mile limit.

Sec.

26.01 Purpose.

26.02 Definitions.

26.03 Radiotelephone required.

26.04 Use of the designated frequency.

26.05 Use of radiotelephone.

26.06 Maintenance of radiotelephone; failure of radiotelephone.

26.07 Communications.

26.08 Exemption procedures.

26.09 List of exemptions.

§ 26.01 Purpose.

(a) The purpose of this part is to implement the provisions of the Vessel Bridge-to-Bridge Radiotelephone Act. This part:

(1) Requires the use of the vessel bridge-to-bridge radiotelephone;

(2) Provides the Coast Guard's interpretation of the meaning of important terms in the Act;

(3) Prescribes the procedures for applying for an exemption from the Act and the regulations issued under the Act and a listing of exemptions.

(b) Nothing in this part relieves any person from the obligation of complying with the rules of the road and the applicable pilot rules.

§ 26.02 Definitions.

For the purpose of this part and interpreting the Act:

"Secretary" means the Secretary of the Department in which the Coast Guard is operating;

"Act" means the "Vessel Bridge-to-Bridge Radiotelephone Act," 33 U.S.C. sections 1201–1208;

"Length" is measured from end to end over the deck excluding sheer;

"Power-driven vessel" means any vessel propelled by machinery;

"Towing vessel" means any commercial vessel engaged in towing another vessel astern, alongside, or by pushing ahead;

"Vessel Traffic Services (VTS)" means a service implemented under Part 161 of this chapter by the United States Coast Guard designed to improve the safety and efficiency of vessel traffic and to protect the environment. The VTS has the capability to interact with marine traffic and respond to traffic situations developing in the VTS area; and

"Vessel Traffic Service Area or VTS Area" means the geographical area encompassing a specific VTS area of service as described in Part 161 of this chapter. This area of service may be subdivided into sectors for the purpose of allocating responsibility to individual Vessel Traffic Centers or to identify different operating requirements.

Note: Although regulatory jurisdiction is limited to the navigable waters of the United States, certain vessels will be encouraged or may be required, as a condition of port entry, to report beyond this area to facilitate traffic management within the VTS area.

§ 26.03 Radiotelephone required.

(a) Unless an exemption is granted under § 26.09 and except as provided in paragraph (a)(4) of this section, this part applies to:

(1) Every power-driven vessel of 20 meters or over in length while navigating;

(2) Every vessel of 100 gross tons and upward carrying one or more passengers for hire while navigating;

(3) Every towing vessel of 26 feet or over in length while navigating; and

(4) Every dredge and floating plant engaged in or near a channel or fairway in operations likely to restrict or affect navigation of other vessels except for an unmanned or intermittently manned floating plant under the control of a dredge.

(b) Every vessel, dredge, or floating plant described in paragraph (a) of this section must have a radiotelephone on board capable of operation from its navigational bridge, or in the case of a dredge, from its main control station, and capable of transmitting and receiving on the frequency or frequencies within the 156–162 Mega-Hertz band using the classes of emissions designated by the Federal Communications Commission for the exchange of navigational information.

(c) The radiotelephone required by paragraph (b) of this section must be carried on board the described vessels, dredges, and floating plants upon the navigable waters of the United States.

(d) The radiotelephone required by paragraph (b) of this section must be capable of transmitting and receiving on VHF FM channel 22A (157.1 MHz).

(e) While transiting any of the following waters, each vessel described in paragraph (a) of this section also must have on board a radiotelephone capable of transmitting and receiving on VHF FM channel 67 (156.375 MHz):

(1) The lower Mississippi River from the territorial sea boundary, and within either the Southwest Pass safety fairway or the South Pass safety fairway specified in 33 CFR 166.200, to mile 242.4 AHP (Above Head of Passes) near Baton Rouge;

(2) The Mississippi River-Gulf Outlet from the territorial sea boundary, and within the Mississippi River-Gulf Outlet Safety Fairway specified in 33 CFR 166.200, to that channel's junction with the Inner Harbor Navigation Canal; and

(3) The full length of the Inner Harbor Navigation Canal from its junction with the Mississippi River to that canal's entry to Lake Pontchartrain at the New Seabrook vehicular bridge.

(f) In addition to the radiotelephone required by paragraph (b) of this section, each vessel described in paragraph (a) of this section while transiting any waters within a Vessel Traffic Service Area must have on board a radiotelephone capable of transmitting and receiving on the VTS designated frequency in Table 26.03(f) (VTS Call Signs, Designated Frequencies, and Monitoring Areas).

Note: A single VHF FM radio capable of scanning or sequential monitoring (often referred to as "dual watch" capability) will not meet the requirements for two radios.

§ 26.04 Use of the designated frequency.

(a) No person may use the frequency designated by the Federal Communications Commission under section 8 of the Act, 33 U.S.C. 1207(a), to transmit any information other than information necessary for the safe navigation of vessels or necessary tests.

(b) Each person who is required to maintain a listening watch under section 5 of the Act shall, when necessary, transmit and confirm, on the designated frequency, the intentions of his vessel and any other information necessary for the safe navigation of vessels.

(c) Nothing in these regulations may be construed as prohibiting the use of the designated frequency to communicate with shore stations to obtain or furnish information necessary for the safe navigation of vessels.

(d) On the navigable waters of the United States, channel 13 (156.65 MHz) is the designated frequency required to be monitored in accordance with § 26.05(a) except that in the area prescribed in § 26.03(e), channel 67 (156.375 MHz) is an additional frequency.

(e) On those navigable waters of the United States within a VTS area, the designated VTS frequency is the designated frequency required to be monitored in accordance with § 26.05.

Note: As stated in 47 CFR 80.148(b), a VHF watch on Channel 16 (156.800 Mhz) is not required on vessels subject to the Vessel Bridge-to-Bridge Radiotelephone Act and participating in a Vessel Traffic Service (VTS) system when the watch is maintained on both the vessel bridge-to-bridge frequency and a designated VTS frequency.

§ 26.05 Use of radiotelephone.

Section 5 of the Act states that the radiotelephone required by this Act is for the exclusive use of the master or person in charge of the vessel, or the person designated by the master or person in charge to pilot or direct the movement of the vessel, who shall maintain a listening watch on the designated frequency. Nothing herein shall be interpreted as precluding the use of portable radiotelephone equipment to satisfy the requirements of this Act.

§ 26.06 Maintenance of radiotelephone; failure of radiotelephone.

Section 6 of the Act states that whenever radiotelephone capability is required by this Act, a vessel's radiotelephone equipment shall be maintained in effective operating condition. If the radiotelephone equipment carried aboard a vessel ceases to operate, the master shall exercise due diligence to restore it or cause it to be restored to effective operating condition at the earliest practicable time. The failure of a vessel's radiotelephone equipment shall not, in itself, constitute a violation of this Act, nor shall it obligate the master of any vessel to moor or anchor his vessel; however, the loss of radiotelephone capability shall be given consideration in the navigation of the vessel.

§ 26.07 Communications.

No person may use the services of, and no person may serve as, a person required to maintain a listening watch under section 5 of the Act, 33 U.S.C. 1204, unless the person can communicate in the English language.

§ 26.08 Exemption procedures.

(a) The Commandant has redelegated to the Assistant Commandant for Marine Safety and Environmental Protection, U.S. Coast Guard Headquarters, with the reservation that this authority shall not be further redelegated, the authority to grant exemptions from provisions of the Vessel Bridge-to-Bridge Radiotelephone Act and this part.

(b) Any person may petition for an exemption from any provision of the Act or this part.

(c) Each petition must be submitted in writing to U.S. Coast Guard, Marine Safety and Environmental Protection, 2100 Second Street, S.W., Washington, D.C. 20593-0001, and must state:

(1) The provisions of the Act or this part from which an exemption is requested; and

(2) The reasons why marine navigation will not be adversely affected if the exemption is granted and if the exemption relates to a local communication system how that system would fully comply with the intent of the concept of the Act but would not conform in detail if the exemption is granted.

§ 26.09 List of exemptions.

(a) All vessels navigating on those waters governed by the navigation rules for the Great Lakes and their connecting and tributary waters (33 U.S.C. 241 et seq.) are exempt from the requirements of the Vessel Bridge-to-Bridge Radiotelephone Act and this part until May 6, 1975.

(b) Each vessel navigating on the Great Lakes as defined in the Inland Navigation Rules Act of 1980 (33 U.S.C. 2001 et seq.) and to which the Vessel Bridge-to-Bridge Radiotelephone Act (33 U.S.C. 1201–1208) applies is exempt from the requirements in 33 U.S.C. 1203, 1204, and 1205 and the regulations under §§ 26.03, 26.04, 26.05, 26.06, and 26.07. Each of these vessels and each person to whom 33 U.S.C. 1208(a) applies must comply with Articles VII, X, XI, XII, XIII, XV, and XVI and Technical Regulations 1–9 of "The Agreement Between the United States of America and Canada for Promotion of Safety on the Great Lakes by Means of Radio, 1973."

Table 26.03(f)

Vessel Traffic Service (VTS) Call Signs, Designated Frequencies and Monitoring Areas

VTS[1] Call Sign	Designated Frequency[2] (Channel Designation)	Monitoring Area
New York[3]		
New York Traffic[4]	156.550 MHz (Ch. 11) and 156.700 MHz (Ch. 14)	The navigable waters of the Lower New York Harbor bounded on the east by a line drawn from Norton Point to Breezy Point; on the south by a line connecting the entrance buoys at the Ambrose Channel, Swash Channel, and Sandy Hook Channel to Sandy Hook Point; and on the southeast including the waters of the Sandy Hook Bay south to a line drawn at latitude 40°25′N.; then west into waters of the Raritan Bay to the Raritan River Rail Road Bridge; and then north including the waters of the Arthur Kill and Newark Bay to the Lehigh Valley Draw Bridge at latitude 40°41.95′N.; and then east including the waters of the Kill Van Kull and Upper New York Bay north to a line drawn east-west from the Holland Tunnel Ventilator Shaft at latitude 40°43.7′N.; longitude 74°01.6′W. in the Hudson River; and continuing east including the waters of the East River to the Throgs Neck Bridge, excluding the Harlem River.
	156.600 MHz (Ch. 12)	Each vessel at anchor within the above areas.
Houston[3]		
Houston Traffic	156.550 MHz (Ch. 11)	The navigable waters north of 29°N., west of 94°20′W., south of 29°49′N., and east of 95°20′W.:
	156.600 MHz (Ch. 12)	The navigable waters north of a line extending due west from the southern most end of Exxon Dock #1 (29°43.37′N., 95°01.27′W.). The navigable waters south of a line extending due west from the southern most end of Exxon Dock #1 (29°43.37′N., 95°01.27′W.).
Berwick Bay		
Berwick Traffic	156.550 MHz (Ch. 11)	The navigable waters south of 29°45′N., west of 91°10′W., north of 29°37′N., and east of 91°18′W.
St. Mary's River		
Soo Control	156.600 MHz (Ch. 12)	The navigable waters of the St. Marys River between 45°57′N. (De Tour Reef Light) and 46°38.7′N. (Ile Parisienne Light), except the St. Marys Falls Canal and those navigable waters east of a line from 46°04.16′N. and 46°01.57′N. (La Pointe to Sims Point in Pataganissing Bay and Worsley Bay).
San Francisco[3]		
San Francisco Offshore Vessel Movement Reporting Service	156.600 MHz (Ch. 12)	The waters within a 38 nautical mile radius of Mount Tamalpais (37°55.8′N., 122°34.6′W.) excluding the San Francisco Offshore Precautionary Area.
San Francisco Traffic	156.700 MHz (Ch. 14)	The waters of the San Francisco Offshore Precautionary Area eastward to San Francisco Bay including its tributaries extending to the ports of Stockton, Sacramento, and Redwood City.
Puget Sound[5]	156.700 MHz (Ch. 14)	The navigable waters of Puget Sound, Hood Canal, and adjacent waters south of a line connecting Marrowstone Point and Lagoon Point in Admiralty Inlet and south of a line drawn due east from the southernmost tip of Possession Point on Whidbey Island to the shoreline.

VTS[1] Call Sign	Designated Frequency[2] (Channel Designation)	Monitoring Area
Seattle Traffic[6]	156.250 MHz (Ch. 5A)	The navigable waters of the Strait of Juan de Fuca east of 124°40'W., excluding the waters in the central portion of the Strait of Juan de Fuca north and east of Race Rocks; the navigable waters of the Strait of Georgia east of 122°52'W.; the San Juan Island Archipelago, Rosario Strait, Bellingham Bay; Admiralty Inlet north of a line connecting Marrowstone Point and Lagoon Point and all waters east of Whidbey Island north of a line drawn due east from the southernmost tip of Possession Point on Whidbey Island to the shoreline.
Tofino Traffic[7]	156.725 MHz (Ch. 74)	The waters west of 124°40'W. within 50 nautical miles of the coast of Vancouver Island including the waters north of 48°N., and east of 127°W.
Vancouver Traffic	156.550 MHz (Ch. 11)	The navigable waters of the Strait of Georgia west of 122°52'W., the navigable waters of the central Strait of Juan de Fuca north and east of Race Rocks, including the Gulf Island Archipelago, Boundary Pass, and Haro Strait.
Prince William Sound[8] Valdez Traffic	156.650 MHz (Ch. 13)	The navigable waters south of 61°05'N., east of 147°20'W., north of 60°N., and west of 146°30'W.; and, all navigable waters in Port Valdez.
Louisville[8] Louisville Traffic	156.650 MHz (Ch. 13)	The navigable waters of the Ohio River between McAlpine Locks (Mile 606) and Twelve Mile Island (Mile 593), only when the McAlpine upper pool gauge is approximately 13.0 feet or above.

Notes:

1. VTS regulations are denoted in 33 CFR Part 161. All geographic coordinates (latitude and longitude) are expressed in North American Datum of 1983 (NAD 83).
2. In the event of a communication failure either by the vessel traffic center or the vessel or radio congestion on a designated VTS frequency, communications may be established on an alternate VTS frequency. The bridge-to-bridge navigational frequency 156.650 MHz (Channel 13) is monitored in each VTS area; and it may be used as an alternate frequency, however, only to the extent that doing so provides a level of safety beyond that provided by other means.
3. Designated frequency monitoring is required within U.S. navigable waters. In areas that are outside the U.S. navigable waters, designated frequency monitoring is voluntary. However, prospective VTS users are encouraged to monitor the designated frequency.
4. VMRS participants shall make their initial report (Sail Plan) to New York Traffic on Channel 11 (156.550 MHz). All other reports, including the Final Report, shall be made on Channel 14 (156.700 MHz). VMRS and other VTS users shall monitor Channel 14 (156.700 MHz) while transiting the VTS area. New York Traffic may direct a vessel to monitor and report on either primary frequency depending on traffic density, weather conditions, or other safety factors. This does not require a vessel to monitor both primary frequencies.
5. A Cooperative Vessel Traffic Service was established by the United States and Canada within adjoining waters. The appropriate vessel traffic center administers the rules issued by both nations; however, it will enforce only its own set of rules within its jurisdiction.
6. Seattle Traffic may direct a vessel to monitor the other primary VTS frequency 156.250 MHz or 156.700 MHz (Channel 5A or 14) depending on traffic density, weather conditions, or other safety factors, rather than strictly adhering to the designated frequency required for each monitoring area as defined above. This does not require a vessel to monitor both primary frequencies.
7. A portion of Tofino Sector's monitoring area extends beyond the defined CVTS area. Designated frequency monitoring is voluntary in these portions outside of VTS jurisdiction, however, prospective VTS users are encouraged to monitor the designated frequency.
8. The bridge-to-bridge navigational frequency, 156.650 MHz (Channel 13), is used in these VTSs because the level of radiotelephone transmissions does not warrant a designated VTS frequency. The listening watch required by 26.05 of this chapter is not limited to the monitoring area.

Questions on the Rules of the Road

1. INLAND ONLY. For the purpose of the Inland Navigation Rules, the term "Inland Waters" includes ___.
   A. the Great Lakes on the United States side of the International Boundary
   B. the water surrounding any islands of the United States
   C. the coastline of the United States, out to one mile offshore
   D. any lakes within state boundaries

2. INTERNATIONAL ONLY. The International Rules of the Road apply ___.
   A. to all waters that are not inland waters
   B. only to waters outside the territorial waters of the United States
   C. only to waters where foreign vessels travel
   D. upon the high seas and connecting waters navigable by seagoing vessels

3. INLAND ONLY. Which term is NOT defined in the Inland Navigation Rules?
   A. Towing light
   B. Vessel constrained by her draft
   C. In sight
   D. Restricted visibility

4. INLAND ONLY. Which statement is TRUE of a power-driven vessel proceeding downbound with the current, when meeting an upbound vessel on the Western Rivers?
   A. She shall not impede the upbound vessel
   B. She shall pass on the port side of the other
   C. She shall propose the manner of passage
   D. All of the above

5. INLAND ONLY. You are navigating in a narrow channel and must remain in the channel for safe operation. Another vessel is crossing the channel ahead of you from your starboard and you doubt whether your vessel will pass safely. Which statement is TRUE?
   A. You must stop your vessel, since the other vessel is the stand-on
   B. You must sound one short blast of the whistle and turn to starboard
   C. You must sound the danger signal
   D. You must stop your engines and you may sound the danger signal

6. INLAND ONLY. Which statement is TRUE concerning narrow channels?
   A. You should keep to that side of the channel which is on your port side
   B. You should avoid anchoring in a narrow channel
   C. A vessel having a following current will propose the manner of passage in any case where two vessels are meeting
   D. All of the above

7. BOTH INTERNATIONAL and INLAND. Which vessel is "underway" under the Rules of the Road?
   A. A vessel at anchor with the engine running
   B. A vessel with a line led to a tree onshore
   C. A vessel drifting with the engine off
   D. A vessel aground

8. BOTH INTERNATIONAL and INLAND. A vessel is "in sight" of another vessel when ___.
   A. she can be observed by radar
   B. she can be observed visually from the other vessel
   C. she can be plotted on radar well enough to determine her heading
   D. her fog signal can be heard

9. BOTH INTERNATIONAL and INLAND. The term "restricted visibility," when used in the Rules, refers to ___.
   A. situations when you can see vessels on radar that you cannot see visually
   B. visibility of less than half a mile
   C. any condition where visibility is restricted
   D. visibility where you cannot see shore

10. BOTH INTERNATIONAL and INLAND. Which factor is listed in the Rules as one that must be taken into account when determining safe speed?
    A. The construction of the vessel
    B. The maneuverability of the vessel
    C. The experience of vessel personnel
    D. All of the above must be taken into account

11. BOTH INTERNATIONAL and INLAND. You are approaching another vessel and are not sure whether danger of collision exists. You must assume ___.
    A. there is risk of collision
    B. you are the give way vessel
    C. the other vessel is also in doubt
    D. All of the above are correct

12. BOTH INTERNATIONAL and INLAND. Which statement is TRUE concerning a vessel equipped with operational radar?
    A. She must use this equipment to obtain early warning of risk of collision
    B. The radar equipment is only required to be used in restricted visibility
    C. The use of a radar excuses a vessel from the need of a lookout
    D. The safe speed of such a vessel will likely be greater than that of vessels without radar

13. BOTH INTERNATIONAL and INLAND. In which situation would you consider a risk of collision to exist?
     A. A vessel is one point on your starboard bow, range increasing, bearing changing slightly to the right
     B. A vessel is broad on your starboard beam, range decreasing, bearing changing rapidly to the right
     C. A vessel is two points abaft your port beam, range decreasing, bearing constant
     D. A vessel is on your starboard quarter, range increasing, bearing is constant

14. BOTH INTERNATIONAL and INLAND. Which procedure(s) shall be used to determine risk of collision?
     A. Watching the compass bearing of an approaching vessel
     B. Systematic observation of objects detected by radar
     C. Long-range radar scanning
     D. All of the above

15. BOTH INTERNATIONAL and INLAND. Which statement is TRUE concerning risk of collision?
     A. The stand-on vessel must keep out of the way of the other vessel when risk of collision exists.
     B. Risk of collision always exists when two vessels pass within one mile of each other.
     C. Risk of collision always exists when the compass bearing of an approaching vessel changes appreciably.
     D. Risk of collision may exist when the compass bearing of an approaching vessel is changing appreciably.

16. BOTH INTERNATIONAL and INLAND. What is a requirement for any action taken to avoid collision?
     A. When in sight of another vessel, any action taken must be accompanied by sound signals.
     B. The action taken must include changing the speed of the vessel.
     C. The action must be positive and made in ample time.
     D. All of the above

17. BOTH INTERNATIONAL and INLAND. When action to avoid a close quarters situation is taken, a course change alone may be the most effective action provided that ___.
     A. it is done in a succession of small course changes
     B. it is not done too early
     C. it is a large course change
     D. the course change is to starboard

18. BOTH INTERNATIONAL and INLAND. Under the Rules, any vessel may slacken her speed, stop, or reverse her engines to ___.
     A. create a crossing situation
     B. allow more time to assess the situation
     C. attract the attention of another vessel
     D. All of the above

19. BOTH INTERNATIONAL and INLAND. When underway in a channel, you should keep to the ___.
    A. middle of the channel
    B. starboard side of the channel
    C. port side of the channel
    D. side of the channel that has the widest turns

20. BOTH INTERNATIONAL and INLAND. You are underway in a narrow channel and are being overtaken by a vessel astern. The overtaking vessel sounds a signal indicating her intention to pass you on your starboard side. If such an action appears dangerous, you should sound ___.
    A. one prolonged followed by one short blast
    B. one prolonged, one short, one prolonged, and one short blast in that order
    C. five short and rapid blasts
    D. three short and rapid blasts

21. BOTH INTERNATIONAL and INLAND. In a traffic separation scheme, when joining a traffic lane from the side, a vessel shall do so ___.
    A. at as small an angle as possible
    B. as nearly as practical at right angles to the general direction of traffic flow
    C. only in case of an emergency or to engage in fishing within the zone
    D. never

22. BOTH INTERNATIONAL and INLAND. A vessel may enter a traffic separation zone ___.
    A. in an emergency
    B. to engage in fishing within the zone
    C. to cross the traffic separation scheme
    D. Any of the above

23. BOTH INTERNATIONAL and INLAND. There are two classes of vessels that do not have to comply with the rule regarding traffic separation schemes, to the extent necessary to carry out their work. One of those is a vessel ___.
    A. engaged in fishing
    B. towing another
    C. servicing a navigational aid
    D. on pilotage duty

24. BOTH INTERNATIONAL and INLAND. An authorized light to assist in the identification of submarines operating on the surface is a(n) ___.
    A. blue rotating light
    B. intermittent flashing amber/yellow light
    C. flashing white light
    D. flashing sidelight

25. BOTH INTERNATIONAL and INLAND. The Rules state that vessels may depart from the requirements of the Rules when ___.
    A. operating in restricted visibility
    B. operating in a narrow channel
    C. necessary to avoid immediate danger
    D. the Master enters it in the ship's log

26. BOTH INTERNATIONAL and INLAND. For the purpose of the Rules, except where otherwise required, the term ___.
    A. "vessel" includes seaplanes
    B. "seaplane" includes nondisplacement craft
    C. "vessel engaged in fishing" includes a vessel fishing with trolling lines
    D. "vessel restricted in her ability to maneuver" includes fishing vessels

27. BOTH INTERNATIONAL and INLAND. The term "power-driven vessel" refers to any vessel ___.
    A. with propelling machinery onboard whether in use or not
    B. making way against the current
    C. with propelling machinery in use
    D. traveling at a speed greater than that of the current

28. BOTH INTERNATIONAL and INLAND. To be considered "engaged in fishing" according to the Rules of the Road, a vessel must be ___.
    A. using fishing apparatus that restricts maneuverability
    B. using trolling lines
    C. power-driven
    D. showing lights or shapes for a vessel restricted in her ability to maneuver

29. BOTH INTERNATIONAL and INLAND. The navigation rules define a "vessel not under command" as a vessel that ___.
    A. from the nature of her work is unable to keep out of the way of another vessel
    B. through some exceptional circumstance is unable to maneuver as required by the rules
    C. by taking action contrary to the rules has created a special circumstance situation
    D. is moored, aground, or anchored in a fairway

30. BOTH INTERNATIONAL and INLAND. A vessel "restricted in her ability to maneuver" is one that ___.
    A. from the nature of her work is unable to maneuver as required by the rules
    B. through some exceptional circumstance is unable to maneuver as required by the rules
    C. due to adverse weather conditions is unable to maneuver as required by the rules
    D. has lost steering and is unable to maneuver

31. BOTH INTERNATIONAL and INLAND. If two sailing vessels are running free with the wind on the same side, which one must keep clear of the other?
    A. The one with the wind closest abeam.
    B. The one with the wind closest astern.
    C. The one to leeward.
    D. The one to windward.

32. BOTH INTERNATIONAL and INLAND. Two sailing vessels are approaching each other as shown in the diagram below. Which statement is correct?

    A. Vessel "I" should stand on because she has the wind on her port side

    B. Vessel "II" should stand on because she has the wind on her starboard side

    C. Neither vessel is the stand-on vessel because they are meeting head-on

    D. Vessel "I" should stand on because she is close-hauled

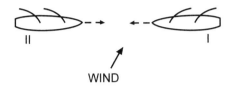

WIND

33. BOTH INTERNATIONAL and INLAND. Which statement is TRUE concerning two sailing vessels?

    A. A sailing vessel with the wind forward of the beam on her port side shall keep out of the way of a sailing vessel with the wind forward of the beam on the starboard side

    B. When both vessels have the wind on the same side, the vessel to leeward shall keep out of the way

    C. A sail vessel with the wind abaft of the beam must keep out of the way of a vessel sailing into the wind

    D. None of the above

34. BOTH INTERNATIONAL and INLAND. You are the watch officer on a power-driven vessel and notice a large sailing vessel approaching from astern. You should:

    A. slow down

    B. sound one short blast and change course to starboard

    C. sound two short blasts and change course to port

    D. hold your course and speed

35. INLAND ONLY. You are on vessel "A," and vessel "B" desires to overtake you on the starboard side as shown in the diagram below. After the vessels have exchanged one blast signals, you should:

    A. alter course to the left

    B. slow your vessel until vessel "B" has passed

    C. hold course and speed

    D. alter course to the left or right to give vessel "B" more sea room

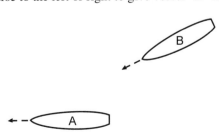

36. BOTH INTERNATIONAL and INLAND. In which situation do the Rules require both vessels to change course?
    A. Two power-driven vessels meeting head-on
    B. Two power-driven vessels crossing when it is apparent to the stand-on vessel that the give-way vessel is not taking appropriate action
    C. Two sailing vessels crossing with the wind on the same side
    D. All of the above

37. BOTH INTERNATIONAL and INLAND. A vessel approaching your vessel from 235° relative is in what type of situation?
    A. Meeting
    B. Overtaking
    C. Crossing
    D. Passing

38. BOTH INTERNATIONAL and INLAND. The Rules state that a vessel overtaking another vessel is relieved of her duty to keep clear when:
    A. she is forward of the other vessel's beam
    B. the overtaking situation becomes a crossing situation
    C. she is past and clear of the other vessel
    D. the other vessel is no longer in sight

39. BOTH INTERNATIONAL and INLAND. Two vessels meeting in a "head-on" situation are directed by the Rules to:
    A. alter course to starboard and pass port to port
    B. alter course to port and pass starboard to starboard
    C. decide on which side the passage will occur by matching whistle signals
    D. slow to bare steerageway

40. BOTH INTERNATIONAL and INLAND. When two power-driven vessels are crossing, the vessel that has the other to starboard must keep out of the way if:
    A. she is the faster vessel
    B. the situation involves risk of collision
    C. the vessels will pass within half a mile of each other
    D. whistle signals have been sounded

41. BOTH INTERNATIONAL and INLAND. Your vessel is NOT making way but is not in any way disabled. Another vessel is approaching you on your starboard beam. Which statement is TRUE?
    A. Your vessel is obligated to stay out of the way
    B. The other vessel must give way, since your vessel is stopped
    C. You should be showing the lights or shapes for a vessel not under command
    D. You should be showing the lights or shapes for a vessel restricted in her ability to maneuver

42. BOTH INTERNATIONAL and INLAND. In the diagram below, vessel "A" is underway and pushing ahead when vessel "B" is sighted off the starboard bow. Which vessel is the stand-on vessel?

    A. Vessel "A" is the stand-on vessel because it is to port

    B. Vessel "A" is the stand-on vessel because it is pushing ahead

    C. Vessel "B" is the stand-on vessel because it is to starboard of vessel "A"

    D. Neither vessel is the stand-on vessel

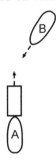

43. BOTH INTERNATIONAL and INLAND. You are approaching another vessel. She is about one mile distant and is on your starboard bow. You believe she will cross ahead of you. She then sounds a whistle signal of five short blasts. You should:

    A. answer the signal and hold course and speed

    B. reduce speed slightly to make sure she will have room to pass

    C. make a large course change, and slow down if necessary

    D. wait for another whistle signal from the other vessel

44. BOTH INTERNATIONAL and INLAND. You are aboard the give-way vessel in a crossing situation. What should you NOT do in obeying the Rules?

    A. Cross ahead of the stand-on vessel

    B. Make a large course change to starboard

    C. Slow your vessel

    D. Back your vessel

45. BOTH INTERNATIONAL and INLAND. A stand-on vessel is:

    A. required to give way in a crossing situation

    B. required to sound the first passing signal in a meeting situation

    C. free to maneuver in any crossing or meeting situation as it has the right-of-way

    D. required to maintain course and speed in a crossing situation but may take action to avoid collision

46. BOTH INTERNATIONAL and INLAND. A stand-on vessel in a crossing situation is allowed to take action when:

    A. on a collision course

    B. the vessel will pass within one mile

    C. it becomes apparent to her that the give-way vessel is not taking appropriate action

    D. the relative speed of the vessels indicates collision in less than six minutes

47. BOTH INTERNATIONAL and INLAND. You are the stand-on vessel in a crossing situation. You may hold your course and speed until:
    A. the other vessel takes necessary action
    B. the other vessel gets to within half a mile of your vessel
    C. action by the give-way vessel alone will not prevent collision
    D. the other vessel gets to within a quarter mile of your vessel

48. BOTH INTERNATIONAL and INLAND. Which requirement must be met in order for a stand-on vessel to take action to avoid collision?
    A. Risk of collision must exist
    B. The give-way vessel must have taken action first
    C. The vessels must be within half a mile of each other
    D. There are no requirements to be met. The stand-on vessel may take action anytime

49. BOTH INTERNATIONAL and INLAND. A power-driven vessel underway shall keep out of the way of a vessel:
    A. not under command
    B. restricted in her ability to maneuver
    C. engaged in fishing
    D. All of the above

50. BOTH INTERNATIONAL and INLAND. You are on a power-driven vessel in fog. Your vessel is proceeding at a safe speed when you hear a fog signal ahead of you. The Rules require you to navigate with caution and, if danger of collision exists:
    A. slow to less than 2 knots
    B. reduce to bare steerageway
    C. stop your engines
    D. initiate a radar plot

51. BOTH INTERNATIONAL and INLAND. You are underway on vessel "A" and sight vessel "B," which is a vessel underway and fishing. Which statement is TRUE? (See diagram below.)
    A. Vessel "A" must keep out of the way of vessel "B" because "B" is to port
    B. Vessel "A" must keep out of the way of vessel "B" because "B" is fishing
    C. Vessel "B" must keep out of the way of vessel "A" because "A" is to starboard
    D. In this case, both vessels are required by the Rules to keep clear of each other

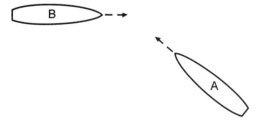

52. BOTH INTERNATIONAL and INLAND. Of the vessels listed, which must keep out of the way of all the others?
   A. A sailing vessel
   B. A vessel restricted in her ability to maneuver
   C. A vessel not under command
   D. A vessel fishing

53. BOTH INTERNATIONAL and INLAND. The Rules state that a seaplane shall:
   A. not be regarded as a vessel
   B. in general, keep well clear of all vessels
   C. proceed at a slower speed than surrounding vessels
   D. when making way, show the lights for a vessel not under command

54. BOTH INTERNATIONAL and INLAND. When navigating in restricted visibility, a power- driven vessel shall:
   A. stop her engines when hearing a fog signal forward of her beam, even if risk of collision does not exist
   B. have her engines ready for immediate maneuver
   C. when making way, sound one prolonged blast at intervals of not more than one minute
   D. operate at a speed to be able to stop in the distance of her visibility

55. BOTH INTERNATIONAL and INLAND. In restricted visibility, a vessel that detects by radar alone the presence of another vessel, shall determine if a close quarters situation is developing or risk of collision exists. If so, she shall:
   A. sound the danger signal
   B. when taking action, make only course changes
   C. avoid altering course toward a vessel abaft the beam
   D. All of the above

56. INLAND ONLY. What shall be used to indicate the presence of a partly submerged object being towed?
   A. A black cone, apex downward
   B. An all-round white light at each end of the tow
   C. A flare-up light
   D. All of the above

57. INLAND ONLY. A vessel of less than 20 meters in length at anchor at night in a "special anchorage area designated by the Secretary" ___.
   A. must show one white light
   B. need not show any lights
   C. must show two white lights
   D. need show a light only on the approach of another vessel

58. BOTH INTERNATIONAL and INLAND. A vessel may exhibit lights other than those prescribed by the Rules as long as the additional lights ___.
   A. do not interfere with the keeping of a proper lookout
   B. are not the color of either sidelight
   C. have a lesser range than the prescribed lights
   D. All of the above

59. BOTH INTERNATIONAL and INLAND. The lights prescribed by the Rules shall be exhibited ___.
    A. from sunrise to sunset in restricted visibility
    B. at all times
    C. from sunset to sunrise, and at no other time
    D. whenever a lookout is posted

60. BOTH INTERNATIONAL and INLAND. An all-round flashing yellow light may be exhibited by a(n) ___.
    A. vessel laying cable
    B. vessel towing a submerged object
    C. vessel not under command
    D. air cushion vessel

61. BOTH INTERNATIONAL and INLAND. You are on a vessel heading due south and see the lights shown one point on the port bow. This vessel could be heading ___. See diagram below.
    A. SW
    B. NW
    C. NE
    D. SE

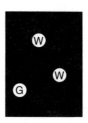

62. INLAND ONLY. What is true of a "special flashing light"?
    A. It may show through an arc of 180°
    B. It flashes at the rate of 120 flashes per minute
    C. It is optional below the Baton Rouge Highway Bridge
    D. All of the above

63. BOTH INTERNATIONAL and INLAND. Dayshapes MUST be shown ___.
    A. during daylight hours
    B. during daylight hours except in restricted visibility
    C. ONLY between 8 A.M. and 4 P.M. daily
    D. between sunset and sunrise

64. BOTH INTERNATIONAL and INLAND. The sternlight shall be positioned such that it will show from dead astern to how many degrees on each side of the stern of the vessel?
    A. 22.5°
    B. 67.5°
    C. 112.5°
    D. 135.0°

65. BOTH INTERNATIONAL and INLAND. Which vessel would exhibit side-lights when underway and not making way?
   A. A vessel towing astern
   B. A vessel trawling
   C. A vessel not under command
   D. A vessel engaged in dredging operations

66. BOTH INTERNATIONAL and INLAND. You see a vessel displaying ONLY the lights in the diagram below. This could be a ___.
   A. vessel engaged in fishing at anchor
   B. pilot vessel on pilotage duty
   C. vessel engaged in launching or recovering aircraft
   D. power-driven vessel underway

67. BOTH INTERNATIONAL and INLAND. A towing vessel pushing a barge ahead and rigidly connected in a composite unit shall show the lights of ___.
   A. a vessel towing by pushing ahead
   B. a power-driven vessel, not towing
   C. a barge being pushed ahead
   D. either answer A or answer B

68. BOTH INTERNATIONAL and INLAND. Which display of lights shown indicates a dredge underway and not dredging? See diagram below.
   A. A
   B. B
   C. C
   D. D

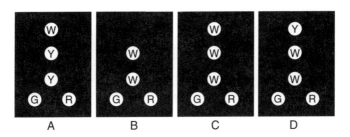

69. BOTH INTERNATIONAL and INLAND. Which of the dayshapes shown would you show on the after end of an inconspicuous, partially submerged vessel or object being towed over 200 meters in length? See diagram below.
    A. A
    B. B
    C. C
    D. No dayshape would be shown

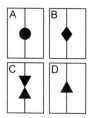

70. BOTH INTERNATIONAL and INLAND. A sailing vessel of over 20 meters in length underway must show a ___.
    A. red light over a green light at the masthead
    B. white masthead light
    C. combined lantern
    D. sternlight

71. BOTH INTERNATIONAL and INLAND. A lantern combining a vessel's navigation lights may be shown on a ___.
    A. 15-meter sailing vessel
    B. 20-meter vessel engaged in fishing and making way
    C. 25-meter power-driven vessel trolling
    D. 25-meter pilot vessel

72. BOTH INTERNATIONAL and INLAND. A sailing vessel underway may exhibit ___.
    A. a red light over a green light at the masthead
    B. a green light over a red light at the masthead
    C. two white lights in a vertical line at the stern
    D. an all-round white light at the bow

73. BOTH INTERNATIONAL and INLAND. A vessel engaged in fishing, and at anchor, shall show ___.
    A. an anchor light
    B. sidelights and a sternlight
    C. three lights in a vertical line, the highest and lowest being red, and the middle being white
    D. None of the above

74. BOTH INTERNATIONAL and INLAND. A vessel trawling will display a ___.
    A. red light over a white light
    B. green light over a white light
    C. yellow light over a red light
    D. white light over a green light

75. BOTH INTERNATIONAL and INLAND. A 60-meter vessel that is trawling is required to show how many white masthead lights at night?
    A. 1
    B. 2
    C. 3
    D. 4

76. BOTH INTERNATIONAL and INLAND. A vessel not under command, underway, but not making way, would show ___.
    A. two all-round red lights in a vertical line
    B. sidelights
    C. a sternlight
    D. All of the above

77. BOTH INTERNATIONAL and INLAND. A vessel will NOT show sidelights when ___.
    A. underway but not making way
    B. making way, not under command
    C. not under command, not making way
    D. trolling underway

78. BOTH INTERNATIONAL and INLAND. A vessel servicing a pipeline during the day shall display ___.
    A. three black shapes in a vertical line; the highest and lowest are balls, and the middle one is a diamond
    B. three shapes in a vertical line; the highest and lowest are red balls, and the middle one is a white diamond
    C. three black balls in a vertical line
    D. two black balls in a vertical line

79. BOTH INTERNATIONAL and INLAND. A vessel restricted in her ability to maneuver shall ___.
    A. turn off her sidelights when not making way
    B. when operating in restricted visibility, sound a whistle signal of two prolonged and one short blast
    C. show a dayshape of two diamonds in a vertical line
    D. keep out of the way of a vessel engaged in fishing

80. BOTH INTERNATIONAL and INLAND. A vessel displaying the dayshapes in the diagram below is ___.
    A. towing astern with a tow greater than 200 meters in length
    B. not under command
    C. dredging
    D. carrying dangerous cargo

81. BOTH INTERNATIONAL and INLAND. During the day, a dredge will indicate the side on which it is safe to pass by displaying ___.
    A. two balls in a vertical line
    B. two diamonds in a vertical line
    C. a single black ball
    D. no shape is shown during the day

82. BOTH INTERNATIONAL and INLAND. Which vessel, when anchored at night, would NOT be required to show anchor lights?
    A. A power-driven vessel
    B. A vessel on pilotage duty
    C. A vessel dredging
    D. A vessel restricted in her ability to maneuver

83. BOTH INTERNATIONAL and INLAND. An anchored vessel on pilotage duty must show which light(s) at night?
    A. A sternlight only
    B. Anchor lights only
    C. A white light over a red light only
    D. A white light over a red light and anchor lights

84. BOTH INTERNATIONAL and INLAND. Which statement is TRUE concerning a vessel of 150 meters in length, at anchor?
    A. She may show an all-round white light where it can best be seen.
    B. She must show an all-round white light forward and a second such light aft.
    C. The showing of working lights is optional.
    D. None of the above

85. INTERNATIONAL ONLY. To indicate that a vessel is constrained by her draft, a vessel may display, in a vertical line, ___.
    A. three 360° red lights
    B. two 225° red lights
    C. three 360° blue lights
    D. two 225° blue lights

86. INLAND ONLY. When you are overtaking another vessel and desire to pass on her left or port hand, you should sound _____.
    A. one short blast
    B. one long blast
    C. two short blasts
    D. two prolonged blasts

87. INLAND ONLY. A flashing blue light is used to identify _____.
    A. law enforcement vessels
    B. U.S. submarines
    C. air-cushion vessels in the nondisplacement mode
    D. dredge pipelines on trestles

88. INLAND ONLY. Your vessel is meeting another vessel head-on. To comply with the rules, you should exchange _____.
    A. one short blast, alter course to the left, and pass starboard to starboard
    B. two short blasts, alter course to the left, and pass starboard to starboard
    C. one short blast, alter course to the right, and pass port to port
    D. two short blasts, alter course to the right, and pass port to port

89. INLAND ONLY. Two vessels in a crossing situation have reached agreement by radiotelephone as to the intentions of the other. In this situation, whistle signals are _____.
    A. required
    B. not required, but may be sounded
    C. required if crossing within half a mile
    D. required when crossing within one mile

90. INLAND ONLY. You are meeting another vessel head-on and sound one short blast as a passing signal. The other vessel answers with two short blasts. What should be your next action?
    A. Pass on the other vessel's starboard side
    B. Sound the danger signal
    C. Pass astern of the other vessel
    D. Hold your course and speed

91. INLAND ONLY. While underway in a harbor you hear a vessel sound a pro-longed blast. This signal indicates that this vessel _____.
    A. desires to overtake your vessel
    B. is at anchor
    C. is backing her engines
    D. is moving from a dock

92. INLAND ONLY. Which light display would mark the opening in a pipeline where vessels could pass through?
    A. Three red lights in a vertical line on each side of the opening
    B. Two red lights in a vertical line on each side of the opening
    C. Three white lights in a vertical line on each side of the opening
    D. Two white lights in a vertical line on each side of the opening

93. BOTH INTERNATIONAL and INLAND. While underway and pushing a barge ahead, your vessel enters a heavy rain storm. You should sound _____.
    A. a prolonged blast every two minutes
    B. two prolonged blasts every two minutes
    C. one prolonged and two short blasts every two minutes
    D. two prolonged and one short blast every two minutes

94. INLAND ONLY. A light used to signal passing intentions must be an _____.
    A. alternating red and yellow light
    B. alternating white and yellow light
    C. all-round white or yellow light
    D. all-round white light only

95. BOTH INTERNATIONAL and INLAND. A 95-meter vessel aground sounds which fog signal?
    A. A rapid ringing of a bell for 5 seconds every two minutes
    B. A whistle signal of one short, one prolonged, and one short blast
    C. A prolonged blast of the whistle at intervals not to exceed one minute
    D. A rapid ringing of a bell for 5 seconds, preceded and followed by three separate and distinct strokes on the bell

96. BOTH INTERNATIONAL and INLAND. You see a vessel displaying the code flag "LIMA" below which is a red ball. The vessel is _____.
    A. trolling
    B. getting ready to receive aircraft
    C. aground
    D. in distress

97. BOTH INTERNATIONAL and INLAND. A vessel may use any sound or light signals to attract the attention of another vessel as long as _____.
    A. white lights are not used
    B. red and green lights are not used
    C. the vessel signals such intentions over the radiotelephone
    D. the signal cannot be mistaken for a signal authorized by the Rules

98. INLAND ONLY. Two vessels are in a starboard to starboard meeting situation and will pass well clear approximately ¼ mile apart. Which action should each vessel take?
    A. Sound a one blast whistle signal and turn to starboard
    B. Maintain course and sound no signal
    C. Sound a two blast whistle signal and maintain course
    D. Sound a three blast whistle signal and turn to port

99. BOTH INTERNATIONAL and INLAND. Each prolonged blast on whistle signals used by a power-driven vessel in fog, whether making way or underway but not making way, is _____.
    A. about one second
    B. two to four seconds
    C. four to six seconds
    D. eight to ten seconds

100. INTERNATIONAL ONLY. You are in sight of another vessel in a crossing situation, and the other vessel sounds one short blast. You are going to hold course and speed. You should _____.
    A. answer with one short blast
    B. answer with two short blasts
    C. sound the danger signal
    D. sound no whistle signal

101. BOTH INTERNATIONAL and INLAND. A continuous sounding of a
fog-signal apparatus indicates _____.
   A. the vessel is in distress
   B. the vessel has completed loading dangerous cargo
   C. it is safe to pass
   D. the vessel is anchored

102. BOTH INTERNATIONAL and INLAND. In restricted visibility, a vessel
fishing with nets shall sound at intervals of two minutes _____.
   A. one prolonged blast
   B. one prolonged followed by two short blasts
   C. one prolonged followed by three short blasts
   D. two prolonged blasts in succession

103. BOTH INTERNATIONAL and INLAND. Five or more short blasts on a ves-
sel's whistle indicates that she is _____.
   A. in doubt that another vessel is taking sufficient action to avoid a
      collision
   B. altering course to starboard
   C. altering course to port
   D. the stand-on vessel and will maintain course and speed

104. BOTH INTERNATIONAL and INLAND. A tug is towing three manned
barges in line in fog. The third vessel of the tow should sound _____.
   A. no fog signal
   B. one prolonged and two short blasts
   C. one prolonged and three short blasts
   D. one prolonged, one short and one prolonged blast

105. BOTH INTERNATIONAL and INLAND. The whistle signal for a vessel op-
erating astern propulsion is _____.
   A. one long blast
   B. one prolonged blast
   C. three short blasts
   D. four or more short blasts

106. BOTH INTERNATIONAL and INLAND. A vessel nearing a bend or an area
of a channel or fairway where other vessels may be hidden by an obstruction
shall _____.
   A. sound the danger signal
   B. sound a prolonged blast
   C. take all way off
   D. post an extra lookout

107. BOTH INTERNATIONAL and INLAND. Which vessel must have a gong, or
other equipment that will make the sound of a gong?
   A. A sailing vessel
   B. Any vessel over 50 meters
   C. Any vessel over 100 meters
   D. A power-driven vessel over 75 meters

108. BOTH INTERNATIONAL and INLAND. Which vessel sounds the same fog signal when underway or at anchor?
  A. A sailing vessel
  B. A vessel restricted in her ability to maneuver
  C. A vessel constrained by her draft
  D. A vessel not under command

109. BOTH INTERNATIONAL and INLAND. At night, a power-driven vessel less than 12 meters in length may, instead of the normal navigation lights, show sidelights and one ___.
  A. white light
  B. yellow light
  C. flashing white light
  D. flashing yellow light

110. INLAND ONLY. Which of the following signals may be exhibited by a vessel trawling in close proximity to other fishing vessels?
  A. Two white lights in a vertical line
  B. A red light over a white light in a vertical line
  C. Two fixed yellow lights in a vertical line
  D. All of the above

111. INTERNATIONAL ONLY. In a crossing situation on international waters, a short blast by the give-way vessel indicates that the vessel _____.
  A. is holding course and speed
  B. is turning to starboard
  C. intends to pass port to port
  D. will keep out of the way of the stand-on vessel

112. BOTH INTERNATIONAL and INLAND. Which statement is TRUE concerning two sailing vessels approaching each other?
  A. The vessel making the most speed is the give-way vessel
  B. A sailing vessel overtaking another is the give-way vessel
  C. A sailing vessel seeing another to leeward on an undetermined tack shall hold her course
  D. All of the above

113. INLAND ONLY. Which is a characteristic of a "special flashing light"?
  A. It is required for all vessels being pushed ahead as part of a composite unit
  B. It must show through an arc of not less than 180° nor more than 225°
  C. It must be of the same character and construction as the masthead light
  D. All of the above

114. BOTH INTERNATIONAL and INLAND. A vessel underway and fishing shall keep out of the way of a:
  A. power-driven vessel underway
  B. vessel not under command
  C. vessel sailing
  D. vessel engaged on pilotage duty

115. BOTH INTERNATIONAL and INLAND. A vessel may exhibit lights other than those prescribed by the Rules as long as the additional lights ___.
    A. are not the same color as either sidelight
    B. have a lesser range of visibility than the prescribed lights
    C. do not impair the visibility or distinctive character of the prescribed lights
    D. All of the above

116. BOTH INTERNATIONAL and INLAND. While you are underway, navigation lights must be displayed on your vessel ___.
    A. during all periods of restricted visibility
    B. at all times
    C. at night only when other vessels may be in the area
    D. at night only when vessels are detected on radar

117. BOTH INTERNATIONAL and INLAND. Dayshapes must be displayed ___.
    A. between sunset and sunrise
    B. only between 8 A.M. and 4 P.M.
    C. during daylight hours in any visibility
    D. during daylight hours in unrestricted visibility only

118. BOTH INTERNATIONAL and INLAND. You are on a vessel heading due north and see the lights shown one point on your port bow. This vessel could be heading ___. See diagram below.
    A. SE
    B. NE
    C. SW
    D. NW

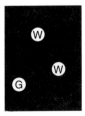

119. BOTH INTERNATIONAL and INLAND. As defined in the Rules, a towing light is a yellow light having the same characteristics as a(n) ___.
    A. masthead light
    B. all-round light
    C. sidelight
    D. sternlight

120. BOTH INTERNATIONAL and INLAND. The lights illustrated in the diagram below are those of a ___.
    A. vessel being towed
    B. power-driven vessel of less than 50 meters in length
    C. fishing vessel at anchor
    D. sailboat

121. BOTH INTERNATIONAL and INLAND. Which statement is TRUE concerning a 75-meter power-driven vessel underway at night?
    A. She must exhibit an all-round white light at the stern
    B. She must exhibit forward and after masthead lights
    C. She must exhibit only a forward masthead light
    D. She may exhibit a red light over a green light forward

122. BOTH INTERNATIONAL and INLAND. A vessel showing a yellow light over a white light at night is a vessel ___.
    A. engaged in piloting
    B. towing astern
    C. engaged in fishing
    D. in distress

123. BOTH INTERNATIONAL and INLAND. A power-driven vessel exhibits the same lights as a ___.
    A. vessel towing, when not underway
    B. vessel towing astern
    C. sailing vessel
    D. pushing vessel and a vessel being pushed, when they are in a composite unit

124. BOTH INTERNATIONAL and INLAND. An inconspicuous, partly submerged vessel or object being towed, where the length of tow is 100 meters, shall show ___.
    A. yellow lights at each end
    B. two red lights in a vertical line
    C. a black ball
    D. a diamond shape

125. BOTH INTERNATIONAL and INLAND. A 20-meter sailing vessel underway must exhibit a ___.
    A. sternlight
    B. combined lantern
    C. red light over a green light at the masthead
    D. All of the above

126. BOTH INTERNATIONAL and INLAND. A lantern combining the two side-lights and sternlight may be shown on a ___.
   A. 10-meter sailing vessel
   B. 20-meter vessel engaged in fishing and making way
   C. 25-meter power-driven vessel engaged in trolling
   D. 25-meter pilot vessel

127. BOTH INTERNATIONAL and INLAND. A sailing vessel is NOT allowed to show the all-round red over green lights on the mast if ___.
   A. she is showing sidelights
   B. her sidelights are combined and shown on the fore and aft centerline of the vessel
   C. she is showing a sternlight
   D. her sidelights and sternlight are combined in one lantern and shown on the mast

128. BOTH INTERNATIONAL and INLAND. Which vessel, when anchored at night, is not required to show anchor lights?
   A. A power-driven vessel
   B. A vessel engaged in survey operations
   C. A vessel engaged on pilotage duty
   D. A vessel engaged in fishing

129. BOTH INTERNATIONAL and INLAND. A vessel engaged in trawling will show identification lights of ___.
   A. a red light over a white light
   B. a white light over a red light
   C. a green light over a white light
   D. two red lights in a vertical line

130. BOTH INTERNATIONAL and INLAND. Which vessel must show a mast-head light abaft of and higher than her identifying lights?
   A. A 55-meter vessel fishing
   B. A 55-meter vessel trawling
   C. A 100-meter vessel not under command
   D. A 20-meter vessel engaged on pilotage duty

131. BOTH INTERNATIONAL and INLAND. A power-driven vessel "not under command" at night must show which lights in a vertical line?
   A. Three red
   B. Two red
   C. Two white
   D. Three white

132. BOTH INTERNATIONAL and INLAND. At night, a vessel shall indicate that she is restricted in her ability to maneuver by showing in a vertical line two ___.
   A. red lights
   B. red lights and two white lights
   C. red lights with a white light in between
   D. white lights with a red light in between

133. BOTH INTERNATIONAL and INLAND. A vessel transferring provisions or cargo at sea shall display during the day ___.
    A. two black balls in a vertical line
    B. three black balls in a vertical line
    C. three shapes in a vertical line; the highest and lowest shall be red balls and the middle a white diamond
    D. three black shapes in a vertical line; the highest and lowest shall be balls and the middle one a diamond

134. BOTH INTERNATIONAL and INLAND. Which lights are shown by a vessel restricted in her ability to maneuver to indicate that the vessel is making way?
    A. Masthead lights, sidelights, and sternlight
    B. Masthead lights and sidelights only
    C. Sidelights and sternlight only
    D. Sidelights only

135. BOTH INTERNATIONAL and INLAND. At night, which lights are required to be shown by a dredge on the side of the dredge which another vessel may pass?
    A. One red light
    B. Two red lights
    C. One white light
    D. Two green lights

136. BOTH INTERNATIONAL and INLAND. You are approaching a vessel dredging during the day and see two balls in a vertical line on the port side of the dredge. These shapes mean that ___.
    A. you should pass on the port side of the dredge
    B. there is an obstruction on the port side of the dredge
    C. the dredge is not under command
    D. the dredge is moored

137. BOTH INTERNATIONAL and INLAND. A rigid replica of the International Code flag "A" may be shown by a vessel ___.
    A. pulling a submarine cable
    B. engaged in diving operations
    C. engaged in underway replenishment
    D. transferring explosives

138. BOTH INTERNATIONAL and INLAND. If you anchor your 25-meter vessel in a harbor, what light(s) must you show?
    A. One all-round white light
    B. Two all-round white lights
    C. One all-round red light
    D. All the deck house lights

139. INTERNATIONAL ONLY. A vessel constrained by her draft may display ___.
    A. three all-round red lights
    B. two 225° red lights
    C. three all-round blue lights
    D. two 225° blue lights

140. INTERNATIONAL ONLY. Which dayshape is prescribed for a vessel constrained by her draft?
    A. A black diamond
    B. A cylinder
    C. A black ball
    D. A black cone, apex upward

ANSWER KEY FOR RULES OF THE ROAD QUESTIONS

1. A	36. A	71. A	106. B
2. D	37. B	72. A	107. C
3. B	38. C	73. D	108. B
4. C	39. A	74. B	109. A
5. C	40. B	75. A	110. A
6. B	41. A	76. A	111. B
7. C	42. C	77. C	112. B
8. B	43. C	78. A	113. B
9. C	44. A	79. A	114. B
10. B	45. D	80. C	115. C
11. A	46. C	81. B	116. A
12. A	47. C	82. C	117. C
13. C	48. A	83. D	118. A
14. D	49. D	84. B	119. D
15. D	50. B	85. A	120. B
16. C	51. B	86. C	121. B
17. C	52. A	87. A	122. B
18. B	53. B	88. C	123. D
19. B	54. B	89. B	124. D
20. C	55. C	90. B	125. A
21. A	56. B	91. D	126. A
22. D	57. B	92. B	127. D
23. C	58. A	93. C	128. D
24. B	59. A	94. C	129. C
25. C	60. D	95. D	130. B
26. A	61. B	96. D	131. B
27. C	62. A	97. D	132. C
28. A	63. A	98. C	133. D
29. B	64. B	99. C	134. A
30. A	65. A	100. D	135. D
31. D	66. D	101. A	136. B
32. A	67. B	102. B	137. B
33. A	68. B	103. A	138. A
34. D	69. B	104. C	139. A
35. C	70. D	105. C	140. B

Study Outline for Rules of the Road

I. Definitions
    A. General—Rule 3
    B. Lights and shapes—Rules 21 through 30
    C. Risk of collision—Rule 7
    D. Narrow channels—Rule 9
    E. Maneuvering situations—Rules 13, 14, 15
    F. Not to impede—Rule 8(f)
    G. Annexes

II. Pecking order of vessels—Rule 18

III. Determination of risk of collision and action to avoid collision—Rules 6, 7, 8

IV. Maneuvering situations
    A. Sailing vessels—Rule 12
    B. Overtaking—Rule 13
    C. Head-on—Rule 14
    D. Crossing—Rule 15

V. Duties of stand-on and give-way vessels
    A. Rule 16
    B. Rule 17
    C. Sound signals for maneuvering—Rules 32, 33, 34

VI. Restricted visibility
    A. Sound signals—Rule 35
    B. Maneuvering—Rule 19

VII. Not to impede—Rule 8(f)
    A. Vessels not to impede—Rules 9, 10, 18
    B. In contrast to "keep out of the way"—Rules 9, 12, 13, 14(d), 15, 17(d), 18

VIII. Narrow Channels—Rule 9
    A. Maneuvers
    B. Sound signals
    C. Not to impede
    D. Western Rivers—Rules 9, 14

IX. Application of lights to maneuvering situations
    A. Running lights—Rule 23
    B. Identification and working lights—Rules 24 through 30

X. Rule of Good Seamanship and General Prudential Rule—Rule 2(a) and (b)

Index

A

Aground vessel lights and sounds, 94, 106
Air-cushion vessel, lights, 74
All-round lights, 70
Alternative compliance, 4, 168-70
Anchoring
  lights and shapes, 94, 143
  narrow channels, 32
  sound signals, 106
  traffic separation schemes, 36
Applicability of Rules, 2
Attracting attention, 108

B

Barges, moored, 139, 143
Bell, 96, 106, 132

C

Channels, narrow, 30
  anchoring, 32
  crossing, 32
  obstruction in, 32, 100
  overtaking in, 32
Collision
  avoidance of, 24, 46, 102
  risk of, 22, 28, 38, 46, 54, 56
  COLREGS Demarcation Lines (33 CFR 80), 144
Compliance, alternative, 168–70
Compliance with Rules, 6
Composite unit
  lights, 78, 143
  sounds (push or tow), 106, 143
Constrained by draft, 50
Crossing situation, 32, 44

D

Danger signal, 32, 98, 100
Demarcation Lines, 144
Departure from Rules, 8
Distress signals, 108, 134
Downbound vessel, 30, 42, 44

E

Dredge pipelines, 141
Dredging operations lights and shapes, 90, 118

Exemptions, 108

F

Fairways. *See* Channels
Fishing vessel
  anchored lights, 86
  defined, 10
  direction indicating lights, 118
  inshore traffic zone, 34
  narrow channels, 32
  not impede passage, 36
  responsibilities, 50
  restricted visibility sound signals, 104
  traffic separation scheme, 36
  trawling lights and shapes, 86, 126
  underway lights and shapes, 86
Flashing light, 70
  special flashing light (yellow), 70

G

General definitions, 8
Give-way vessel, 44, 48
Gong, 96, 106, 132
Great Lakes
  defined, 14
  lights, 74
  narrow channels, 30
  power-driven vessel lights, 74, 82
  right of way, 42, 44

H

Head-on situation, 42
High-speed craft, 124

I

Inland Interpretative Rules (33 CFR 90), 143
Inland Rules, 2, 16

Inland waters, 14, 170
Inshore traffic zone, 34
International Interpretative Rules (33 CFR 82), 143
International Regulations, 16
International Rules, 2

L

Light signals, 100
Lights
    all-round, 70, 116, 118
    color specification, 120
    exception, 82
    flashing, 70, 100, 102
    general, 56
    horizontal positioning and spacing, 116
    horizontal sectors, 122
    intensity of, 120
    intensity of nonelectric, 124
    maneuvering, 124
    masthead (white), 68
    sidelights (green and red), 68, 116
    special flashing (yellow), 70
    sternlight (white), 68
    table (summary) of responsibilities, 59
    towing (yellow), 68
    unlighted vessel, 82
    vertical positioning and spacing, 114
    vertical sectors, 122
    visibility, 70, 72
Look-out, 16

M

Maneuvering signals, 98
Masthead light (white), 68
Mineclearance operations lights and shapes, 88, 92
Moored barges, 139, 143

N

Noncompliance, 4
Nonmaneuverable vessel
    defined, 10
    lights and shapes, 88
    sounds, 104
    traffic separation schemes, 36
Not to impede, 28, 30, 32, 36
Not under command vessel
    defined, 10
    lights and shapes, 88, 143
    sound signals, 104

O

Overtaking
    defined, 40
    power-driven vessels, 32

P

Partly submerged vessel lights, 80
Penalty provisions, 164
Pilot rules, 137–41
Pilot vessel lights, shapes, and sounds, 92, 108
Pipelines, dredge, 141
Power-driven vessel
    anchored, sounds, 106
    crossing, 44, 46, 98
    defined, 10
    head-on situation, 42
    making way sounds, 104
    narrow channels, 30
    overtaking, 32, 100
    pushing ahead lights and sounds, 78, 104
    responsibilities, 50
    restricted visibility, 52, 104
    sound signals, 98, 104
    towing alongside lights and sounds, 78, 80, 104
    towing astern lights and shapes, 76
    underway, but stopped sounds, 104
    underway lights, 72
Prolonged blast, 96, 102, 104
Purse seiners, 126

R

Radar, 20, 22, 54
Radiotelephone, 102, 171
Responsibility, 6
Restricted visibility
    defined, 14, 52
    sound signals, 104

S

Safe passage, 28, 98
Sailing vessel
    defined, 10
    inshore traffic zone, 34
    narrow channels, 30
    responsibilities, 50
    restricted visibility sound signals, 104
    safe passage (with visibility), 38
    underway lights and shapes, 84
Screens for sidelights, 118
Seaplane
    defined, 10
    lights and shapes, 96
    responsibilities, 52
Searchlight, 82, 84, 108
Secretary
    defined, 14
    waters specified by, 170
Shapes, 118
Short blast, 96, 104

Sidelights (green and red), 68
Signals
    attract attention, 108
    distress, 108, 134
    fog, 56
    purse seiners, 126
    trawlers, 126
Speed, safe, 20
Stand-on vessel, 46
Sternlight (white), 68
Study outline, 203
Submarine cable, 12, 36

T

Towing light (yellow), 68
Towing sound signals, 104
Traffic separation schemes, 4, 34
    anchoring, 36
    crossing, 34, 36
Trawling lights and shapes, 86, 126

U

Underwater operations lights and shapes, 90, 118
Underway, 12
Upbound vessel, 30, 42, 44

V

Vessel, defined, 8. *See also* each type of vessel
Vessel Bridge-to-Bridge Radiotelephone
    Regulations, 171–77
Vessel less than 7 meters, 74, 84
Vessel less than 12 meters
    exemption, 92
    masthead light, 68
    sidelights, 68
    sound signalling, 98, 106
    visibility of lights, 72, 74

Vessel less than 20 meters
    exemptions, 110
    impede passage, 36
    inshore traffic zone, 34
    narrow channels, 30
    sidelights, 68
    sound signals, 108
    special anchorage area lights, 96
    traffic separation scheme, 36
    underway lights, 84
Vessel under oars, 84
Violations of rules
    inland, 165–67
    international, 164–65
Visibility
    any condition of, 16
    defined, 14
    in sight of one another, 38
    lights, 70, 72
    See also Restricted visibility

W

Warning signals, 98
Western Rivers
    defined, 14
    narrow channels, 30
    pushing ahead lights, 82
    right of way, 42, 44
    towing alongside lights, 82
Whistle
    defined, 96
    expressing doubt, 102
    technical details of, 128–32
Wing-in-Ground (WIG) craft
    defined, 14
    lights, 74
    responsibilities, 52

Bibliography

Allen, Craig. *Farwell's Rules of the Nautical Road.* Annapolis: Naval Institute Press, 2005.

Cahil, R. A. *Collisions and Their Causes.* London: The Nautical Institute, 2002.

Cockcroft, A. N. and J. N. F. Lameiger. *Collision Avoidance Rules.* Oxford: Butterworth-Heinemann, 1996.

Llana, Christopher and George Wisneskey. *Handbook of the Nautical Rules of the Road.* Annapolis: Naval Institute Press, 1991.

About the Authors

B. A. Farnsworth graduated from the United States Merchant Marine Academy in 1971 with a bachelor of science degree in marine transportation and served as a Coast Guard marine inspector for four years. From 1975 to 1990, he worked in the Coast Guard licensing program. He presently pastors an independent Baptist Church in Oklahoma and works for the Federal Aviation Administration's Civil Aviation Registry in Oklahoma City as a program analyst in the Airmen Certification Branch.

Larry C. Young is a graduate of the United States Coast Guard Academy and holds a master's degree in business administration from Oklahoma City University. He served as officer of the deck and navigator aboard the USCGC *Jarvis* before joining the United States Coast Guard Institute in 1976. After leaving the institute, he moved into the testing and training field. He was involved in revamping the training program for the Coast Guard Auxiliary. He left the Coast Guard and took the position of manager, military testing, for the American Council on Education, becoming involved in GED testing internationally. He now operates Knowledge Assessment Service, a consulting company specializing in test preparation courses.

Captain Steve Browne holds a U.S. Coast Guard license as Master Mariner, Any Gross Tons Upon Oceans. He was awarded a bachelor's degree in computer studies and a master's degree in engineering management, both from Northwestern University in Evanston, Illinois. He served for several years as a surface warfare officer in the U.S. Navy and was Master of the M/V *Doulos,* a passenger vessel of 6,804 gross registered tons. He is currently an Assistant Professor of Marine Transportation at the California Maritime Academy in Vallejo, California. He also works as a maritime legal consultant specializing in the Rules of the Road.

CORNELL MARITIME PRESS

American Merchant Seaman's Manual
William B. Hayler, Editor in Chief, 978-0-87033-549-5

Applied Naval Architecture
Robert B. Zubaly, 978-0-87033-475-7

Behavior and Handling of Ships
Henry H. Hooyer, 978-0-87033-306-4

Business of Shipping
Lane C. Kendall and James J. Buckley, 978-0-87033-526-6

Cornell Manual, The
John M. Keever, 978-0-87033-559-4

Dictionary of Maritime and Transportation Terms
Jeffrey W. Monroe and Robert Stewart, 978-0-87033-569-3

Diesel Engines
Leo Block, P.E., 978-0-87033-418-4

Formulae for the Mariner
Richard M. Plant, 978-0-87033-361-3

Handbook of Rights and Concerns for Mariners
Roberto Tiangco and Russ Jackson, 978-0-87033-530-3

Marine Cargo Operations
Robert J. Meurn and Charles L. Sauerbier, 978-0-87033-550-1

Marine Engineering Economics and Cost Analysis
Everett C. Hunt and Boris S. Butman, 978-0-87033-458-0

Marine Radionavigation and Communications
Jeffrey W. Monroe and Thomas L. Bushy, 978-0-87033-510-5

Marine Refrigeration and Air-Conditioning
James A. Harbach, 978-0-87033-565-5

Master's Handbook on Ship's Business
Tuuli Anna Messer, 978-0-87033-531-0

Modern Marine Engineer's Manual, Volume I
Everett C. Hunt, Editor in Chief, 978-0-87033-496-2

Modern Marine Engineer's Manual, Volume II
Everett C. Hunt, Editor in Chief, 978-0-87033-537-2

Modern Marine Salvage
William I. Milwee, Jr., 978-0-87033-471-9

Modern Towing
John S. Blank, 3rd, 978-0-87033-372-9

Primer of Towing
George H. Reid, 978-0-87033-563-1

Real Time Method of Radar Plotting
Max H. Carpenter and Wayne M. Waldo, 978-0-87033-204-3

Shiphandling for the Mariner
Daniel H. MacElrevey and Daniel E. MacElrevey, 978-0-87033-558-7

Shiphandling with Tugs
George G. Reid, 978-0-87033-354-5

Stability and Trim for the Ship's Officer
William E. George, 978-0-87033-564-8

Survival Guide for the Mariner, 2nd Edition
Robert J. Meurn, 978-0-87033-573-0

Tanker Operations
Mark Huber, 978-0-87033-528-0

U.S. Regulation of Ocean Transportation
Gerald H. Ullman, 978-0-87033-470-2

Vessel Security Officer
Joseph Ahlstrom with David W. Narby and Joseph Tenaglia, 978-0-87033-570-9

Vessel Traffic Systems
Charles W. Koburger, Jr., 978-0-87033-360-6

Watchstanding Guide for the Merchant Officer
Robert J. Meurn, 978-0-87033-409-2

ISBN-13: 978-0-87033-578-5

54000